AD 508 Source Book

Heidi Heiks

TEACH Services, Inc.
www.TEACHServices.com

Copyright © 2011 TEACH Services, Inc.
ISBN-13: 978-1-57258-631-4
Library of Congress Control Number: 2011924419

Published by
TEACH Services, Inc.
www.TEACHServices.com

**To
Robin**

**My constant helpmate,
and best friend.**

CONTENTS

FOREWORD

Brother Heiks has spent many years of research studying the primary documents of church and political history that surround the important developments towards the end of the fifth century A. D. and the beginning of the sixth century. This was a time of immense political changes and those political changes directly influenced the course of church history. The research done by Heiks has turned up new material not previously recognized from this period and there have also been major revisions in the history of the period by scholars studying the religious and political history of the times. Central to this period is the year 508 which has significance for students of prophetic history who follow the historicist view of interpretation, as this is a pivotal date for one of the time periods at the end of the book of Daniel, along with the other time periods closely related to it. We appreciate the fine work that Brother Heiks has done in collecting and analyzing much of this obscure material. Students of political, religious and prophetic history are in his debt for this very useful work.

William H. Shea, MD, Ph.D.
Former Professor: Old Testament Department
Seminary, Andrews University
Former Associate: Biblical Research Institute
General Conference of Seventh-day Adventists

* * * * * * *

Heidi Heiks has produced and completed as promised a most thorough and timely study on the historical/prophetic dimensions of these four years. In many respects it is an original contribution, anchoring with great scholarly precision the reliability of the significance of these four dates.

It will be a great read, not only for fellow scholars across the academic landscape, but equally so for the thoughtful layperson that enjoys documentation that guarantees deeper assurance in critical biblical study. It surely will not compete with anything else on the market.

Anyone familiar with historical research will be gratified with the author's care and devotion to unvarnished facts and his articulateness in translating from the original languages. Perhaps someone somewhere will take issue with some aspect of this research. But if so, he would have to demolish the brick-by-brick structure that the author has constructed—and that seems to be an unlikely achievement.

I was especially grateful for his writing style—his force, careful transitions, and absence of pretentiousness. This is an unexpected achievement in the world of scholarship. I predict that many teachers and pastors will use these three volumes as a basis for many church-sponsored study groups. I can't imagine an Adventist church that will overlook the power flowing through these pages.

One of the most impressive features that make these books so timely and relevant is the linkage of the historical facts with the biblical anchorage and Ellen White's commentary. I found this three-fold connection to be rewarding and gratifying—not because I had hoped to find it so, but to see how deep this linkage is.

Many good men and women have supported the century-old interpretation that the "daily" refers to paganism, rather than Christ's ministry in heaven. They have seen, for them, good reasons for this position. However, it seems to me that they will find this understanding worthy of further consideration.

I am a wiser man after reading these books, not only for clearer reasons to see validity in 508, 538, 1798 and 1843, but also for the careful details describing the temporary demise of the papacy in 1798.

Herbert Edgar Douglass, Th.D.
Professor, Pacific Union College,
President, Atlantic Union College
Associate editor, Review and Herald
Vice President, Pacific Press
Publishing Association.
Lincoln Hills, California

* * * * * *

The apocalyptic books of Daniel and Revelation have received a variety of interpretations throughout church history. Of the three major schools of interpretation, historicism, futurism and preterism, historicism is the oldest, and until the nineteenth century it was the dominant school of interpretation. It can be traced back to some of the church fathers like Irenaeus, Hippolytus, and Jerome. It was taught by Joachim of Floris (1130-1202) in the twelfth century and became the standard interpretation of expositors until the time of the Counter Reformation.

Historicists believe in the divine inspiration of the book of Daniel, that it was written in the sixth century B.C., and that its main prophecies cover the period from the Babylonian Empire to the second coming of Christ. Historicists generally agree that the four empires of Daniel 2 and 7 represent the kingdoms of Babylon, Medo-Persia, Greece, and Rome, and that the Little Horn in Daniel 7 is the papacy. A third factor common to all is their use of the year-day principle in interpreting most, if not all, the time prophecies in Daniel? A last point on which there is general agreement among historicists is the prophecy in Daniel 9:24-27. All historicist commentators agree that the focus of this prophecy is Jesus Christ and that He fulfilled it in His incarnation.

Because historicists believe that the prophecies of Daniel and Revelation are fulfilled throughout the history, and particularly throughout the history of the Christian church, historical sources confirming the fulfillment of these prophecies are extremely important to historicist interpreters. The three volumes by Heidi Heiks contain not only a large amount of primary source material illustrating how the prophecies of Daniel and Revelation were fulfilled in history, they also provide important background information.

The backbone for the interpretation of the time prophecies found in Daniel and Revelation (3½ times, 1260, 1290, 1335 days and 42 months) is the year-day principle.

The main points in support of it can be summarized as follows:[1]

1) Since the visions in Daniel 7 and 8 are largely symbolic, with a number of different beasts representing important historical empires (7:3-7; 8:3-5, 20-21), the time periods (7:25; 8:14) should also be seen as symbolic.

2) The fact that the visions deal with the rise and fall of known empires in history which existed for hundreds of years indicates that the prophetic time periods must also cover long time periods.

---

[1] See Desmond Ford, Daniel (Nashville: Southern Publishing Association, 1978), 300-305 and William H. Shea, Selected Studies on Prophetic Interpretation, Revised edition, DARCOM, 7 vols. (Silver Spring, MD: Biblical Research Institute, 1992), 1:67-104.

3) In Daniel 7 the four beasts which together account for a reign of at least one thousand years are followed by the little horn power. It is the focus of the vision since it is most directly in opposition to God. Three and a half literal years for the struggle between the little horn and the Most High are out of proportion to the comprehensive scope of salvation history portrayed in this vision. The same applies to Revelation 12:6 and 14 where the one thousand and two hundred and sixty prophetic days or three and a half times cover most of the history between the First and Second Advents

4) According to the context, the expressions "time, times, and half a time" (Dan 7:25; 12:7; Rev 12:14), "forty-two months" (Rev 11:2; 13:5), and "one thousand two hundred and sixty days" (Rev 11:3; 12:6) all apply to the same time period, but the natural expression "three years and six months" is not used once.

The Holy Spirit seems, in a manner, to exhaust all the phrases by which the interval could be expressed, excluding always that one form which would be used of course in ordinary writing, and is used invariably in Scripture on other occasions, to denote the literal period. This variation is most significant if we accept the year-day system, but quite inexplicable on the other view[2]

5) The prophecies in Daniel 7-8, and 10-12 lead up to the "time of the end" (8:17; 11:35, 40; 12:4, 9) which is followed by the resurrection (12:2) and the setting up of God's everlasting kingdom (7:27). Literal time periods of a few years are not capable of reaching anywhere near the time of the end. Therefore, these prophetic time periods should be seen as symbolic, standing for long periods of actual time

6) In Numbers 14:34 and Ezekiel 4:6 God deliberately used the day for a year principle as a teaching device.

7) In Dan 9:24-27 the 70-week time prophecy met its fulfillment at the exact time, if we use the year-day principle to interpret it. Many interpreters, who in other apocalyptic texts do not use the year-day principle, recognize that the 70 weeks are in fact "weeks of years" reaching from the Persian period to the time of Christ. Thus the pragmatic test in Daniel 9 confirms the validity of the year-day principle.

The historicist method of interpretation is used by the angel in Daniel 7 and 8, explaining the various beast symbols as representing a sequence of political powers in history. Hence, it rests on a solid biblical and historical foundation; and in spite of what some may claim, it is not an outdated method belonging to the past but a valid principle of interpreting apocalyptic prophecies today. Heidi Heiks has put together an impressive array of historical material. One may disagree with his comments and

---

[2] T.R. Birks, *The Two Later Visions of Daniel: Historically Explained* (London: Seeley, Burnside, and Seeley, 1846), 352.

interpretations of the sources, but one can hardly argue with the historical material itself. Students of prophetic history will find an abundance of information to facilitate the interpretation of the apocalyptic prophecies of Daniel and Revelation.

Gerhard Pfandl Ph.D.

Associate Director: Biblical Research Institute
General Conference of Seventh-day Adventists

* * * * * * *

PREFACE

"In the great final conflict, Satan will employ the same policy, manifest the same spirit, and work for the same end as in all preceding ages. That which has been, will be, except that the coming struggle will be marked with a terrible intensity such as the world has never witnessed. Satan's deceptions will be more subtle, his assaults more determined."[3]

Inspiration has informed us that the same cause will produce the same effect except that the coming struggle will be marked with a terrible intensity such as the world has never witnessed. For the Christian, then, the following history should take on a whole new meaning as we brace for the coming crisis and a better understanding of the steps to be taken for the resurrection of the beast:

"For six thousand years that mastermind that once was highest among the angels of God has been wholly bent to the work of deception and ruin. And all the depths of satanic skill and subtlety acquired, all the cruelty developed, during these struggles of the ages, will be brought to bear against God's people in the final conflict. And in this time of peril the followers of Christ are to bear to the world the warning of the Lord's second advent; and a people are to be prepared to stand before Him at His coming, "without spot, and blameless." 2 Peter 3:14. At this time the special endowment of divine grace and power is not less needful to the church than in apostolic days."[4]

It should be of the utmost interest to all Christians to see how the beast power came to be, for in so doing we will better understand the process through which she will accomplish her resurrec-

---

[3]   Ellen White, *The Great Controversy*, (Nampa, ID: Pacific Press, 1911), xi.

[4]   Ibid., x

xiii

tion and the wiles we must shun in order to escape her snares as foretold in Revelation chapter 13 and 17. Let us never forget, then, that the same cause will produce the same effect and that to be forewarned is to be forearmed. History will be repeated. The image to the beast found in Revelation 13:14 will be an exact replica of the beast itself except it will attack with an intensity such as the world has never before witnessed:

> "The founders of the nation [America] wisely sought to guard against the employment of secular power on the part of the church, with its inevitable result—intolerance and persecution."[5]

Professor Bertrand Fauvarque shares how the opening of the believed millennium in the sixth century with the loss of the empire, wars and rumors of war, epidemics, not to mention how the economy was in shambles, brought about fears in the people that the world was coming to an end. Fauvarque thus states:

> "The fall of the Roman Empire in the Occident with its cortege of barbarian invasions, of devastation, and of epidemics were indeed conductive to these fears."[6]

> "We think we are able to put into evidence that Clovis' baptism was devised by the clerks, who organized it as the best antidote possible for the ambient fears. For in their minds, it signified not the end of the world but the entrance into a new millennium, not the end of the Empire."[7]

Taking advantage of the said circumstances of the time, Clovis no doubt used every means to unite the Gallo-Roman society into one for the sole purpose of securing his political agenda. The church was fully united behind Clovis and thereby secured her ecclesiastical agenda, as well. Thus, the people were led to concede to the wishes of the powers that be:

---

[5] Ibid., 442-3.

[6] C'est ce context que nous avons etudie en detail dans la these de Doctorat: Fin de Rome, fin du monde? Levolution des conceptions eschatologiques de la fin de Rome de Marc Aurele a Anastase, ANRT, 1996.

[7] Rouche, Michel, ed. *Clovis, Histoire et Mémoire* (Actes du Colloque international d'historie de Reims), 2 vols. Paris: Univ. of Paris-Sorbonne Press, 1997, 1:271. (Bertrand Fauvarque, Le bapteme de Clovis, ouverture du millenaire des saints, [Clovis' Baptism The beginning of the saint's millennium], 1:271.)

"Through Gemellus, he addressed himself "to all the provincials of the Gauls returned to Roman society, delivered to former freedom. Conduct yourself as citizens worthy of wearing the toga. Reject barbarity and ferocity. *Is there nothing better than living under a regime of the law, to be protected by laws and to have nothing to fear?* The law protects the weak, creates civilization. The barbaric domination, it, is characterized by individual whim" (ibid., III, 17). This anti-Frank diatribe illustrates the tactic of him who took himself to be the emperor of the Occident: to play the card of the pro-Gothic Roman party and to make everyone forget his own Germanic origins. He was the example of integration. . . ."[8]

This assimilation concept that all must be of one accord would most naturally strike down any one person or group of people heralding anything else as being divisive, and they would be accused of disaffection toward the government. This assimilation concept was actually put into law prohibiting certain identities. Thus the stage was set:

"The fines concerning the murder of a Roman or of a Franc were identical, an enormous sum: one hundred to two hundred coins. Therefore, there was no one conquering people, the Franks, imposing its supremacy on the conquered, the Romans. The law was the same for everyone. It sought to establish peace and eradicate violence by transforming the people."[9]

---

[8] Rouche, Michel. Clovis. Fayard, France, 1996, 324.

[9] Ibid., 333.

INTRODUCTION

In this study, I have focused on a Seventh-day Adventist readership ranging from academia to local churches to whom these several topics are not unfamiliar. It is hoped that the information presented will lead to unity among us. The research has been presented before the most versed, scholarly minds of our faith in order to demonstrate that the applications made on the combined basis of historical and prophetic literature will stand the test of investigation. This gathering and compilation of the primary historical sources, with its translation of the Latin, Greek French, German and Italian, will serve Seventh-day Adventism with the needed Biblical integrity she must display to the world as she is commissioned to present the last invitation of mercy to a perishing world. Our Biblical and historical interpretation will provide Seventh-day Adventism with a solid foundation for the four prophetic periods of Daniel, so we may boldly, correctly and without reserve proclaim the Four Angels' messages of Revelation 14:6-12, 18:1-5. Furthermore, we believe all the necessary information has been provided in these three volumes (Vol. 1, *A.D. 508 Source Book*, Vol. 2, *A.D. 538 Source Book*, and Vol. 3, *A.D. 1798 1843 Source Book*) to forever eliminate long-standing error and confusion within Seventh-day Adventism regarding those dates and the prophetic events linked to them. When all doubt is removed, unanimity is attainable. Then, with a unified front, we can present to the world a united message.

"A.D. 508", largely a reference work with commentary citing primary and secondary sources, is designed to meet the need of establishing the commencement of the 1290/1335-day/year prophecy of Daniel 12:11-12. This thesis uses the day-for-a-year principle for interpreting prophecy which is supported by Ezekiel 4:6 and Numbers 14:34. Due to space limitations and a bibliography of over one hundred pages, I must refer the reader to my website at www.the sourcehh.org to view the sources used for these three volumes. One will there find all the sources listed in PDF format under their appropriate designated year in alphabetical order along with translated papal letters of the 5th and 6th century, primary documents, books, maps, articles and so much more. However, the reader will find in the footnotes of this book a most thorough description of the source cited, as well. All emphasis is mine. Scripture references are taken from the King James Version of the Bible.

Roman Christianity in the first three centuries was far different from Roman Catholic Christianity of the fourth century and onward. This change occurred after the state recognized Christianity for the first time under the reign of Constantine the Great and Pope Sylvester I. Roman Christianity was established on the Biblical New Testament principle of complete religious liberty:

> "Though the Apostles were deeply imbued with the conviction that they must transmit the deposit of the Faith to posterity undefiled, and that any teaching at variance with their own, even if proclaimed by an angel of Heaven, would be a culpable offense, yet St. Paul did not, in the case of the heretics Alexander and Hymeneus, go back to the Old Covenant penalties of death or scourging (Deut., xiii, 6 sqq.; xvii, 1 sqq.), but deemed exclusion from the communion of the Church sufficient (1 Tim., i, 20; Tit., iii, 10). In fact to the Christians of the first three centuries it could scarcely have occurred to assume any other attitude towards those who erred in matters of faith. Terullian (*Ad. Scapulam*, c. ii) lays down the rule:
>
> Humani iuris et naturalis potestatis, unicuique quod putaverit colere, nec alii obest aut prodest alterius religio. Sed nec religionis est religionem colere, quae sponte suscipi debeat, non vi.
>
> In other words, he tells us that the natural law authorized man to follow only the voice of individual conscience in the practice of religion, since the acceptance of religion was a matter of free will, not of compulsion. Replying to the accusation of Celsus, based on the Old Testament, that the Christians persecuted dissidents with death, burning, and torture, Origen (C. Cels., VII, 26) is satisfied with explaining that one must distinguish between the law which the Jews received from Moses and that given to the Christians by Jesus; the former was binding on the Jews, the latter on the Christians. Jewish Christians, if sincere, could no longer conform to all of the Mosaic law; hence they were no longer at liberty to kill their enemies or to burn and stone violators of the Christian Law.
>
> St. Cyprian of Carthage, surrounded as he was by countless schismatics and undutiful Christians, also put aside the material sanction of the Old Testament, which punished with death rebel-

lion against priesthood and the Judges. "Nunc autem, quia circumcisio spiritalis esse apud fideles servos Dei coepit, spiritali gladio superbi et contumaces necantur, dum de Ecclesia ejiciuntur" (Ep. lxxii, ad Pompon., n. 4)-religion being now spiritual, its sanctions take on the same character, and excommunication replaces the death of the body. Lactantius was yet smarting under the scourge of bloody persecutions, when he wrote his *Divine Institutes* in A.D. 308. Naturally, therefore, he stood for the most absolute freedom of religion. He writes:

Religion being a matter of the will, it cannot be forced on anyone; in this matter it is better to employ words than blows [verbis melius quam verberibus res agenda est]. Of what use is cruelty? What has the rack to do with piety? Surely there is no connection between truth and violence, between justice and cruelty . . . . It is true that nothing is so important as religion, and one must defend it at any cost [summâ vi] . . . It is true that it must be protected, but by dying for it, not by killing others; by long-suffering, not by violence; by faith, not by crime. If you attempt to defend religion with bloodshed and torture, what you do is not defense, but desecration and insult. For nothing is so intrinsically a matter of free will as religion. (*Divine Institutes* V:20)

The Christian teachers of the first three centuries insisted, as was natural for them, on complete religious liberty. . . ."[10]

Roman Catholic Christianity did not really come into focus until after the Edict of Milan (A.D. 313) and the toleration of Galerius and the policy of Constantine and Licinius. After the victorious battle of Chrysopolis, Constantine's holy war against Licinius which established Constantine as the sole ruler of the entire Roman Empire, something occurred that was totally unexpected. Instead of depriving the pagans of their rights, Constantine declared "peace and quiet should be enjoyed by those who err as much as by believers. For this will bring them to the true faith. . . ." Toleration was largely the policy of Constantine (contrary to the teachings of some) and under his rule the Christian church was recognized as such for the first time by the State. It was not until after this event that we were to witness the first union of church and state in the Roman Empire. However, the Catholic religion did not become the official religion of the Roman Empire until the Edict of

---

[10] "Inquisition" *The Catholic Encyclopedia*, (New York, The Encyclopedia Press, Robert Appleton Company, 1910), 8:26-7.

the *Emperors Gratian, Valentinian II and Theodosius I,* establishing Catholicism as the State Religion on February 28, 380.[11]Ever since the church received recognition by the State under Constantine, history has shown that the church has waged a fierce battle for supreme control through the Theodosian law code and the church canons in order to overthrow Pagans, Jews, Arians, Manichaeans, Donatists, Montanists, Priscillianists and any other sect that she considered competition. These were labeled as Heretics in order to drive them out of the empire by exile or death. For Sabbatians [sic] being branded as heretics in the Theodosian law code, as well, see 16.5.59. April 9, 423.[12]

Now with the union of church and state established in the fourth century, the church's spirit of intolerance is revealed for the first time by the mass number of legal Imperial Edicts and Constitutions found in the Theodosian law code and the church canons. Ever since the church removed the plain bloodstained garments of Christ and put on the haunty kingly robes of a monarch, she has demonstrated the utmost contempt for even the mildest infringement upon her authority:

> "53. The same Augustuses to Felix, Prefect of the City.
>
> The complaint of the bishops deplores the fact that Jovinianus holds sacrilegious meetings outside the walls of the most sacred City. Therefore, We command that the aforesaid person shall be arrested and beaten with leaden whips and that he shall be forced into exile along with the remaining adherents and ministers. He himself, as the instigator, shall be transported with all haste to the island of Boa; the rest, as seems best, provided only that the band of superstitious conspirators shall be dissolved by the separation of exile, shall be deported for life to solitary islands situated at a great distance from each other. Moreover, if any person with obstinate depravity should repeat such forbidden and condemned acts, he shall know that he will incur a more severe sentence."[13]
>
> *Given on the day before the nones of March at Milan in the year of the ninth consulship of Honorius Augustus and the fifth consulship of Theodosius Augustus. AD 412, March 6; AD 398.*

---

[11] Original Latin text in Mommsen, *Theodosiani libri XVI,* vol. 1-2, "De fide catholica," p. 833.

[12] Pharr, Clyde, trans. *The Theodosian Code and Novels and the Sirmondian Constitutions.* Union, NJ: Lawbook Exchange, 2001, 461.

[13] Ibid., 16.5.53. 459-460

This is only one of the many edicts. That others were far more severe against Heretics and may be witnessed from *The Theodosian Law Code* of the fourth and fifth centuries. The same spirit of intolerance was also demonstrated to be the case with the legal backing of the so-called one and only true faith:

"The Pontificy of Leo the Great also showed how helpful the imperial legislation, finally supported on the old Roman *ius publicum*, was for the fortification of the papal thought of the primacy. According to the view of the Emperor Valentine III., the support of the Roman church lay very publicly in the interest of *res Romana*, whose care belonged to him. The means to the exercise of this care lay ready in the public law. With the help of the Roman church he could effectively confront the Arianist risk in the German-occupied or threatened areas.

Two imperial edicts deserved observation. Both are similarly the protection of the Roman-church unity in they are of the western leadership. The *ratio legis* of both edicts,—even though laid on completely different levels-concerned the protection of the interests, which were necessary for the inner peace. Both edicts flowed out from the imperial charge of care, whose reference point, the *res Romana*, had freely fundamentally altered itself: it was no longer a religious element that held the structure of the *res Romana* together. With that, the ecclesiastic standpoint found entrance in constitutional law. It is the equation or "coincidence" of Roman law and Christian law that made the imperial legislation of Valentine III. understandable. The support and protection of the *res Romana* by the Emperor was concurrent with the support and protection of the *ecclesia Romana* and, according to contemporary view, Christianity in general."[14]

The Edict of the Emperors Valentinian III and Theodosius II which recognized the Pope as head of the Western Church in 445 is just another such example.[15]

"Of very special interest, however, is the view of the Pope

---

[14] About that, consider also W. ESSLIN: *Valentinianus III.* 2243 f. A. MANDOUZE: *Die Kirche* 207 throws out, that both were "bound insolubly for better or for worse": Roman law and Christian law were conflated in other words." Ullman, Walter von. *Päpste und Papsttum [Popes and Papacy]: Gelasius I. (492–496).* Bd. 18. Stuttgart: Anton Hiersemann, 1981, 62.

[15] Original Latin text in Migne, *Patrologia Latina*, vol. LIV, col. 636.

reigning in this time, *Leo the Great*, on the relation of state and church.[16]That the Caesar should have the right and the duty to take care of ecclesiastical affairs, and in particular to protect pure doctrine, fight splits within the church, and take steps against false doctrines and their followers, was, for Leo, self-understood. He explicitly challenged the Caesars not seldom to proceed against heretics, he *wanted* them to be prosecuted with secular means of power, and in particular that they be banished. In the question whether the *death-penalty* should be applied in the case of heretics, Leo did not take a consistent position. On the one hand he *approved* of it that Priscillian had been executed earlier as a heretic,[17] but on the other he expressed the desire that the Caesar *not* apply the death-penalty in his sallies against religious unrest in Palestine.[18] Leo, however, obviously did *not* imagine things as though the secular power was simply the executive organ of the church in the sense that the Caesar was only allowed to interfere in ecclesiastical matters according to the directions of the church. According to the writings of the Pope there can hardly be any doubt that he recognized an *independent* right of the Caesar to interfere in the ecclesiastical area. For him the Caesar is the *"protector of the faith,"* who unites Caesarian power and priestly zeal in his person,[19] he is to be counted amongst the *preachers of Christ*, his power is not transferred to him merely for reign over the world but foremost for the protection of the church. His care for the church is inspired by God's spirit [*Gottes Geist*], God has selected him as protector of the Catholic faith, he is filled with priestly spirit. However many of such phrases must be attributed to the account of the normal flattering and devoted tone with regard to the Caesar, the actual viewpoint of the Pope will have been the result in the view that the ruling-rights of the Caesar reached beyond the wordly and covered even the *religious-ecclesiastical*, that he possesses an *independent* right conferred on him by *God* to take active part for the good of the church and the protection of the pure faith."[20]

---

[16] Cf. here *Kissling*, Sacerdotium and Imperium p. 16 ff.

[17] To be precise, Priscillian was not judged because of heresy but because of magics (maleficium).

[18] Leonis magni epist. 15 and 118, *p. et H. Ballerini*, Sancti Leonis Magni Rom. Pontif. Opera T I (1753) p. 696 and 1211, Migne p. l. 54, 679 ff. and 1040.

[19] Epist. 115 c. 1, 135 c. 1, Ballerini I p. 1201 and 1277, Migne p. l. 54, 1031 ff. and 1097.

[20] Voigt, Karl. *Staat Und Kirche Von Konstantin Dem Grossen Bis Zum Ende Der Karolingerzeit. [State and Church from Constantine the Great to the End of the*

While it is not our intent here to disclose the vast amount of civil/ ecclesiastical legislation during the era of A.D. 100-475, this may be viewed on my website, www.thesourcehh.org. The purpose here is simply to establish the existence, work, and character of the Church of Rome, "the little horn," as specified in the book of Daniel prior to the prophetic role she was to fulfill after the demise of the Western Roman Empire in A.D. 476. When one considers the description, reign and character of the "little horn" in the book of Daniel, the careful student of prophecy quickly notices that the Bible does not deny the existence of the "little horn" prior to A.D. 476. In fact, Paul tells us in 2 Thessalonians 2 that the "mystery of iniquity" was already at work in his own day, but counseled the brethren at that time that his appearing was yet to be in the future. John, however, narrows that appearing to a specified event:

> Revelation 17:3 "So he carried me away in the spirit into the wilderness: and I saw a woman sit upon a scarlet coloured beast. . . ."

A woman in prophecy denotes a church. Revelation 12:1-6 signifies the true church of Christ while Revelation 17:3 pictures the church of Satan, the apostate church, sitting upon a scarlet colored beast or political power, as Daniel 7:17 confirms. This is another Biblical description of the union of church and state. Three times in Revelation chapter 17 we are told that this beast power is to have a resurrection after it receives a deadly wound and that this resurrection cannot and will not take place until there is a union of church and state. In fact, the Bible does not even recognize the first beast prior to her deadly wound until there has been this union of church and state. We have documented that the first appearing of this beast power or oppressive union of church and state transpired in the fourth century. This beast power is said to be diverse from all the others (Daniel 7:24) in that it is a political-religious entity. However, the prophecy takes us beyond the fourth century and focuses our attention on the "little horn" after the fall of the Western Roman Empire in A.D. 476 because the ten horns (kingdoms, Daniel 7:8, 20, 24) do not and cannot come on the stage of action until the demise of the Western Roman Empire. That did not officially take place until Augustulus, Emperor of the West, was forced by Odoacer to a formal resignation before the Senate, and

---

Carolingian Period]. New printing of Stuttgart ed., 1936. Aalen, Scientia Verlag, 1965, 76-77

the Senate to the declaration that the Western Empire was extinct. The year was A.D. 476. Some just-come-lately historians are trying to suggest this demise of the Western Roman Empire really never happened and certain text books are trying to change history in order to deceive. This is being done because the enemies of Biblical truth know that A.D. 476 is a Biblical cornerstone that has been set for the appearing of the ten horns. This, in turn, pinpoints the era for the commencement of these prophetic periods and provides the required time span of the "little horn" to meet all those Biblical specifications. This means that the Antichrist of Daniel and Revelation and all its prophetic issues does not come into focus until sometime after A.D. 476 when the new world and new law codes were to be introduced. This would be followed by a union of church and state, (Daniel 2:40-45; 7:8, 20, 24-28) a world of multiple nations, some strong as "iron" and others pictured as "weak." These multiple nations would exist as such until the second coming of Jesus Christ.[21]

The three uprooted horns (kingdoms) in Daniel 7:8, 20, 24 have no direct bearing on the 1290/1335-day/year prophecy of Daniel 12:11-12 because the original Hebrew of those verses does not demand the plucking up of the three horns as necessary before the 1290/1335-day/year prophecy can begin. We will be fully

---

[21] Joseph MCcabe was born in 1867 and became a Franciscan monk at the age of nineteen. Gifted with the ability of the original languages and highly educated but disgusted with his fellow monks and the deceptions of Christianity and her doctrines,, he left the priesthood for good on February 19, 1896. His experience with Catholicism left him bitter against Christianity and rendered him an infidel but his exposing of Catholicism has proven to be honest and accurate when he analyzes and translates from the primary sources. On those grounds I highly recommend the reader to visit my website at www.thesourcehh.org and read the three short articles I compiled in one PDF file I named, *J. MCcabe X3*, about the true nature, rise, and history of the papacy during the first six centuries that has been so whitewashed by Roman sympathizers. Remember, deception is the watchword when analyzing church history.

[1.] McCabe, Joseph, *The Truth About the Catholic Church*, (Girard, Kansas, Haldeman-Julius Company, 1926), 7-16, (Big Blue Book, No. B-27), chapters 1-2.

[2.] McCabe, Joseph, *St. Augustine and His Age*, (New York, G. P. Putnam's Sons, 1902). 431-435, 456-460.

[3.] The Contemporary Review, *St. Augustine and the Roman Claims*, Joseph MCcabe, (London, Horace Marshall & Son, Temple House, Temple Avenue, and 125 Fleet Street, E.C; Volume 82. July-December, 1902), 685-695.

documenting and confirming this claim from the scriptures as well as addressing all the issues related to the three uprooted horns and the emerging ten horns into the new world. These horns are generally addressed under the 1260-day/year prophecy and will be discussed fully in my *A.D. 538 Source Book.*

In discussing Clovis, King of the Franks, we know absolutely nothing of his civil administration; however, his ecclesiastical policies are illuminating. It is inevitable that his baptism would be a topic that merits extensive dialogue, especially as it does among European historians. Over the years, I have combed through an extensive number of European books, journals, and articles on Clovis and on his baptism and have translated hundreds of pages on this topic with an open mind and have weighed the arguments for and against the year of 496 declared by Gregory of Tours to have been the year of the baptism of Clovis. Other dates frequently suggested for the baptism of Clovis have been 498, 499, 506, 507, and 508. Disputes of whether this baptism took place in Tours or Reims have had nearly an equal amount of dialogue. Reims receives the most support and has mine, as well. But why is there a dispute over the date of 496 by Gregory of Tours, the authority on Clovis?

"It was early recognized[22] that as far as these questions are concerned, the Ps.-Fredegar (line 642) and the *Hist. gentis Franc.* (line 727) draw from Gregory of Tours, *HF.*, II, 29-31 (line 575). In providing the elements of a chronology of the life and works of Boethius, Cassiodorus and Ennodius, the philologist H. Usener remarked as early as 1877 that the letter Cassiodorus, *Var.* II, 41, which Theodoric the Great (the Ostrogothic king, master of Italy) addressed to Clovis about his victory against the Alamanni, dates from before 501. At that time, the baptism of the Frankish king was fixed in 496 based on Gregory; for this date seemed to be confirmed by the letter of congratulation from Pope Anastasius (Nov. 24, 496-Nov. 17, 498), and the connection between the

---

[22] However God. KURTH, *Et. crit. sur le "Gesta regum Franc."* [Critical Study of the "Gesta regum Franc"], BULLETIN ACAD. DE BELGIQUE, 3rd series, v. XXIII (1889), p. 261-291 and *L'histoire de Clovis d'après Frédégaire* [The History of Clovis According to Fredegar], REVUE DES QUESTIONS HISTORIQUES, v. 47 (1890), p. 60-100, still had to defend the superiority of the *H. F.* over these two sources, to which, for the history of Clovis, even a Leopold von RANKE, *Weltgesch.*, v. IV, 2 (1883), p. 350 ss. continued to give preference. –On the current state of discussions, cf. S. HELLMANN, *Das Fredegarproblem*, HIST. VIERTELJAHRSCHR., v. 39 (1934), p. 36-92.

battle and the conversion by the letter of congratulation from the metropolite of Burgundy, Avit (*solutus adhuc nuper populus captivus*, would refer to the Alamanni)."[23]

Since 1877, criticisms have increased and the cracks in the chronology by Gregory of Tours on Clovis have since widened to craters. Dialogue among European historians regarding the inconsistencies of Gregory of Tours raged in the 1930's and 40's as the works of Van de Vyver[24] and others reveal to the present day. As recognized then as well as now, it has been shown and so stated that Gregory of Tours has, indeed, lied to us:

> "The father of French history, whatever his intentions, became for Halphen the father of lies. . ."[25]

This statement was considered by some as a mortal sin, for this was a man who was held by some to be infallible and these treated his writings as if they were the Bible. The facts support the claims of those honest historians, so the integrity of Gregory of Tours falls by the wayside. Those who still wish to cling to the traditional view of 496 after viewing the facts against it do so with the aid of the straw man. What then is the accepted year for Clovis's baptism? The best scholarly and uncontested work on this topic today is the work found in the following journal: "Early Medieval Europe, 1998, Volume 7, Issue 1, Pages 29–57 by Blackwell Publishers, by, Danuta Shanzer, titled, *"Dating the baptism of Clovis: the bishop of Vienne vs the bishop of Tours."*

I spoke with Danuta Shanzer early in 2008 and she confirmed that since Blackwell Publishers published her 29-page article in 1998 that no one has contested or yet proven her dating of the baptism of Clovis on Christmas Day of A.D. 508 to be in error.

---

[23] Van de Vyver, Andre. "L'unique victoire contre les Amalans et la Conversion de Clovis en 506" [The single victory against the Alamanni and the conversion of Clovis in 506]. Pts. 1–3. *Revue Belge de Philologie et D'Histoire* [*Belgian Review of Philology and History*] (1936): 859–860.

[24] van de Vyver, Andre. "L'unique victoire contre les Amalans et la Conversion de Clovis en 506" [The single victory against the Alamanni and the conversion of Clovis in 506]. Pts. 1–3. *Revue Belge de Philologie et D'Histoire* [*Belgian Review of Philology and History*] (1936): 859–914; 16, nos. 1–2, (January–June 1938): 35–94; 17, nos. 3–4 (July–December 1938): 793–814.

[25] Halphen, 'Gregoire de Tours', pp. 243-4. Quoted by, Danuta Shanzer, *Dating the baptism of Clovis: the bishop of Vienne vs the bishop of Tours*, 29.

This evidence is so overwhelming that even the 2008 Encyclopedia Britannica has cited her work, as well as that of others, and supports the 508 date for the baptism of Clovis:

"According to Avitus, it is also likely that Clovis was baptized rather late in life, possibly at Christmas in 508, only three years before his death."[26]**Appendix**[27]

"The feasts of the temporal cycle can be divided into two groups: those which refer to Christmas and are fixed in the Roman calendar, and those which refer to Easter whose date must be computed separately for each year, according to the lunar calendar."[28] Since most of the Merovingian sacramentaries fix the beginning of the year on the 25th of December, *Missale Gothicum* 3; *Missale Gallicanum Vetus* 7; *Gelasianum* I;1. This will be my starting point as well. [62] NATIVITAS/NATALIS (Christmas): The feast commemorating the birth of Christ was celebrated on the 25th December by a vigil and mass,[29] and it was one of the three most important feast mentioned by the Church councils and Caesarius of Arles.[30]

Professor Danuta Shanzer's full article titled *"Dating the baptism of Clovis: the bishop of Vienne vs the bishop of Tours"* is <u>highly recommended</u> and may be purchased from Blackwell Publishers, UK at: http://www3.interscience.wiley.com/journal/119131132/issue **Appendix**[31]

For those who do not read the original languages, see Alex-

---

[26] "Clovis I" *Encyclopedia Britannica*. Ultimate Reference Suite. Chicago: Encyclopedia Britannica, 2008.

[27] For an English translation of the letter by Bishop Alcimus Ecdicius Avitus of which is the only contemporary document that speaks of the baptism of Clovis see **APPENDIX I**, pg. 111.

[28] The point of departure was the Jewish Passover which was celebrated on the night between the 14 and the 15 of the first lunar month (Nisan). On the computation of the days see: C.Vogel, *Medieval Liturgy*, pp. 305-8; T.J. Talley, *The Origins of the Liturgical Year* (New York, 1986), pp. 1-70; A.Adam, *The Liturgical Year*, tr., J.O'Connell, (New York, 1981).

[29] Caesarius, *Sermon* 190; *VSM* II:25; *GM* 86; *VP* 8:11.

[30] "For the Christmas masses see: *Missale Gothicum* 3-4; *Missale Gallicanum Vetus* 9-11; *Gelasianum* I: 1-4; *Luxeuil* 7-8; *Bobbio* 64-79." Hen, Yitzhak. *Culture and Religion in Merovingian Gaul A.D. 481–751*. Leiden: E. J. Brill, 1995, 61-62.

[31] For concluding remarks of Professor Danuta Shanzer's article see **APPENDIX II**, pg. 114.

ander Murray, ed., trans. *From Roman to Merovingian Gaul*. Peterborough, Ontario: Broadview Press, 2000, for an excellent source on the history of Gaul and an English translation of many letters and primary sources, including those on Clovis.

Regarding the conversion of Clovis to Catholicism in 508 by other credible sources, we submit the following:

"In agreement with events reported by Gregory and by Nicetius, and in agreement with the arguments in explanation of Gregory's suppression of important historical facts, it is now submitted that:

(a) After Clovis' campaign against the Visigoths, which with its reduction of Tours came to an end in 508, he proceeded to Tours where he communicated to Clotilde [his wife] his decision to join the Orthodox Church [Catholic];

(b) From Tours, the queen (not the king) secretly sent for St. Remi to settle matters arising out of the king's decision—more especially the need of the king's preparation;

(c) After secret meetings with St. Remi, Clovis on November 11th made public his decision to undergo baptism. The decision was announced by a vow made over St. Martin's tomb in St. Martin's church on the day of the Feast of St. Martin. It is on this occasion that Clovis offered his generous gift of treasure to St. Martin's church;

(d) At Christmas of the same year (508) Clovis went to St. Martin's church solemnly to signify his acceptance and to don the costume of the Imperial honour conferred upon him by the Emperor of Byzantium.

(e) Still clothed in his Imperial robes of office he proceeded from the Church of St. Martin to the cathedral there to be baptized;

(f) He subsequently left Tours for Paris which he had chosen thenceforth to be his royal capital."[32]

---

[32] Francis Oppenheimer, *Frankish Themes and Problems* (London: Faber and Faber, 1952), 62.

"In order to disprove the 508 dating it would be necessary to find another context which fitted all the contemporary evidence more clearly."[33]

"This premise stands securely to this day."[34]

It all began in 1877 when the philologist H. Usener began to unmask some of the discrepancies of Gregory of Tours. Ironically, it was another philologist, Danuta Shanzer, who has supplied us with the best scholarship thus far for dating the baptism of Clovis on December 25, 508.

Having said all this however, the baptism of Clovis is not one of the specifications of identification of this prophecy. Interrelated perhaps, but baptism does not "set up" or establish either political or religious entities. That union foretold in Daniel 11:31 and 12:11 was cemented by civil and ecclesiastical legislation which we shall shortly establish.

My previous book entitled *508 538 1798 1843 Source Book (Preliminary)* revealed that the central issue which took preeminence after the demise of the Western Roman Empire in A.D. 476 was indeed a religious war that was to decide whether the Catholic or Arian creed would be followed in Western and Eastern Europe. Under the Theodosian Law code and church cannons of the fourth and fifth century, the Catholic Church was successful in eliminating the threat of paganism. The Jewish threat was largely removed, as well, and the precedent was set for future generations. The roots of Jewish anti-Semitism originated with the church and this ongoing tirade of legal enactments, church cannons and published propaganda did not cease its baleful work until the seeds sown reaped their natural outcome in Nazi Germany. However, the greatest threat to the Catholic Church after the demise of the Western Roman Empire according to Saint Caesarius of Arles was the threat of Arianism. With Clovis coming into power and ascending to the Catholic faith, Theodore the Great, the Arian King of the West, decreed between the years 507-511 a most remarkable decree. This decree was honored by the Arians but was diametrically opposed to the principles and government of the Catholic Church:

---

[33] Ian N. Wood, *Revue Belge de Philologie Et D'Histoire* (Brussels: n.p., 1985), 63:271. To date, no one has countered the evidence he set forth in that article as well.

[34] For another scholarly source for the baptismal date of 508, see Weiss, Rolf. *Chlodwigs Taufe* [Baptism]: *Reims 508*. Bern: Verlag Herbert Lang, 1971.

".... We cannot order a religion, because no one is forced to believe against his will."[35]

While the Arian Christians of the West and East were not at all free from some entanglements of church and state as we know and understand today, nevertheless, they never crossed the red line by resorting to force in religious matters against the will of an individual whether he be of the Arian or Catholic faith. This could hardly be said of the Catholic Church. It is here, in the issue of *religious liberty*, that the war between two completely different ideologies materializes. This has been the best kept secret of the Dark Ages. Theodore Mommsen dates Theodore the Great's Book II, 27, law code between 507–511, and no one disputes the dating of his letters of Cassiodorus. The central players in this controversy were the Catholic Church, the Catholic King Clovis, King of the Franks (French), the Visigoths, and Theodoric the Great, the Arian Christian King of the Ostrogoths. By contrasting the two ideologies and the characters of each warring faction through their civil/ecclesiastical laws and theological understandings, the reader will finally have the facts from the primary sources to see what actually happened and the process that led up to the commencement or the "setting up" of the 1290/1335-day/year prophecies that began concurrently in A.D. 508. This "setting up" process will reveal to the reader the steps taken by the Papacy as she was aiming to re-establish her authority in the new world. Clovis, King of the Franks (France), the first king of the ten symbolic horns in the new world to incorporate the principles or government of popery through legislation, ushers in the forbidden union of church and state. The denial of religious liberty was now in place, legislating the so-called "one and true Catholic faith" and thereby setting up Catholic principles. This Pontifical government that denies freedom of conscience in religious matters is in sharp contrast to the Arians who rejected that concept. These considerations, as well as the removal of the "tamid" or the "daily," will be of the primary concerns addressed, and we will fully document that they fulfill the exact specifications of the prophecy.

It must be kept in mind, however, that 508 was only the "setting up" of the papal government in the new world. The principles brought about from this union of church and state in the new world were yet to be more forcefully defined and contrasted against the Arian faith's central ideology of *religious liberty*, (albeit in its primi-

---

[35] Cassiodorus, Magnus Aurelius, Hodgkin, Thomas, *The Letters of Cassiodorus*. London: Henry Frowde, 1886, Book II, 27.

tive state). As will be shown, ever since the battle of Vougle in 508 when Clovis fought as a Catholic defeating Alaric II, the King of the Visigoths, the true characters of these two ideologies have been fully revealed. This warfare over religious liberty was to come to its climax in one of the biggest battles of the history of the dark ages in the year of A.D. 538. This foundational premise of religious liberty, one of the main *keys* that unlock our understanding in rightly interpreting the four prophetic periods of Daniel in relationship to the government of God verses the government of Satan, will be presented in our *A.D. 538 Source Book* when the Pontifical government will be shown to have come into full confrontation with the government of God. The new world was to learn what the purposes of Rome really were only when it would be too late to escape her snare.

I am forever indebted to Darcie Litton, my copy editor, for all her endless hours of critique and constructive criticism which gave this work its final veracity.

Special gratitude to Gerhard Pfandl Ph.D., Associate Director of the Biblical Research Institute of the General Conference of Seventh-day Adventists, for his critique and valuable suggestions.

I also want to thank Rabbi Doshia Parrott, an excellent teacher and friend, for the innumerable hours of instruction in Biblical Hebrew.

I humbly confess that without the aid of the Holy Spirit and the direct working of my guardian angel this massive project would have never been completed. I could spend hours giving an account of heaven's direct intervention throughout these past six years during which I gained a living experience that will stay with me for the rest of my life. It is, therefore, my hope and sincere prayer that the information provided will be a confirmation and fortification for all in the coming crisis.

Heidi Heiks, former international Christian editor, college educator, and speaker for *The People of the Book* radio program, has written numerous articles and books.

Heidi Heiks
✳✳✳✳✳✳✳

The Rise of the Antichrist

Our study will begin with an exposition that will address each and every specification of the scriptures that introduces and centers on the commencement of the A.D. 508 prophetic period. This study will fully justify the validity of the 508 date under inquiry, proving it to be trustworthy and true. Therefore, we must diagnose carefully the given specifications and clauses of the prophetic time period emerging after A.D. 476 that are related to the "little horn" in the book of Daniel. In doing so, we must contend with the given text of the Bible that directly introduces our topic. Our first work is to identify and interpret aright each clause of the following scriptures directly related to A.D. 508:

Daniel 8:11 "Yea, he magnified[1431] *himself* even to[5704] the prince[8269] of the host,[6635] and by[4480] him the daily[8548] *sacrifice* was taken away,[7311] and the place[4349] of his sanctuary[4720] was cast down."[7993]

Daniel 8:12 "And a host[6635] was given[5414] *him* against[5921] the daily[8548] *sacrifice* by reason of transgression,[6588] and it cast down[7993] the truth[571] to the ground;[776] and it practiced,[6213] and prospered."[6743]

Daniel 11:31 "And arms[2220] shall stand[5975] on his part,[4480] and they shall pollute[2490] the sanctuary[4720] of strength,[4581] and shall take away[5493] the daily[8548] *sacrifice*, and they shall place[5414] the abomination[8251] that maketh desolate."[8074]

Daniel 12:11 "And from the time[4480, 6256] *that* the daily[8548] *sacrifice* shall be taken away,[5493] and the abomination[8251] that maketh desolate[8074] set up,[5414] *there shall be* a thousand[505] two hundred[3967] and ninety[8673] days."[3117]

Daniel 12:12 "Blessed[835] *is* he that waiteth,[2442] and co-meth[5060] to the thousand[505] three[7969] hundred[3967] and five[2568] and thirty[7970] days."[3117]

It is true that prophecy not only separates the sheep from the goats, but it also measures one's true worth; however, it serves yet another purpose:

"And now I have told you before it come to pass, that, when it is come to pass, ye might believe." John 14:29

It serves to strengthen our faith in a God who "declares the end from the beginning and from ancient times the things that are not yet done" (Isaiah 46:9-10). Ellen White takes us yet further behind the scenes into the high intelligences of the heaven with whom we have to do:

"God had a knowledge of the events of the future, even before the creation of the world. He did not make His purposes to fit circumstances, but He allowed matters to develop and work out. He did not work to bring about a certain condition of things, but He knew that such a condition would exist."[1]

If ever we, as a people, need to have our faith strengthened, it most certainly is in this hour of the world's history. We need to become so fortified that we cannot be moved. This can be accomplished only by first identifying each clause of the previously listed scriptures with their intended interpretations clearly revealed. Then we will confirm those interpretations with the primary historical sources. Since humanity cannot change the course of past events (although some have tried), the following illustrated history will most certainly and firmly establish one's personal faith in our historic timelines, but as Seventh-day Adventists it will bring a higher sense of responsibility to our message and confirm the integrity of the Lord's last day prophet in ways that we have never before witnessed. We will now address each clause of the given scripture with the appropriate resources; multiple proofs will be illustrated in a reference format. For the benefit of the reader, we will begin in Daniel 8:8-9 because we want all to see and understand the solid foundation heaven has established for A.D. 508:

---

[1] Nichol, F. D. *The Seventh-day Adventist Bible Commentary*, (Review and Herald Publishing Association, 1978; 2002), 6:1082.

Daniel 8:8–9 reads:

> 8. "Therefore the he goat waxed very great: and when he was strong, the great horn was broken; and for it came up four notable ones toward the four winds of heaven. 9. And out of one of them came forth a little horn, which waxed exceeding great, toward the south, and toward the east, and toward the pleasant land."

From where does the little horn come? Does the antecedent for the pronoun "them" favor "out of the winds" or "out of the horns"? What saith the scriptures? In comparison of scripture, we find the following:

> Matthew 24:31 "And he shall send his angels with a great sound of a trumpet, and they shall gather together his elect from the four winds, from one end of heaven to the other."

> Revelation 7:1 "And after these things I saw four angels standing on the four corners of the earth, holding the four winds of the earth, that the wind should not blow on the earth, nor on the sea, nor on any tree."

As we will see, the little horn comes out of one of the four winds of heaven, which represent the four compass directions. Since there has been confusion on this issue, and since proponents of the Antiochus Epiphanes position largely supply words here to sustain their grossly invalid interpretation, we, therefore, shall let Brother William Shea, MD. Ph.D., writing for the Biblical Research Institute, further address this issue for us:

> "The English translation, 'Out of one of them' . . . obscures and smoothes out the actual Hebrew construction. The sentence actually opens with two prepositional phrases. Translated literally the sentence reads, 'and *from* the one *from them* . . .', etc. The reason why it is important to notice this literal construction is that it provides a precise parallel to the gender of the elements found in the last phrase of v 8. This can best be shown by transposing the first phrase of v 9 to line up beneath the last phrase of v 8 with these elements in parallel columns. Such a procedure presents the following alignment:

	Fem.	Masc.
v8	to the four winds	of the heavens'
	le arba ruhot	hasamayim
	min-ha ahat	mehem
v9	'from the one	from *them*'

"When this procedure is carried out, it can be seen that the gender of the first two elements in v 9 ('one/them') lines up perfectly with the gender of the last two elements at the end of v 8 ('winds/heavens').

"In writing his visions Daniel simply broke up the construct chain at the end of v 8 ('the four winds *of* the heavens') and distributed its two *elements* to two separate prepositional phrases at the beginning of v 9 ('from the one/from them'). This is not poetic parallelism; it is syntactic parallelism in which the gender of the elements in the second statement parallels the gender of the elements in the first, or preceding, statement.

"Thus the antecedent of 'them' in the phrase 'from them' (v 9), is neither 'winds' nor 'horns,' but 'heavens.' Since 'heavens' is masculine by gender and treated as a plural in biblical Hebrew, according to the verbs and adjectives used with it, there is perfect agreement in gender and number with the masculine plural pronoun 'them.' It is not necessary to resort to emendations to bring the text into line with one's preconceptions about where the little horn came from. The feminine 'one' of v 9 refers back to the feminine 'winds' of v 9. The text discloses the origin clearly enough: it came from one of the four winds of the heavens, that is, from one of the directions of the compass.

"From this understanding of the syntax in vs 8-9, it is evident that when the little horn came onto the scene of action, it did not come from the Seleucid horn nor from the other three. In the pictorial vision it is simply seen as coming from one of the compass directions. Thus the syntax of this statement does not support the contention that the little horn developed from the Selucid horn/kingdom."[2]

For further study on verses 8–14 and this issue, see Biblical Research Institute, *Symposium on Daniel*, Vol. 2. We highly recom-

---

[2] William H. Shea, MD, Ph.D., Biblical Research Institute of the General Conference of Seventh–day Adventist, *Selected Studies on Prophetic Interpretation*, 1:42–3, emphasis original.

mend this book for the serious student of prophecy, for the brethren have indeed done a superb job on the book of Daniel, from which we shall glean.

Clearly, then, the "little horn" moves forth from one of the compass directions on a horizontal plane and expands to other such directions. The direction of the compass from which the "little horn" moved forth can only be from the west.

This brings us to another point of confusion. Is the "little horn" represented by heaven as denoting both pagan and papal Rome? Indeed, pagan and papal Rome are counted as one entity in Daniel and Revelation, as others have so recognized. In Daniel 7:8, 20, 24, the little horn (the papacy) is represented as coming out of the fourth beast (pagan Rome). It is a continuation or part of pagan Rome. In Daniel 8 the little horn power finds its fulfillment only in pagan and papal Rome combined. Heaven counts them as one. In Daniel 11, the king of the north represents both pagan and papal Rome. Both are termed "the king of the north." In Revelation 12:3–4, the dragon power that endeavors to destroy the Christ child was *pagan* Rome. However, verses 13–16 reveal that during the 1260 years, the dragon cast a flood of water out of its mouth to sweep away the woman. This was during the reign of *papal* Rome. Thus, the dragon power of Revelation 12 is also both pagan and papal Rome. This will be important to remember when studying Revelation 17.

All generally recognize that the "little horn" in Daniel 8:9 has two phases, yet is counted as one in the eyes of heaven. In verse 9, we have only a brief introduction in which is described the expansion of *pagan* Rome on a horizontal plane. Her detailed atrocities, including the crucifixion, are recorded in Daniel 9. Remember that in Eastern mindset, effect precedes its cause; in Western mind set, we follow from cause to effect. In other words, Daniel describes in Daniel 7 the ultimate effect: Christ is pictured as King or King of Kings. In Daniel 8 Christ is pictured as Priest. In Daniel 9 Christ is presented as the Messiah. Thus the focus and theme of each chapter is clear.

Daniel 8:10 reads:

> "And it waxed great, even to the host of heaven; and it cast down some of the host and of the stars to the ground, and stamped upon them."

The "host⁶⁶³⁵ of heaven" is the people of God:

> Exodus 12:41 "And it came to pass at the end of the four hun-
> dred and thirty years, even the selfsame day it came to pass, that
> all the hosts⁶⁶³⁵ of the LORD went out from the land of Egypt."

And "the stars" represent the leaders of the host:

> Revelation 1:20 "The mystery of the seven stars which thou
> sawest in my right hand, and the seven golden candlesticks. The
> seven stars are the angels of the seven churches: and the seven
> candlesticks which thou sawest are the seven churches."

In Daniel 8:10, the focus of the warfare of the little horn shifts
to a vertical plane, against heaven. We are introduced to the persecution of the "host" and of the "stars" of "heaven" at the hands of
papal Rome. Those being persecuted are God's people, described
by Philippians 3:20 as having their citizenship in heaven. The interpretation of Daniel 8:10, 12 by the angel interpreter in Daniel
8:24 declares that the power that is to "prosper and practice" is the
same power that "shall destroy the mighty and the holy people" of
God. We will fully document this application after we disclose to
the reader that the power in verse 12 that was to have "practiced
and prospered" is none other than papal Rome. In fact, this vertical plane continues all the way to the end of verse 14.

Believing Daniel 8:10 is largely self-explanatory, we shall move
directly to verse 11, since this is where our subject of the "daily" is
introduced.

Daniel 8:11 reads:

> Daniel 8:11 "Yea, he magnified¹⁴³¹ *himself* even to⁵⁷⁰⁴ the
> prince⁸²⁶⁹ of the host,⁶⁶³⁵ and by⁴⁴⁸⁰ him the daily⁸⁵⁴⁸ *sacrifice* was
> taken away,⁷³¹¹ and the place⁴³⁴⁹ of his sanctuary⁴⁷²⁰ was cast
> down."⁷⁹⁹³

A literal translation reads thus:

> "And he made himself great even to the prince of the host, and
> from him was taken away the continuance, and the foundation of
> his sanctuary was thrown down."

"Yea, *he*" has been regarded as significant in that the Hebrew in Daniel 8 makes a definite gender change from the feminine "little horn" in verse 9 to the masculine gender "he" in verse 11. However, one should not push this point too far. Scholars have noted that a dual gender in a noun can be seen elsewhere without significance. The context and the angel's interpretation of verses 23–25 will make clear the power being designated after we analyze verses 11-12.

First, though, we want to establish the meaning of several words in Daniel 8:11. We'll begin with the word "magnified"[1431] (*gadal*). Usage: AV—magnify 32, great 26, grow 14, nourish up 7, grow up 6, greater 5, misc 25; 112 verses, 115 hits. In Daniel 8:25, we have the interpretation of verse 11 of the vision by the angel, and it will clearly settle which phase of Rome does the "magnifying":

> Daniel 8:25 "And through his policy also he shall cause craft to prosper in his hand; and he shall magnify himself in his heart, and by peace shall destroy many: he shall also stand up against the Prince of princes; but he shall be broken without hand."

Who is this power that magnifies himself and thinks to stand up against the Prince of princes? The angel declares it will be the power that shall be broken without hand. "Broken without hand" is a clear reference from Daniel to the Second Coming of Christ:

> Daniel 2:44–45 "And in the days of these kings shall the God of heaven set up a kingdom, which shall never be destroyed: and the kingdom shall not be left to other people, but it shall break in pieces and consume all these kingdoms, and it shall stand for ever. Forasmuch as thou sawest that the stone was cut out of the mountain without hands, and that it brake in pieces the iron, the brass, the clay, the silver, and the gold; the great God hath made known to the king what shall come to passhereafter: and the dream is certain, and the interpretation thereof sure."

II Thessalonians 2:8 makes the inescapable connection between Jesus' return and the end of papal Rome:

> "And then shall that Wicked be revealed, whom the Lord shall consume with the spirit of his mouth, and shall destroy with the brightness of his coming."

Ellen White agrees with Paul, but is at odds with William Miller. By quoting 2 Thessalonians 2:7–8, she proclaims that which is to be taken out of the way is the papacy at our Lord's second coming, not paganism:

> "'The mystery of iniquity doth already work; only he who now letteth [hindereth] will let [hinder], until he be taken out of the way. And then shall that Wicked be revealed, whom the Lord shall consume with the spirit of his mouth, and shall destroy with the brightness of his coming.' The prophet Daniel, describing the same power, says, 'He shall speak great words against the Most High, and shall wear out the saints of the Most High, and think to change times and laws.' How strikingly have these prophecies been fulfilled by the Romish Church! . . . The mystery of iniquity, which had already begun to work in Paul's day, will continue its work until it be taken out of the way *at our Lord's second coming.*"[3]

Therefore, the presumptuous power brought to view in verse 11 that is to be "broken without hand" in the interpreting of verse 25 cannot be pagan Rome, for it had ceased to exist many centuries before. The only logical answer to our question regarding the identity of that power is that it is none other than papal Rome. It is papal Rome, continuing until Jesus' Second Advent, which shall be destroyed by Christ, the Rock that is "cut out of the mountain without hands."

Uriah Smith has erroneously applied the crucifixion of Christ by pagan Rome to the following clause[4]:

> Daniel 8:25 "He shall also stand up against the Prince of princes."

However, neither the context nor the antecedent of the "he" in the very next clause supports that application:

> Daniel 8:25 "But he shall be broken without hand."

The "he" that "shall be broken without hand" is the same "he" that "also [stands] up against the Prince of princes." This is fulfilled only in papal Rome.

Continuing our word study in Daniel 8:11, we next investigate

---

[3] Ellen White, *Signs of the Times*, June 12, 1893.
[4] Uriah Smith, *Daniel and the Revelation*, 159.

the meaning of "the Prince[8269] of the host." "Prince" (*sar*) often designates a heavenly being (Daniel 8:11, 25; 10:13, 21; 12:1). The
expression "Prince of the host" is never used to designate a high
priest in the Old Testament. To the contrary, Joshua clearly designates the "Prince of the host of Yahweh":

> Joshua 5:14–15 "And he said, Nay; but as captain of the host
> of the LORD am I now come. And Joshua fell on his face to the
> earth, and did worship, and said unto him, What saith my lord
> unto his servant? And the captain of the LORD'S host said unto
> Joshua, Loose thy shoe from off thy foot; for the place whereon
> thou standest is holy. And Joshua did so."

Further study would show that in Daniel 12:1 Michael is "the
great Prince," and in Jude 9 Michael is identified with Christ. In
other words, the "Prince of the host" is none other than Jesus
Christ.

Regarding "by[4480] him" (*mimmennu*), those who have the KJV
with a marginal reading will notice that the translators recognized
that the word "by" should perhaps be translated "from." Turning to
The Complete Word Study Dictionary, we look for the true meaning
of *mimmennu*:

> "A preposition used to indicate from, out of, away from; more
> than; after, since, immediately; because of, since; so that; without;
> direction as southward, etc. . . Its basic meaning is from, away
> from, out of."[5]

We quote from another credible source:

> "The Hebrew expression *mimmennu* is not to be translated
> 'by him' but 'from him.' Who is the antecedent of 'him'? Gram-
> matically, the nearest and most natural antecedent is 'the Prince
> of the host.' This is supported in the ancient versions."[6]

One day I asked my Hebrew teacher[7] of twenty-six years' teaching experience, "Should the Hebrew word *mimmennu*[4480] be trans-

[5] Warren Baker and Eugene Carpenter, The *Complete Word Study Dictionary: Old Testament*, Chattanooga, Tennessee: AMG Press, 2003, p. 625.
[6] Frank B. Holbrook, Ed; *Symposium on Daniel*, Washington D.C. Biblical Research Institute of Seventh-day Adventist, 2:404.
[7] Rabbi Doshia Parrott.

literated as "by" or "from?" Her immediate response was:

> "*Mimmennu* is never translated 'by;' it is always translated
> 'from.'"

Thus, three authoritative sources speak with one voice. The
text will now read "from him," as a reference to the "Prince of the
host."

Next, we consider the meaning of the "<u>daily</u>"[8548] (*tamid*). Usage: AV- continually 53, continual 26, daily 7, always 6, alway 4,
ever 3, perpetual 2, continual employment 1, evermore 1, never
1; 103 verses, 104 hits. The following study on the "daily" will be
a major abridgement in contrast to my already published book on
this topic. For the most complete and thorough work on this topic
to date which will answer every legitimate and historical objection to the "daily" being the Ministry of Christ with rewards for
evidence contrary to the facts, see my book.[8] Let us now turn to
our first reference to the "daily" in the book of Daniel. It is in this
first usage of the term that we understand its context, theme and
its intended definition.

In the Hebrew of the Old Testament, the "daily" is the *tamid*
(#8548 in *Strong's* or Old Testament lexicons). The context of its
usage gives certain light as to its meaning. The theme and context
in which the "daily" finds its home in the book of Daniel is none
other than that of the sanctuary. As we look at the following texts,
it will become abundantly clear to the reader that the prophets had
one thought in mind and one only: the "daily" was always used
in connection with the ministerial work of the priest in the first
apartment. As will be shown in the following Biblical verses, never
was the "daily" attributed to the work of the priest in the second
apartment or to anything else. In every case, the underlined word,
each one written in the context of the sanctuary, has the very same
reference number "8548" as does the "daily" in Daniel 8:11. Without
question, then, the meaning of the "daily" is synonymous with the
meaning of these words:

> Exodus 29:38 "Now this is that which thou shalt offer upon
> the altar; two lambs of the first year day by day <u>continually</u>."

> Exodus 29:42 "This shall be a <u>continual</u> burnt offering

---

[8] *The "Daily" Source Book*, published by, Teach Services, N.Y. that may be obtained
at www.thesourcehh.org.

throughout your generations at the door of the tabernacle of the congregation before the LORD: where I will meet you, to speak there unto thee."

Exodus 30:8 "And when Aaron lighteth the lamps at even, he shall burn incense upon it, a perpetual incense before the LORD throughout your generations."

Turning now to the book of Hebrews, we find total consistency from the Old Testament prophets to the New:

Hebrews 7:3 "Without father, without mother, without descent, having neither beginning of days, nor end of life; but made like unto the Son of God; abideth a priest continually."

Hebrews 7:27 "Who needeth not daily, as those high priests, to offer up sacrifice, first for his own sins, and then for the people's: for this he did once, when he offered up himself."

Hebrews 9:6 "Now when these things were thus ordained, the priests went always into the first tabernacle, accomplishing the service of God."

Hebrews 10:1 "For the law having a shadow of good things to come, and not the very image of the things, can never with those sacrifices which they offered year by year continually make the comers thereunto perfect."

Hebrews 10:11 "And every priest standeth daily ministering and offering oftentimes the same sacrifices, which can never take away sins."

Here we see perfect harmony between the Old and New Testaments. Let us now inquire if Ellen White is in harmony with the rule of faith:

"After His ascension, our Saviour was to begin His work as our High Priest. Says Paul, 'Christ is not entered into the holy places made with hands, which are the figures of the true; but into heaven itself, now to appear in the presence of God for us.' Hebrews 9:24. As Christ's ministration was to consist of two great divisions, each occupying a period of time and having a distinctive place in the heavenly sanctuary, so the typical ministration consisted of two divisions, the <u>daily</u> and the yearly service, and to each a department of the tabernacle was devoted. As Christ at His ascension appeared in the presence of God to plead His blood in behalf of penitent believers, so the priest in the <u>daily</u> ministration sprinkled the blood of the sacrifice in the holy place in the sinner's behalf."[9]

"The ministration of the earthly sanctuary consisted of two divisions; the priests ministered daily in the holy place, while once a year the high priest performed a special work of atonement in the most holy, for the cleansing of the sanctuary. Day by day the repentant sinner brought his offering to the door of the tabernacle and, placing his hand upon the victim's head, confessed his sins, thus in figure transferring them from himself to the innocent sacrifice. . . . Such was the work that went on, day by day, throughout the year. The sins of Israel were thus transferred to the sanctuary, and a special work became necessary `for their removal."[10]

Once again, we see perfect harmony. Those three harmonious sources clearly demonstrate the following principle, stated variously:

Genesis 41:32 "And for that the dream was doubled unto Pharaoh twice; it is because the thing is established by God. . . ."

1 Corinthians 14:29 "Let the prophets speak two or three, and let the other judge."

2 Corinthians 13:1 "This is the third time I am coming to you. In the mouth of two or three witnesses shall every word be established."

From nowhere in the entire Bible has anyone been able to produce even one text that says the "daily" is paganism—*not one!*—despite rewards offered for such evidence found in my *"Daily" Source Book.* That's because the Bible nowhere endorses that premise. That interpretation is alien to the Bible and the prophets, and so is its doctrine. With no Biblical support, one does not have a Bibli-

---

[9] Ellen White, *Patriarch and Prophets* (Nampa, Idaho: Pacific Press, 1958), 357
[10] Ellen White, *The Great Controversy* (Nampa, Idaho: Pacific Press, 1911), 418.

cal doctrine and should not advocate it as such. And what other authority could be claimed? When the "daily" is used in the context of the sanctuary, it is always the work of the priest in the first apartment of the sanctuary. Never was the "daily" attributed to the work of the priest in the second apartment, or to anything else in that context.

We leave the reader with a well-defined summary of the "daily" by William H. Shea, MD, Ph.D.:

"About 1900 L. R. Conradi, W. C. White, A. G. Daniells and W. W. Prescott developed the "so called new view of the daily" that it represents the heavenly high priestly ministry of Christ. In contrast to the so called old view of the daily by W. Miller that the daily was paganism which was taken out of the way to make room for the rise of the papacy. One of the defendants of the so called old view was S. N. Haskell, he went to Ellen G. White to settle the matter and that was when she told him that God had not given her any light on the daily. The new view of the daily was developed by close attention to the biblical text, especially Dan 8. It is like a three legged stool with three lines of proofs in support of the so called new view and they are:

1. **Lexical.** Word study of tamid shows that it is used about 30 times in connection with the sanctuary in addition to other uses. It is never used of a foreign invader or pagan religion.

2. **Context.** There is a shift in the arena of action in Dan 8 at v. 10 the shift is from earthly conquests—to the east the south and the glorious land, by pagan Rome, to an attack upon heaven. First the stars, persecuted saints, then an attack upon the Prince who is Christ in heaven, then an attack upon "his" sanctuary, the one that belongs to him in heaven, and finally upon the tamid or the daily ministry carried on there. The focus of the climax of Dan 8 is upon the true versus the false sanctuary and the plans of salvation and the climax comes when the judgment makes clear where the true sanctuary and the true plan of salvation was located, in heaven with Christ.

3. **Parallels with Leviticus.** In the earthly sanctuary service there was the daily in the holy place for which tamid is used for various aspects of service, the lamps, the incense and the shewbread. This was followed at the end of the religious year by the

yearly service in the most holy place on the Day of Atonement. This two phase ministry is the type for which the heavenly is the antitype therefore one would expect a day (from the ascension) ministry to be carried on and then at the end of the prophetic time, the 2300 day years, the yearly ministry of judgment would be added to it.

So these three lines of evidence, lexical, context in Dan 8 and type-antitype parallels with Leviticus all show that the interpretation of the "daily" in Daniel 8 is the heavenly high priestly ministry of Christ; it is not in any sense of the word paganism."[11]

"*Sacrifice*," is a supplied word and does not belong in the text.

"Taken away" [7311] (*rum*). Usage: AV—(lift, hold, etc. . .) up 63, exalt 47, high 25, offer 13, give 5, heave 3, extol 3, lofty 3, take 3, tall 3, higher 2, misc 24; 184 verses, 194 hits.

Nevertheless, let us look again, a little closer, at the phrase "take away," *rum*,[7311] as found in Daniel 8:11. When the Hebrew word *rum* is used in the context of the sanctuary, the action of the verb is described as "take away" or "remove." Notice how this is done in the following verses:

Leviticus 2:9 "And the priest shall take[7311] from the meat offering a memorial thereof, and shall burn it upon the altar: it is an offering made by fire, of a sweet savour unto the LORD."

Leviticus 4:8 "And he shall take[7311] off from it all the fat of the bullock for the sin offering; the fat that covereth the inwards, and all the fat that is upon the inwards,"

Leviticus 4:10 "As it was taken[7311] off from the bullock of the sacrifice of peace offerings: and the priest shall burn them upon the altar of the burnt offering."

Leviticus 4:19 "And he shall take[7311] all his fat from him, and burn it upon the altar."

Leviticus 6:10 "And the priest shall put on his linen garment, and his linen breeches shall he put upon his flesh, and take[7311] up [to remove] the ashes which the fire hath consumed with the

---

[11] William H. Shea, MD, Ph.D., Sent to the author in a personal letter.

burnt offering on the altar, and he shall put them beside the altar."

Leviticus 6:15 "And he shall take[7311] of it his handful, of the flour of the meat offering, and of the oil thereof, and all the frankincense which is upon the meat offering, and shall burn it upon the altar for a sweet savour, even the memorial of it, unto the LORD."

This meaning of "take away" or "remove" is especially true of Daniel 8:11, as the action of the verb is universally acknowledged by the following:

"It can have the sense of removing something, abolishing it (Dan. 8:11)."[12]

The research of Brother Gerhard Pfandl Ph.D., Associate Director of the Biblical Research Institute, General Conference of Seventh-day Adventists, will settle the matter most effectively. We quote from his findings about *rum's* meaning:

"Peters . . . argues that in Daniel 8:11 it should also be translated 'lifted up' (see above). However, there is a reason for this exception in Daniel 8:11. The verbal root *rum* in Hiphil/Hophal, the basic meaning of which is "bring aloft, raise up, lift up" (HALOT, 3:1204), takes on a specific meaning in clauses with the preposition *min* (from) and a direct or prepositional object. Proebstle has made a study of the twenty-three passages where *rum* appears with the preposition *min* and direct or prepositional objects (Lev 2:9; 4:8, 10, 19; 6:8; Num 17:2; 18:26, 28, 29, 30, 32; 31:28, 52; 1 Sam 2:8; 1 Kgs 14:7; 16:2; Isa 14:13; 57:14; Ezek 45:1; Ps 75:7; 89:20; 113:7; Dan 8:11; all references are according to the Hebrew Bible) and has come to the following conclusions:

"1. If the object is not personal, i.e., a physical object or part of a (dead) animal, *rum* designates the activity of removing or setting aside something from a larger group of which that object was a part (See Lev 2:9; 4:8, 10, 19; 6:8; Num 17:2; 18:26, 28, 29, 30, 32; 31:28, 52; Isa 14:13; 57:14; Ezek 45:1). To illustrate this point I will quote a few texts:
"Lev 2:9 'the priest shall take [*rum*] from [*min*] the grain of-

---

[12] Warren Baker and Eugene Carpenter, The *Complete Word Study Dictionary: Old Testament* (Chattanooga, Tennessee: AMG Press, 2003), 1042.

fering'

"Num 17:2 'Tell Eleazar . . . to pick up [*rum*] the censers out of [*min*] the blaze'

"Ezek 45:1 'when you divide the land by lot into inheritance, you shall set apart [*rum*] a district for the LORD, a holy section of [*min*] the land'

"2. If the object is a person, the activity of separation or removal expressed by *rum* takes on the additional notion of exaltation. A person is separated from a group to a higher status, usually by God Himself (See 1 Sam 2:8; 1 Kgs 14:7; 16:2; Ps 75:7; 89:20; 113:7).

"1 Sam 2:8 '[God] lifts [*rum*] the beggar from [*min*] the ash heap, To set them among princes'

"Ps 113:7 'I have exalted [*rum*] one chosen from [*min*] the people.'

"In other words, in a cultic context [i.e., in a context of a system of religious worship] *rum* in Hiphil/ Hophal means 'to set aside' or 'to remove,' whereas when the context refers to social status it means 'to exalt.' Parallel expressions to *rum*, e. g., *sur* 'remove' (Lev 4:9, 31, 35; Ezek 21:31; 45:9) and *badal* in Niphal 'separate [oneself]' (Num 8:14; 16:21) provide clear support for the conclusion that *rum* in a cultic context always means 'to set apart, remove.'

"Applying what we have just learned to Daniel 8:11 b we come to the following conclusions:

"1. In Daniel 8:11, in a cultic context, the object is impersonal. The word *rum*, therefore, designates the activity of removing or setting aside the *tamid*.

"2. The preposition *min* indicates from whom the *tamid* is removed. And as indicated above, the person from whom the tamid is removed is the Prince of the Host and not the little horn."[13]

As we continue our word study of Daniel 8:11, we next want to scrutinize the noun "place"[4349] (*makon*) from the clause "the place of his sanctuary was cast down." (An important distinction is that the sanctuary itself was not cast down; rather, the "place" of his sanctuary was cast down.) Usage of "place:" AV- place 14, habitation 2, foundations 1; 17 verses, 17 hits. Those who advocate the paganism view of "place" do nothing more than echo Uriah Smith and endorse his construction of "place's" meaning:

---

[13] Gerhard Pfandl, *Evaluation of "The Mystery of 'The Daily'" by John W. Peters.* July 2005, p. 6–7.

"Pagan Rome was remodeled into papal Rome. 'The place of his sanctuary,' or worship, the city of Rome, was cast down. The seat of government was removed by Constantine to Constantinople, A. D. 330. This same transaction is brought to view in Revelation 13:2, where it is said that the dragon, pagan Rome, gave to the beast, papal Rome, his seat, the city of Rome."[14]

Let us analyze those sentences of Uriah Smith for historical accuracy. Was the pagan city of Rome, which Smith interprets as being the "place of his sanctuary," truly "cast down" in AD 330? No, it was not. Smith based his flawed interpretation on a document known by historians as the *Constitutum Domni Constantini Imperatoris*, "The agreement of the lord Constantine the emperor," or better known as the *Donation of Constantine*, in which Constantine allegedly conferred on the papacy extensive privileges and possessions. However, that specious document is just another forgery in the history of the early and medieval church and is recognized as such by scholars throughout the world. Even the Catholic Church readily admits to this fact:

"This document is without doubt a forgery, fabricated somewhere between the years 750 and 850. As early as the fifteenth century its falsity was known and demonstrated."[15]

But the inaccurate historical foundation of Smith's position does not stop there. Smith and other paganism-view adherents tell us, as previously seen in his excerpt:

"The seat of government was removed by Constantine to Constantinople. . . . This same transaction is brought to view in Revelation 13:2. . . ."

Is it true that the same event is referred to in Revelation 13:2? Turning to Inspiration, we have this quote from Ellen White:

"In the sixth century the papacy had become firmly established. Its seat of power was fixed in the imperial city, and the bishop of Rome was declared to be the head over the entire

[14] Uriah Smith, *Daniel and the Revelation*, 161
[15] "Donation of Constantine," *The Catholic Encyclopedia* (New York: Appleton, 1909), 5:119.

church. Paganism had given place to the papacy. The dragon had given to the beast 'his power, and his seat, and great authority.' Revelation 13:2. And *now began* the 1260 years of papal oppression foretold in the prophecies of Daniel and the Revelation. Daniel 7:25; Revelation 13:5–7."[16]

When did the 1260 years of papal oppression begin? AD 330 or 538? Of course, 538—hence, another error. Smith's first misunderstanding about the *Donation* led to a second one here revealed. A third error will now be exposed.

Uriah Smith and the advocates of paganism tell us that the meaning of the word "place" in Daniel 8:11 is "'the place of his sanctuary' or worship, the city of Rome. . . .'" They claim that in AD 330, Rome was "cast down," thus, they say, indicating the demise of paganism in that year. How was this accomplished, according to them?

> "The seat of government was removed by Constantine to Constantinople, A. D. 330."[17]

While it is true that the capitol was moved to Constantinople, history unanimously reports it was done for political expediency and was not the result of any attempt to undermine or vanquish paganism. Nor did it result in the historical demise of paganism in that year. More importantly, though, Smith's comprehension of the event, based as it is on the forged *Donation of Constantine*, completely misses the true understanding of "place."

So what is the "<u>place</u>"[4349] in Daniel 8:11 that was "cast down"? For clearest light and understanding on the true meaning of the "place"[4349] (*makon*) of his sanctuary," we turn to the scriptures to see what the Bible says:

> 2 Chronicles 6:30 "Then hear thou from heaven thy dwelling <u>place</u>,[4349] and forgive, and render unto every man according unto all his ways, whose heart thou knowest; (for thou only knowest the hearts of the children of men.)"

> 2 Chronicles 6:33 "Then hear thou from the heavens, even from thy dwelling <u>place</u>,[4349] and do according to all that the stranger calleth to thee for; that all people of the earth may know

---

[16] Ellen White, *The Great Controversy* (Nampa, Idaho: Pacific Press, 1911), 54
[17] Uriah Smith, *Daniel and the Revelation*, 161

thy name, and fear thee, as doth thy people Israel, and may know that this house which I have built is called by thy name."

2 Chronicles 6:39 "Then hear thou from the heavens, even from thy dwelling place,[4349] their prayer and their supplications, and maintain their cause, and forgive thy people which have sinned against thee."

We know that "from him the daily *sacrifice* was taken away, and the place of his sanctuary was cast down." We see from these verses that the "place" referred to is where prayers are heard and sins are forgiven, i.e. the heavenly sanctuary. That heavenly "place" has been cast down—removed from men's remembrance—by the same entity that "took away" the "daily" *from* Christ by interposing an earthly counterfeit of His "daily" ministration in the sanctuary. Without question, these scriptures reveal that the little horn has taken on a priestly attire and presumes to perform priestly functions. The horn's plain intention continues to be deflecting men's interest in heaven and God's interaction with humanity by inserting himself between man and his interceding Savior. He imposes himself in the place of Christ. It was not *pagan* Rome but *papal* Rome who dared and dares to attempt to usurp the prerogatives of God who alone can answer prayers and forgive sins. *That* is the significant event paganism proponents miss or dismiss.

To expand upon our Biblical study of "place," as well as for confirmation of our understanding, we ask again, "What is God's dwelling place[4349] (*makon*)?" The answer comes:

Psalm 89:14 "Justice and judgment are the habitation[4349] (*makon*) of thy throne: mercy and truth shall go before thy face."

Psalm 97:2 "Clouds and darkness are round about him: righteousness and judgment are the habitation[4349] (*makon*) of his throne."

Righteousness, judgment and justice are said to be the *makon*, the "place of his sanctuary." They constitute the "basis" or "foundation" of His throne. That meaning of "foundation" is also used in connection with the Jerusalem temple and in one instance designates the whole site or area of Mt. Zion (Ezra 2:68; Isaiah 4:5). Of the remaining ten verses out of the seventeen times the Bible uses this word *makon* in the Old Testament, we find in Psalm 104:5

the only instance in which *makon* is not employed as a reference to the sanctuary. That singular usage refers in metaphorical language to God's act of establishing the *earth* "upon its foundations." Otherwise, seven times *makon* is used for the designation of God's "place of dwelling:" 1 Kings 8: 39, 43, 49; 2 Chronicles 6:2, 30, 33, 39. These texts show His "place of dwelling" is in heaven: 1 Kings 8: 39, 43, 49; 2 Chronicles 6:30, 33, 39; Psalm 33:14. Three times it is used for His earthly "place of dwelling," namely, His earthly sanctuary (1 Kings 8:13; 2 Chronicles 6:2; Exodus 15:17). The context of Isaiah 18:4 could allow *makon* to be either the heavenly or earthly "dwelling." Never, though, is the *makon* said to represent a pagan sanctuary nor does it ever even allude to anything of a pagan or of a sinful nature. For further confirmation by Ellen White that this word is used solely to represent a divine sanctuary, see below.[18]

These scriptures bring us again to the settled Biblical fact that it was the heavenly "foundation" of His throne that the little horn thought to cast down to the ground [earth]. In no instance is this term connected with the idea of contamination or defilement. The horn's act of throwing down the *makon* ("foundation" or "place") of the sanctuary in heaven is an interference with God's hearing the prayers of His people and an interference with the forgiveness that is the basis and foundation of God's sanctuary in heaven.

We now progress to the interpretation of the second noun in the phrase "the place of his sanctuary:" sanctuary[4720] (*miqdash*). Usage: AV- sanctuary 69, holy place 3, chapel 1, hallowed part 1; 72 verses, 74 hits. Let us examine this word's application in the Bible.

> Exodus 15:17 "Thou shalt bring them in, and plant them in the mountain of thine inheritance, in the place,[4349] O LORD, which thou hast made for thee to dwell in, in the Sanctuary,[4720] O Lord, which thy hands have established."

Here we have His "foundation" (*makon*) and His "sanctuary" (*miqdash*) all in the same verse. The Bible says that our God dwells in the *miqdash* of the earthly sanctuary. This is nothing less than "the pattern" of the great original where God Himself dwells in the heavenly sanctuary:

> Exodus 25:8, 9 "And let them make me a sanctuary;[4720] that I may dwell among them. According to all that I show thee, after

---

[18] Ellen White, *Prophets and Kings* (Nampa, Idaho: Pacific Press, 1943), 41–2.

the pattern of the tabernacle, and the pattern of all the instruments thereof, even so shall ye make it."

Miqdash may refer to God's sanctuary/temple in the earth specifically on the great Day of Atonement:

> Leviticus 16:33 "And he shall make an atonement for the holy sanctuary,[4720] and he shall make an atonement for the tabernacle of the congregation, and for the altar, and he shall make an atonement for the priests, and for all the people of the congregation."

It may refer to God's sanctuary/temple on earth:

> Psalm 68:35 "O God, thou art terrible out of thy holy places:[4720] the God of Israel is he that giveth strength and power unto his people. Blessed be God."

And *miqdash* may refer to God's sanctuary/temple on earth and in heaven in the same verse:

> Psalm 96:6 "Honour and majesty are before him: strength and beauty are in his sanctuary."[4720]

It is true that *miqdash* can refer to a sanctuary of Satan, while *qodesh* solely refers to the sanctuary of the Lord. But those who are looking for a pagan sanctuary will not find it here in the context of Daniel 8:11. This position will be cemented even further as we progress in our study, but the Bible does tell us the term heaven uses to describe "pagan holy places" or a "pagan sanctuary:" "place"[4725] (*maqom*). Usage: AV- place 391, home 3, room 3, whithersoever 2, open 1, space 1, country 1; 379 verses, 402 hits.

Let's view the word "place" (*maqom*) as it appears in Deuteronomy:

> Deuteronomy 12:2 "Ye shall utterly destroy all the places,[4725] wherein the nations which ye shall possess served their gods, upon the high mountains, and upon the hills, and under every green tree":

> Deuteronomy 12: 3"And ye shall overthrow their altars, and break their pillars, and burn their groves with fire; and ye shall hew down the graven images of their gods, and destroy the names

of them out of that <u>place</u>."[4725]

It is this word *maqom*, clearly alluding to places of pagan religious activity, which Daniel would have used if the sanctuary
in 8:11 was a pagan sanctuary. Again, we present evidence that
maqom is used when referring to pagan sanctuaries:

> Ezekiel 6:13 "Then shall ye know that I am the LORD, when
> their slain men shall be among their idols round about their al-
> tars, upon every high hill, in all the tops of the mountains, and
> under every green tree, and under every thick oak, the <u>place</u>[4725]
> where they did offer sweet savour to all their idols."

According to 2 Corinthians 13:1, the meaning of the *maqom* is
established by two or three witnesses of scriptures. Without question, then, Daniel would have used *maqom*[4725] if he had a pagan
sanctuary in mind. Instead, he used *makon*. [4349]

Now we move forward to a determination of the meaning of
"<u>cast down</u>"[7993] (*shalak*). Usage: AV- cast 77, cast out 15, cast away
11, cast down 11, cast forth 4, cast off 2, adventured 1, hurl 1,
misc 3; 121 verses 125 hits. While the little horn, the papacy, only
"thinks to change times and laws," it has indeed "cast down" the
continuance of divine services for man's salvation in that for centuries its usurpation and blasphemous priestly claims have blinded
the eyes of too many who knew or presently know nothing of the
heavenly mediation available to them. Through church law and
through exaltation of the counterfeit worship system so vividly portrayed in 2 Thessalonians 2:4, the truth has been concealed so as
to deny or otherwise block access to the forgiveness freely offered.
This deliberate obscuring or "casting down" attacks the very foundational intent of God's sanctuary, and we will now confirm this
very premise from the writings of Mrs. White herself. Ellen White
understood, just as Daniel did, that there was a very real and precise point in the history of the Papacy when the "daily" priestly ac-
tivities of Christ were to be taken away or usurped from the minds
of the people by human laws and the masses were made to look to
fallible, erring, and cruel men acting as priestly intercessors:

> "The accession of the Roman Church to power marked the
> beginning of the Dark Ages. As her power increased, the dark-
> ness deepened. *Faith was transferred [usurped] from Christ, the
> true foundation, to the pope of Rome.* Instead of trusting in the

Son of God for forgiveness of sins and for eternal salvation, the people looked to the pope, and to the priests and prelates to whom he delegated authority. They were taught that the pope was their earthly mediator and that none could approach God except through him; and, further, that he stood in the place of God to them and was therefore to be implicitly obeyed. *A deviation from his requirements was sufficient cause for the severest punishment to be visited upon the bodies and souls of the offenders.* Thus *the minds of the people were turned away [taken away] to fallible, erring, and cruel men, nay, more, to the prince of darkness himself, who exercised his power through them.* Sin was disguised in a garb of sanctity. When the Scriptures are suppressed, and man comes to regard himself as supreme, we need look only for fraud, deception, and debasing iniquity. *With the elevation of human laws and traditions* was manifest the corruption that ever results from setting aside the law of God.

"Those were days of peril for the church of Christ. The faithful standard–bearers were few indeed. Though the truth was not left without witnesses, yet at times it seemed that error and superstition would wholly prevail, and *true religion would be banished from the earth. The gospel was lost sight of,* but the forms of religion were multiplied, and the people were burdened with rigorous exactions. They were taught not only to look to the pope as their mediator, but to trust to works of their own to atone for sin."[19]

The scriptures and Ellen White confirm that the "daily" was indeed "taken away" as the pope presumed to supplant Christ as humanity's intercessor. This, as we will soon show, was legally enacted in the year A.D. 508. Faith was transferred or cast down from heaven to the earth. "Thus *the minds of the people were turned away to fallible, erring, and cruel men, nay, more, to the prince of darkness himself, who exercised his power through them.*"

In Revelation 10, in the eating of the little book lying open in the angel's hand, John the Revelator foresaw that this suppression of truth regarding Christ being humanity's true intercessor, would end after the Great Disappointment of 1844 described so vividly in chapter 10. Following this great disappointment, the Remnant Church was given this commission:

Revelation 10:11 "And he said unto me, Thou must prophesy

---

[19] Ellen White, *The Great Controversy*, (Nampa, Idaho: Pacific Press, 1911), 55.

again before many peoples, and nations, and tongues, and kings."

Revelation 11:1 supplies us with the additional understanding that followed in the church's commission of Revelation. 10:11:

> Revelation 11:1 "And there was given me a reed like unto a rod: and the angel stood, saying, Rise, and measure the temple of God, and the altar, and them that worship therein."

What was to be understood when the church was told to take a reed and measure the temple and the altar? The word "reed" in the Greek is kanon, from which we get our word "canon." Canon means "rule" or "law," or, as Webster defines it, "a standard used in judging something; criterion." For the sake of clarity, criterion means "a standard, rule, or test by which a judgment of something can be formed." The Greek word for measure, when it is applied to a building or object, means to "preserve" or "restore" it. In other words, we are to use the Bible, the canon or rule of scripture, in our work of examining and restoring the temple and the altar. The temple and altar were to be restored because Daniel had previously said it was going to be taken away. While the Protestant Reformation did emphasize the priesthood of believers, it did not restore the truth concerning the heavenly sanctuary or the "daily," Christ's ministration and function at the altar in that sanctuary.

As we have already seen in Daniel 8:11, the "daily" would be taken away, and the place of his sanctuary would be cast down. The papacy took away the "daily" and cast down the "place" (His foundation, to hear and answer prayers and to forgive sins) of His (Christ's) sanctuary by setting up a counterfeit priesthood, sanctuary and altar. The altar that was to be measured or restored is the altar of incense. The altar of incense in the earthly sanctuary was especially connected with the ministry of the priest in the first apartment. When the Roman Catholic system developed, the world was deceived into looking to the Catholic system of priesthood for its salvation. The great truths of Christ's heavenly sanctuary and of His mediation before the altar in that sanctuary were cast down, lost or, better stated, usurped:

> "God has never given a hint in His word that He has appointed any man to be the head of the church. The doctrine of papal supremacy is directly opposed to the teachings of the Scriptures. *The pope can have no power over Christ's church except by usurpa-*

tion. . . . In order for Satan to maintain his sway over men, and establish the authority of the *papal usurper*, he must keep them *in ignorance of the Scriptures.*"[20]

Since 1844, the ignorance of the Scriptures regarding these grand truths of Christ and his ongoing Priestly ministerial work in heaven has been restored to the world through the Remnant Church. The following letter from L. R. Conradi to J. N. Loughborough succinctly summarizes the "continual's" relevance to Seventh-day Adventism. It verifies that, historically, no denomination, no minister, no theologian and no commentary had the right idea of the sanctuary service or any knowledge of the true, divine service in heaven, until after the great disappointment of 1844:

". . . But there is one thing that is continual, and will continue, and that is the true, divine service of God. When, about the year 508, the Roman Catholic Church through the so-called conversion of King Chlodwick [Clovis] of France, received its moral support from kings, and later on, in consequence, from the emperor of Eastern Rome, that church did away with the true sanctuary service of God so completely that its true meaning was entirely lost on the earth. The church established its own sanctuary service, its own priesthood, even professing to continue the Levitical, and establish its own acrifice in the mass; and to show how completely the knowledge of the true sanctuary service has been done away, we need only to remark that no denomination and no minister and no theologian and no commentary had any more the right idea of the sanctuary service, or any knowledge of the true, divine service in heaven, until, after the 1844 movement, Seventh-day Adventists, in view of the disappointment, searched in the Bible until the Spirit of God enlightened them, and since that time, the true 'continual' service is being again assigned its proper place.

". . . We arrive at a consistent and reasonable explanation, full of harmony, and we arrive at this by comparing Scripture with Scripture.

"I know that different ones have written you about this matter. I do not even question that you are fully convinced that the theory held up to the present time is the right one; but after having read your article, I felt it my duty as a brother to set before you what I believe to be the teaching of the Word of God—an

---

[20] Ellen White, *The Great Controversy*, (Nampa, Idaho: Pacific Press, 1911), 51

exposition that only strengthens the reasons for our existence as a denomination."[21]

In the eyes of heaven, these daring acts of the Romish Church to interfere with or prohibit mankind's access to the holy sanctuary are viewed as an attack on God Himself. It should be no marvel that Daniel 8:25 tells us the little horn's interference and audacious claims to the prerogatives of God will end in the ultimate consequence: "He shall be broken without hand." We are now ready to analyze Daniel 8:12:

> Daniel 8:12 And a host[6635] was given[5414] *him* against[5921] the daily[8548] *sacrifice* by reason of transgression,[6588] and it cast down[7993] the truth[571] to the ground;[776] and it practiced,[6213] and prospered.[6743]

A literal translation of this verse reads thus:

> "And a host will be given over the continuance causing transgression, and it throws the truth down to the earth; and it practiced, and prospered."

"And an <u>host</u>"[6635] (*tsaba*). Usage: AV—host 393, war 41, army 29, battle 5, service 5, appointed time 3, warfare 2, soldiers 1, company 1, misc 5; 485; 461 verses 485 hits. Who is the "host" of verse 12? We have already shown in verse 11 how the little horn (papal Rome) has taken on priestly attire. The only other entity presented in Daniel 8:11 was "the prince of the host" whom we have also seen was none other than Christ Himself. So, it should not be a hard matter for one to recognize that the "host" in verse 12 that is to be set over or given over the "daily" is the one and same "host" in verse 11 that has taken away the "daily" and cast down the "place" of "his" (Christ's) sanctuary in hearing and answering prayers and forgiving sin. Therefore, the causing of or the conception of transgression has its origin in verse 11, by the heinous illegal acts perpetuated by papal Rome.

At this point, all we need to do is verify if heaven uses the term "host" to identify a priesthood of believers or a group of people in religious garb, thus representing themselves to be priestly intercessors:

---

[21] Letter from L. R. Conradi to J. N. Loughborough, April 16, 1907.

Numbers 4:2–3 "Take the sum of the sons of Kohath from among the sons of Levi, after their families, by the house of their fathers, From thirty years old and upward even until fifty years old, all that enter into the host,[6635] to do the work in the tabernacle of the congregation."

Clearly, these sanctuary priests were the "host," so we find heaven, indeed, uses "host" in a context of religious ministry. Thus, the host of verse 12 finds its fulfillment only in papal Rome. In the context of Daniel 8:11–12, the supposition that the "host" is in reference to the barbarians that invaded and subverted the Roman Empire has no Biblical or historical support whatsoever.

It is of interest to mention that Pope Symmachus (AD 498–514), the bishop of Rome who reigned through the time period of 508, has been recognized by Catholic historians for one of his great feats. During his pontificate, through ordination, he created:

> "One hundred and seventeen bishops, ninety-two priests, and sixteen deacons."[22]

Such an accomplishment no previous pope had equaled. A. T. Jones rightfully declared:

> "It was 'by reason of transgression,' that is, by reason of sin, that this power gained 'the host' that was used to cast down the truth to the ground, to shut away from the church and the world Christ's priesthood, His ministry, and His sanctuary; and to cast it all down to the ground and tread it underfoot."[23] Indeed, "a host was given him."

Continuing with verse 12, we come to the word "transgression"[6588] (*pesa*). Usage: AV—transgression 84, trespass 5, sin 3, rebellion 1; 90 verses 93 hits. This transgression is one committed by human beings. Notice how the Bible introduces this Hebrew word and its context:

---

[22] The Chevalier Artaud De Montor, "Pope Symmachus" [A.D. 498-514], *The Lives and Times of the Popes* (n.p.: Catholic Publication Society, 1911), 1:150. Imprimatur.

[23] A. T. Jones, The Consecrated Way to Christian Perfection, *(Boise, Idaho: The Upward Way, 1988), Chapter 13, The Transgression and Abomination of Desolation, 64.*

Genesis 31:36 "And Jacob was wroth, and chode with Laban: and Jacob answered and said to Laban, What is my trespass?[6588] what is my sin, that thou hast so hotly pursued after me?"

Genesis 50:17 "So shall ye say unto Joseph, Forgive, I pray thee now, the trespass[6588] of thy brethren, and their sin; for they did unto thee evil: and now, we pray thee, forgive the trespass[6588] of the servants of the God of thy father. And Joseph wept when they spake unto him."

Thus far in Daniel 8:11 and in this first clause of verse 12, "And a host will be given over the continuance [or "daily"] causing transgression." Indeed, this priestly host has transgressed because it has "cast down the truth to the ground." However, the Bible now moves us forward to a new time period in the career of the papacy when she was to practice and prosper:

Daniel 8:12 "And it cast down the truth to the ground; and it practiced, and prospered."

This new time period, introduced to us from the remainder of Daniel 8:12, brings us to the year A.D. 538 which we will conclude and confirm in our A.D. 538 study, for it serves no further purpose here.

Our next scripture of interest that has need of interpretation is found in Daniel 12:

Daniel 12:11 "And from the time[4480, 6256] *that* the daily[8548] *sacrifice* shall be taken away,[5493] and the abomination[8251] that maketh desolate[8074] set up,[5414] *there shall be* a thousand[505] two hundred[3967] and ninety[8673] days."[3117]

Our first and most obvious reading of this text reveals the following: from verse 11, the commencement of the 1290-year prophecy is clearly established when two things take place simultaneously. The "daily" is being taken away at the same time the abomination that maketh desolate is "set up." Both clauses have the same starting point in verse 11. This leaves us with two clauses yet to be ascertained. The "daily" that is to be "taken away" is the same "daily" as we have seen in Daniel 8:11 and it repeats and enlarges our understanding here because the "daily" that is to be taken away coincides with the "abomination that maketh desolate" being "set up." Contextually, Daniel 12:11 and 11:31 are the same with Daniel 11:31 providing more details. Since the same two clauses and prophetic time periods are found in Daniel 11:31, let us turn our attention there for its intended interpretation:

> Daniel 11:31 "And arms[2220] shall stand[5975] on his part,[4480] and they shall pollute[2490] the sanctuary[4720] of strength,[4581] and shall take away[5493] the daily[8548] *sacrifice*, and they shall place[5414] the abomination[8251] that maketh desolate."[8074]

Daniel 11:31 is a key text in understanding A.D. 508 aright. The first clause we want to identify is "arms":

> Arms: "[2220]. זְרוֹעַ **zerôaͅ**:: A common noun referring to arm, power, strength, might."[24]

Usage: AV—arm 83, power 3, shoulder 2, holpen 1, mighty 1, strength 1; 84 verses 91 hits.

The following texts reveal that the primary meaning of "arms" used in the context of Daniel 11:31 is political or military power of a given civil entity:

> Daniel 11:6 "And in the end[7093] of years[8141] they shall join themselves together;[2266] for the king's[4428] daughter[1323] of the south[5045] shall come[935] to[413] the king[4428] of the north[6828] to make[6213] an agreement:[4339] but she shall not[3808] retain[6113] the power[3581] of the <u>arm</u>;[2220] neither[3808] shall he stand,[5975] nor his <u>arm</u>:[2220] but she[1931] shall be given up,[5414] and they that brought[935] her, and he that begot[3205] her, and he that strengthened[2388] her in *these* times."[6256]

> Daniel 11:15 "So the king[4428] of the north[6828] shall come,[935] and cast up[8210] a mount,[5550] and take[3920] the most fenced[4013] cities:[5892] and the <u>arms</u>[2220] of the south[5045] shall not[3808] withstand,[5975] neither his chosen[4005] people,[5971] neither[369] *shall there be any* strength[3581] to withstand."[5975]

> Ezekiel 30:22 "Therefore[3651] thus[3541] saith[559] the Lord[136] GOD;[3069] Behold,[2009] I *am* against[413] Pharaoh[6547] king[4428] of

---

[24] Warren Baker and Eugene Carpenter, *The Complete Word Study Dictionary: Old Testament*, s.v. "abomination" (Chattanooga: AMG Publishers, 2003), 302.

Egypt,[4714] and will break[7665] [(853)] his <u>arms</u>,[2220] [(853)] the strong,[2389] and that which was broken;[7665] and I will cause [(853)] the sword[2719] to fall[5307] out of his hand."[4480, 3027]

Ezekiel 30:24 "And I will strengthen[2388] [(853)] the <u>arms</u>[2220] of the king[4428] of Babylon,[894] and put[5414] [(853)] my sword[2719] in his hand:[3027] but I will break[7665] [(853)] Pharaoh's[6547] <u>arms</u>,[2220] and he shall groan[5008] before[6440] him with the groanings[5009] of a deadly wounded[2491] *man*."

Ezekiel 30:25 "But I will strengthen[2388] [(853)] the <u>arms</u>[2220] of the king[4428] of Babylon,[894] and the <u>arms</u>[2220] of Pharaoh[6547] shall fall down;[5307] and they shall know[3045] that[3588] I[589] *am* the LORD,[3068] when I shall put[5414] my sword[2719] into the hand[3027] of the king[4428] of Babylon,[894] and he shall stretch it out[5186, (853)] upon[413] the land[776] of Egypt."[4714]

Jeremiah 48:25 "The horn[7161] of Moab[4124] is cut off,[1438] and his <u>arm</u>[2220] is broken,[7665] saith[5002] the LORD."[3068]

Ezekiel 30:21 "Son[1121] of man,[120] I have broken[7665] [(853)] the <u>arm</u>[2220] of Pharaoh[6547] king[4428] of Egypt;[4714] and, lo,[2009] it shall not[3808] be bound up[2280] to be healed,[5414, 7499] to put[7760] a roller[2848] to bind[2280] it, to make it strong[2388] to hold[8610] the sword."[2719]

Our next word study is:

Stand: "[5975]. צָמַר‎ *ǎmad:* A verb meaning to stand, to rise up; to take one's stand."[25]

Usage: AV—stood 171, stand 137, (raise, stand . . .) up 42, set 32, stay 17, still 15, appointed 10, standing 10, endure 8, remain 8, present 7, continue 6, withstand 6, waited 5, establish 5, misc 42; 496 verses 521 hits.

The following texts will reveal that the primary meaning of "stand" used in the context of Daniel 11:31 is to defend or to protect:

Daniel 11:1 "Also I[589] in the first[259] year[8141] of Darius[1867] the

---

[25] Warren Baker and Eugene Carpenter, *The Complete Word Study Dictionary: Old Testament*, s.v. "abomination" (Chattanooga: AMG Publishers, 2003), 843.

Mede,[4075] *even* I, <u>stood</u>[5975] to confirm[2388] and to strengthen[4581] him."

Daniel 11:3 "And a mighty[1368] king[4428] shall <u>stand</u> up,[5975] that shall rule[4910] with great[7227] dominion,[4474] and do[6213] according to his will."[7522]

Daniel 11:6 "And in the end[7093] of years[8141] they shall join themselves together;[2266] for the king's[4428] daughter[1323] of the south[5045] shall come[935] to[413] the king[4428] of the north[6828] to make[6213] an agreement:[4339] but she shall not[3808] retain[6113] the power[3581] of the arm;[2220] neither[3808] shall he <u>stand</u>,[5975] nor his arm:[2220] but she[1931] shall be given up,[5414] and they that brought[935] her, and he that begot[3205] her, and he that strengthened[2388] her in *these* times."[6256]

Daniel 11:21 "And in[5921] his estate[3653] shall <u>stand</u> up[5975] a vile person,[959] to[5921] whom they shall not[3808] give[5414] the honor[1935] of the kingdom:[4438] but he shall come in[935] peaceably,[7962] and obtain[2388] the kingdom[4438] by flatteries."[2519]

Daniel 11:25 "And he shall stir up[5782] his power[3581] and his courage[3824] against[5921] the king[4428] of the south[5045] with a great[1419] army;[2428] and the king[4428] of the south[5045] shall be stirred up[1624] to battle[4421] with a very[5704, 3966] great[1419] and mighty[6099] army;[2428] but he shall not[3808] <u>stand</u>:[5975] for[3588] they shall forecast[2803] devices[4284] against[5921] him."

Our next word study is:

Pollute: "[2490]. חָלַל *ḥālal*: A verb meaning to pierce, to play the pipe, to profane. This word has three distinct meanings. The first meaning is to pierce or wound, either physically unto death (Isa. 53:5; Ezek. 32:26) or figuratively unto despair (Ps. 109:22). The second meaning of this word is to play the pipe, which is used only twice in the Old Testament (1 Kgs. 1:40; Ps. 87:7). The third meaning is to profane or to defile, which is used primarily of the ceremonial objects of worship (Ex. 20:25; Ezek 44:7; Dan. 11:31); of the Sabbath (Ex. 31:14; Neh. 13:17; Ezek. 23:38); of God's name (Lev. 18:21; Jer. 34:16); of God's priests (Lev. 21:4, 6). However, it also refers to sexual defilement (Gen. 49:4; Lev. 21:9); the breaking of a covenant (Ps. 89:31[32], 34[35]; Mal. 2:10); and making a vineyard common (Deut. 20:6; 28:30). In the causative form of this verb, it means to begin (Gen. 4:26; 2 Chr. 3:2)."[26]

Usage: AV—begin 52, profane 36, pollute 23, defile 9, break 4, wounded 3, eat 2, slay 2, first 1, gather grapes 1, inheritance 1, began men 1, piped 1, players 1, prostitute 1, sorrow 1, stain 1, eat as common things 1; 132 verses 141 hits.

The following texts will reveal that the primary meaning of "pollute" used in the context of Daniel 11:31 is synonymous with pollute or to defile:

> Revelation 13:6 "And he opened his mouth in <u>blasphemy</u> against God, to blaspheme <u>his name</u>, and <u>his tabernacle</u>, and them that dwell in heaven."

> Psalms 74:7 "They have cast fire into <u>thy sanctuary</u>, they have <u>defiled</u> by casting down the dwelling place of <u>thy name</u> to the ground."

> Leviticus 20:3 "And I will set my face against that man, and will cut him off from among his people; because he hath given of his seed unto Molech, to <u>defile my sanctuary</u>, and to <u>profane my holy name</u>."

His name and His sanctuary are synonymous. If you defile one, you pollute the other:

> Hebrews 10:29 "Of how much sorer punishment, suppose ye, shall he be thought worthy, <u>who hath trodden under foot the Son of God,</u> and hath counted the blood of the covenant, wherewith he was sanctified, an unholy thing, and hath done despite unto the Spirit of grace?"

If we, as individuals, may be found to have "trodden underfoot the Son of God" spiritually, then how much more is the distinct reality that a system of either a civil or a religious nature may yet be capable of the same?

We submit this further point of information about the sanctuary. The *miqdash*[4720] (sanctuary) in Daniel 8:11and the *miqdash*[4720] (sanctuary) in Daniel 9:17 are both designated as the Lord's by

---

[26] Warren Baker and Eugene Carpenter, *The Complete Word Study Dictionary: Old Testament*, s.v. "abomination" (Chattanooga: AMG Publishers, 2003), 342

Daniel (emphasis below added):

> Daniel 9:17 "Now[6258] therefore, O our God,[430] hear[8085, 413] the prayer[8605] of thy servant,[5650] and his supplications,[8469] and cause thy face[6440] to shine[215] upon[5921] <u>thy sanctuary</u>[4720] that is desolate,[8076] for the Lord's sake."[4616, 136]

The *miqdash*[4720] (sanctuary) in Daniel 11:31, i.e., "<u>the sanctuary of strength</u>," and the *miqdash*[4720] (sanctuary) in Psalm 96:6 are also one and the same, the Lord's. The word <u>strength</u> in both texts is from the same root of 5810:

> Psalms 96:6 "Honor[1935] and majesty[1926] *are* before[6440] him: <u>strength</u>[5797] and beauty[8597] *are* in <u>his sanctuary.</u>"[4720]

> Daniel 11:31 "And arms[2220] shall stand[5975] on his part,[4480] and they shall pollute[2490] <u>the sanctuary</u>[4720] of strength,[4581] and shall take away[5493] the daily[8548] *sacrifice*, and they shall place[5414] the abomination[8251] that maketh desolate."[8074]

Our next word study is:

> Abomination: "[8251]. שִׁקּוּץ *šiqqûṣ*, שִׁקֻּץ *šiqqûṣ*: A masculine noun meaning a detestable thing, an abomination, and an idol. This Hebrew word identifies an object that is abhorrent or blasphemous. It is used to denote filth (Nah. 3:6); forbidden food (Zech. 9:7); and a blasphemous activity (Dan. 9:27). <u>Most often, it is used as a synonym for an idol or idolatry</u> (Jer. 7:30; Hos. 9:10)."[27]

Usage: AV—abomination 20, detestable things 5, detestable 1, abominable filth 1, abominable idols 1; 26 verses 28 hits.

Our next word study is:

> Desolate: "[8074]. שָׁמֵם *šāmēm*: A verb meaning to be desolated, to be destroyed. The desolation or destruction that this verb refers to can be used of both people (2Sam. 13:20; Lam. 1:13, 16); and places Lev. 26:31, 32; Isa. 61:4; Ezek. 35:12) and is used in both its simple and causative forms. A second meaning of this verb, which is extremely common, is to be appalled or astonished and is used

---

[27] Warren Baker and Eugene Carpenter, *The Complete Word Study Dictionary: Old Testament*, s.v. (Chattanooga: AMG Publishers, 2003), 1193.

in the simple, passive, and passive causative stems (Job 18:20; Isa. 52:14; Jer. 18:16). The connection between these two meanings is not entirely clear; yet they are both used with great frequency. When this verb is used in the second meaning, it often describes a person's reaction on seeing desolation and destruction. For example, in 1 Kings 9:8, the reaction of people to a destroyed land was described with this verb. A much less common use of this verb is in the reflexive stem. Here it meant to be disheartened or dismayed (Ps. 143:4)."[28]

Usage: AV—desolate 49, astonished 20, desolation 7, waste 5, destroy 3, wondered 2, amazed 1, astonishment 1, misc 4; 85 verses 92 hits.

"And *"arms"* shall *"stand"* on *"his part."* With confidence we can say and will further document our claims from historical and academic sources that it was the *"arms"* of Clovis, King of the Franks, the state's political and military strength that was to *"stand"* with or ally itself on *"his part"* which was that of Catholicism. "And *"they"* (Clovis and Catholicism) "shall *"pollute"* (symbiosis of church and state) "the *sanctuary of strength."* The *"sanctuary"* as we have already witnessed is the sanctuary of Christ. *"Of strength"* should read *"The Rock"* (masculine singular future tense), as it is rightly translated in the Hebrew. *"The Rock,"* of course, is none other than Jesus Christ (1 Corinthians 10:4), so the phrase *"sanctuary of strength"* can be interpreted *"the sanctuary of Christ."* Ironically, those who say this is a pagan sanctuary have never been able to explain how one *"pollutes"* a pagan sanctuary. "And shall take away the *daily."* As we have already witnessed, the little horn had usurped the prerogatives of Christ's ministry in hearing prayers and forgiving sins. As we will soon see, the "daily" was taken away or usurped from the minds of the people, taken away by human laws, and the masses were made to look to fallible, erring, and cruel men acting as priestly intercessors. *"Sacrifice"* is a supplied word and does not belong in the text. "And *"they"'* (church and state) "shall *"place"* the *"abomination"* that" maketh desolate."'

Thus far, ten of the thirteen segments of Daniel 11:31 have been interpreted. The eleventh through thirteenth parts now become our focus as a biblical and inspired basis is sought for a correct understanding of "shall *place* the *abomination* that *maketh deso-*

---

[28] Warren Baker and Eugene Carpenter, *The Complete Word Study Dictionary: Old Testament,* s.v. "abomination" (Chattanooga: AMG Publishers, 2003), 1164-5.

late." These three remaining italicized segments will be revisited and concluded after we disclose our historical documentation, fully establishing the following historical narrative that will be seen to perfectly align with the scriptural account. Note that the "abomination of desolation" is not only "placed" in Daniel 11:31, but "set up" in Daniel 12:11:

> "And they shall *place* the *abomination* that *maketh desolate.*"

> "And *they* [Clovis and Catholicism] shall *place* [or *set up,* Daniel 12:11] the *abomination.*"

> "Abomination," by its very nature, is sin. It is abhorrent to God, disgusting to Him, "espec. *idolatry* or (concr.) an *idol."* (See *Strong's* #8251, #8441.) In this case, as will be shown, the "sin" is idolatry, manifested in spiritual adultery. The *placement* or the *setting up* of the *abomination* or *sin* that *desolates* is done jointly by the term, *"they."*

Due to the ominous role of the "abomination," it is prudent to examine that word closely for full understanding. "Abomination," when used prophetically, applies to both pagan and papal Rome. It is employed three times in the book of Daniel:

1. Daniel 9:27 "And for the overspreading of abominations he shall make it desolate, even until the consummation, and that determined shall be poured upon the desolate."

This refers to the pagan Romans with their idolatrous standards in the siege, capture and destruction of Jerusalem. This is the Old Testament source to which Jesus referred in Matthew 24:15.

2. Daniel 11:31 "And they shall place the abomination that maketh desolate."

This refers to papal Rome.

3. Daniel 12:11 "And the abomination that maketh desolate set up."

This is a repetition and enlargement of Daniel 11:31 and also refers to papal Rome.

Each usage in Daniel is #8251 in concordances and lexicons. It is defined as something that is "abhorrent or blasphemous," or even a "blasphemous activity. . . . Most often it is used as a synonym for an idol or idolatry."[29] Before applying that meaning to pagan and papal Rome, however, the word's six uses in the New Testament should be considered in conjunction with its Old Testament usage:

1. Matthew 24:15 "When ye therefore shall see the abomination of desolation, spoken of by Daniel the prophet, stand in the holy place. . . ."

The "abomination" spoken of here refers to the pagan Roman armies surrounding Jerusalem with their idolatrous standards. Ellen White, in commenting on this, connects "abomination" with Rome's idolatry:

> "When the idolatrous standards of the Romans should be set up in the holy ground which extended some furlongs outside of the city walls, then the followers of Christ were to find safety in flight."[30]

2. Mark 13:14 "But when ye shall see the abomination of desolation, spoken of by Daniel the prophet, standing where it ought not, (let him that readeth understand). . . ."

This is applied to the same action by the same power as in Matthew 24:15.

3. Luke 16:15 "Ye are they which justify yourselves before men; but God knoweth your hearts: for that which is highly esteemed among men is abomination in the sight of God."

This refers to things men permit or seek that are in competition with their loyalty and homage to God—things that God, therefore, hates. It indirectly refers to idolatry.

---

[29] Warren Baker and Eugene Carpenter, *The Complete Word Study Dictionary: Old Testament*, s.v. "abomination" (Chattanooga: AMG Publishers, 2003), 1193.

[30] Ellen White, *The Great Controversy*, (Nampa, Idaho: Pacific Press, 1911), 26.

4.   Revelation 17:4 "And the woman was arrayed in purple and scarlet colour, and decked with gold and precious stones and pearls, having a golden cup in her hand full of abominations and filthiness of her fornication."

This applies to papal Rome.

5.   Revelation 17:5. "And upon her forehead was a name written, MYSTERY, BABYLON THE GREAT, THE MOTHER OF HARLOTS AND ABOMINATIONS OF THE EARTH."

This again is applied to papal Rome.

6.   Revelation 21:27. "And there shall in no wise enter into it anything that defileth, neither whatsoever worketh abomination, or maketh a lie. . . ."

This is applied to all idolaters.

Thus twice in the New Testament, "abomination"946 is specifically applied to pagan Rome and twice to papal Rome. In each case, its meaning is defined as something detestable—specifically, idolatry or idolatrous worship.

In the book of Daniel, that same meaning is once applied to pagan Rome and twice to papal Rome. Idolatry is rejection of God, defection from His law and His principles, a preference for another ruler—even self—whose influence, power and values are preferred above God's.

This is the significance and application of the term "abomination," the particular "sin" referred to in these prophetic Scriptures.

Exactly how this idolatry manifested itself in the "abomination" of prophecy, within the documented historical context of a counterfeit worship system and the growing symbiosis of church and state, can be seen in an investigation of a related term of equal significance—that of spiritual fornication or spiritual adultery. A church can be guilty of the sin of spiritual fornication or spiritual adultery in three ways:

1.   By the worship of idolatrous images which is spiritual unfaithfulness to Christ:

Ezekiel 16:17 "Thou has made to thyself images of men [idols] and did commit whoredom [fornication] with them."

By worshiping images, ancient Israel was unfaithful to God: Jeremiah 3:6, 9 "She committed adultery with sticks and stones."

2. By the church becoming friendly with the degenerate world:

James 4:4 "Ye adulterers and adulteresses, know ye not that the friendship of the world is enmity with God?"

3. By the union of church and state:

Romans 13:7 "Render therefore to all their dues: tribute to whom tribute is due; custom to whom custom; fear to whom fear; honour to whom honour."

By illicit or forbidden union, the church commits spiritual adultery. In Scripture, the spiritual husband of the church is Jesus Christ. If a church unites with or receives favors from one who is not her husband, she commits spiritual adultery or spiritual fornication. That unlawful union occurs when the kings, rulers or civil powers of the state unite with the church and/or support the church's interests and aims. It occurs when the church forsakes its dependence upon divine grace and power preferring instead earthly power which is usually expressed in legislative decrees. She thus devotes her energies and priorities to a mutual relationship with someone or something other than the One who deserves such attention. It is spiritual unfaithfulness, spiritual adultery, in the sight of God. Her unlawful act is a form of idolatry.[31] In sum, the "abomination" or "sin" of idolatry that is spoken of in Daniel 11:31 and 12:11 refers to the amalgamation or union of church and state. That is the specific sin referred to in those verses of Daniel's prophetic vision. The church had committed spiritual adultery and had married herself to one other than her spiritual husband, Jesus Christ.

In this study of "abomination" in the Old and New Testaments, in the context being addressed, Rome's role in prophetic history is thus firmly established. Rejecting Christ, the Church of Rome had transferred her dependence, welcomed the influence of and given

---

[31] Pastor Austin P. Cooke, with many thanks for his portions of information.

her undue affection and allegiance to the state, thereby crossing a forbidden line into idolatry.

Having allowed the scriptures to interpret themselves, it is at this point that we will sustain our said claims with the necessary historical documentation. Having largely collected over the years all the primary documents pertaining to Clovis and the church in and around the beginning of the 6th century, we have chosen to present this evidence to our readership through some of the world's most renowned and respected European historians of this historical era. For the sake of integrity, this unbiased approach will serve the truth in the best possible way, establishing definitive references for scholars, pastors, evangelists and the serious layman. These are acknowledged by European scholarship, thereby confirming the illustrated translations from the primary sources to be accurate, as well. Authors' bibliographies are given for the benefit of the reader and are only a partial list of those who will be cited and whose works still speak with authority among European historians today.[32]

---

[32] For some of the *authors' bibliographies* see **APPENDIX III**, pg. 119.

2

Clovis and Catholicism Embrace

Clovis was the first King in the new world after A.D. 476 that embraced the Catholic faith:

> "It is observable that Clovis was, at this time, the only Catholic Prince in the known world, as the word Catholic was then understood. . . . Clovis was not only the sole Catholic Prince at this Time in the World; but the first King that ever embraced the Catholic Religion; which has procured to the French king the Title of the Most Christian, and that of the Eldest Son of the Church. But were we to compare the Conduct and Actions of Clovis, the Catholic, with those of the Arian King Theodoric, such a comparison would no-ways redound to the honor of the Catholic faith."[33]
>
> ". . . The Franks were heavily recruited into the Roman army and a segment known as the Salians was settled in what is now the Netherlands. In the early 6th C., the Franks were united politically by Clovis (Chlodovechus, 481^1/2-511), who extended Frankish rule over the whole of Roman Gaul with the exception of Septimania and Provence. Clovis also converted to Orthodox [Catholic] Christianity, the first barbarian king to do so. This conversion and his victory over the VISIGOTHS (508) contributed to a Byz. perception of the Franks as potential allies against the Arian Gothic kingdoms and later the Lombards in Italy. Merovingian kings from Clovis onward were frequently honored by Constantinople with the titles consul and patrikios."[34]

The talk of war in AD 507 between Clovis and Alaric was authentic as confirmed by the letters sent by Theodoric to Alaric,

---

[33] Archibald Bower, *The History of the Popes* (London: n.p., 1750), 2:248.

[34] *The Oxford Dictionary of Byzantium*, s.v. "Franks" (New York: Oxford University Press, 1991), 2:803.

King of the Visigoths[35] as well as to Clovis, King of the Franks[36] as Theodoric was trying to sooth the tensions between the two. The possibility of the war commencing in late 507 exist, however, like the just quoted *Oxford Dictionary of Byzantium*, the latest in academic scholarship has contested that the battle of Vougle fought against the Visigoths by Clovis was ultimately in the year AD 508. The following primary document dated June 24, 508 gives strong support to this conclusion:

King Theodoric to all the Goths

"To the Goths a hint of war rather than persuasion to the strife is needed, since a warlike race such as ours likes to prove its courage. In truth, he shuns no labor who hungers for the renown of valour. Therefore with the help of God, whose blessing along brings prosperity, we design to send our army to the Gaul's for the common benefit of all, that you may have an opportunity of promotion, and we the power of testing your merits; for in time of peace the courage which we admire lies hidden, and when men have no chance of showing what is in them, their relative merits concealed. We have therefore given our Sajo,[37] Nandius, instructions to warn you that on the eighth day before the calends of next July, you move forward to the campaign in the name of God, sufficiently equipped according to your old custom, with horses, arms, and every requisite for war. Thus will ye at the same time show that the old valour of your sires yet dwells in your hearts, and also successfully perform your Kings command. Bring forth your young men for the discipline of Mars. Let them see you do deeds which they may love to tell their children. For an art not learned in youth is an art missing in our riper years. The very hawk, whose food is plunder, thrusts her still weak and tender young ones out of the nest, that they may prove to be such in the future as her maternal fondness can be proud of. Do you therefore, lofty by nature, and stimulated yet more by the love of fame, study to leave such sons behind you as your fathers have left in

---

[35] Cassiodorus, Magnus Aurelius, Hodgkin, Thomas, *The Letters of Cassiodorus.* London: Henry Frowde, 1886, Book III-I, 196-19

[36] Cassiodorus, Magnus Aurelius, Hodgkin, Thomas, *The Letters of Cassiodorus.* London: Henry Frowde, 1886, Book III-4, 198-199.

[37] See for the Office of the Sajo, note on ii. 13.

leaving you.

[*We can hardly be wrong in referring this stirring proclamation to the year 508, when Theodoric sent troops into Gaul to save remnants of the Visigothic Monarchy from the grasp of Clovis.* The first sentence recalls the expression 'certaminis gaudia.' which Jordanes no doubt borrowed from Cassiodorus. For the simile at the end of the letter, cf. Deuteronomy xxxii, 'As an eagle stirreth up her nest'.]"[38]

---

[38] Cassiodorus, Magnus Aurelius, Hodgkin, Thomas, *The Letters of Cassiodorus*. London: Henry Frowde, 1886, Book I-24, 157-158.

3

Clovis takes his Crown in the Year
A.D. 508

Professor Rouche hosted the 1996 International History Conference which was held in Reims, France to commemorate the
baptism of Clovis. On this occasion, Pope John Paul II was able to
meet and talk with historians, researchers and scientists gathered
around the issue. The proceedings of the symposium were then
made available in two volumes (in French). Following are a few
small excerpts from the various historians that participated in that
conference. Professor Rouche is to be congratulated for providing
us with the latest scholarship on Clovis which defines many issues.
We take note how this conference confirms the Kingship of Clovis
and the fusion of a Gallo-Roman Christianity that took place in
A.D. 508 when Clovis was crowned King:

[392] "On this point, the solemn entry into Tours, in 508, after
the battle of Vouille, was very significant; the report from Gregory
of Tours contains particularly suggestive indications.[339] This ceremony was the reflection of the entries of emperors into Rome
or to Constantinople or simply[40] those of victorious generals into
the provincial cities, it possesses essential elements that show
that perfect agreement, in northern and central Gaul, between
the population, the notables, and a barbaric monarch can only
be made on certain conditions, reunited here: the *adventus* of the
victorious was covered with *paludamentum* and distributed its
largesse in gold and silver along the cortege's path. Simply, the
path is deeply Christianized because its point of departure is the
atrium of Saint

---

[39] Greg. Tours, *HF*, II, 38. P. Courcelle, *BSNAF*, 1948-1949, p. 46-57
[40] As M. Mac Cormick thinks, *op. cit.*, p. 336.

[393] Martin and its completion was at the Tours cathedral, Saint Gatian. This *adventus*, at once traditional and Christian, in the right line of what other barbarians had already done, could only affirm in everyone's eyes the legitimacy of Clovis' power. He was a Christian sovereign who had preserved the most ancient of traditions to show that God protected him and gave him victory. The title of consul, honorary, was given to Anastasius, and could only reinforce this impression. In front of such perfection, we can be surprised that some Gallo-Romans from Tours also gave him the name of *Augustus*. Clovis, for the inhabitants of Tours, was similar to the emperor. This result was acquired thanks to the conversion and the integration into Romanness.

The Christian barbaric people from the West were at the origin of that fusion between the Victory and the will of God. They integrated the idea of the Victory by linking it to their conversion to Christianity and, by using Roman rites; they made a first step towards the acceptance of the submissive people. The best example is Clovis at his entry into Tours in 508: the Gallo-Roman society of Tours recognized that his victory was due to his and his people's conversion to Christianity."[41]

"For the following chapter, number 38, the title in the index announces, *De patriciatu Chlodovechi regis*, that is to say, "Concerning" or "About the noble King Clovis" The text continues with Clovis' visit to Tours in 508 in the following manner:

Then he received from emperor Anastasius the consulate's codicils and having covered in the basilica the blessed Martin in a purple tunic (*tunica blattea*) and a mantle, he put a diadem on his head. Then mounting his horse, he distributed with great generosity gold and silver on the path between the vestibule's door (in the basilica) and the city church[42] and they then from his own hand to the people who were present, and from this day he was called consul or emperor (*tamquam consul aut augustus*). Then he left Tours to come to Paris and made that the royal seat.[43]

---

[41] Rouche, Michel, ed. *Clovis, Histoire et Mémoire* (Actes du Colloque international d'historie de Reims), 2 vols. Paris: Univ. of Paris-Sorbonne Press, 1997, 1:392-3. (Jean-Pierre Martin, *The Mystique of the Victory in the Low Empire*, University of Paris IV-Sorbonne, 1:392-3.)

[42] That is to say, the cathedral that is within the city walls; Martin's basilica is outside of the walls.

[43] "*Igitur ab anastasio imperatore codicillos de consolato accepit, et in basilica beati Martini tunica blattea indutus et clamide, inponens vertice diademam, tunc ascenso*

[316] "Clovis was therefore considered a type of vice-emperor, recognized as such by Anastase. The ritual ovations made by the army and the people placed him above Theodoric, for this latter was acclaimed by the honor of Flavius, a name that dates only to Vespasian (69-79) and not to Augustus (27 BC-14 AD). This implies that, following the example of Augustus, who had refused all royal pomp and circumstance, the king of the Franks was also *princeps*, that is to say, the first in the Senate, apt to prescribe laws. Clovis, as we will see, used this faculty to create laws, notably the Salic Law. In his dual with Theodoric, the king of the Franks began to find himself on par with the king of the Ostrogoths. . . . [319] His sense of maneuver allowed him to eliminate, at all costs, the Visigoths from Gaul. This policy of small steps made him, as of the grand consular ceremony in Tours, the founder of Roman-Christian and Germanic unity . . .

While the war was not finished and the Burgunds held onto their kingdom more strongly than ever, Clovis was going to take on the construction of a Christian and Roman kingdom."[44]

"A.D. 508. A short time after these events, Clovis received the titles and dignity of Roman Patricius and consul from the Greek Emperor Anastasius. . . ."[45]

"In the same year [508] . . . he was invested with the diadem

---

(Cont.)

equite, aurum argentumque in itinere illo, quod interportam atque [ms. atrii] ecclesiam civitatis est, praesentibus populis manu propria spargens, voluntate benignissima erogavit, et ab ea die tamquam consul aut augustus est vocitatus, egressus autem a torons, Parisiis venit ibique cathedram regni constituit" (Greg. Tur. *HF* 2.38; tr. LATOUCHE, *ibid.* p. 132-133). For a summary, see *LHF* 17, with a *"corona aurea"* rather than the diadem. One finds a later version in *V. Remigii* 20 *(MGH SRM* 3.311-312): *"per idem tempus ab Anastasio imperatore codicellos Hludowicus.*

Rouche, Michel, ed. *Clovis, Histoire et Mémoire* (Actes du Colloque international d'historie de Reims), 2 vols. Paris: Univ. of Paris-Sorbonne Press, 1997, 1:395. (Ralph Mathisen, *Clovis, Anastasius, and Gregory of Tours: consul, patrician, and king,* University of South Carolina, United States, 1:395.

[44] Rouche, Michel. *Clovis.* Fayard, France, 1996, 316, 319.

[45] Walter C. Perry, *The Franks* (London: Longman, Brown, Green, Longmans, and Roberts, 1857), 88. Perry quotes from Gregory of Tours' *The History of the Franks,* trans. O. M. Dalton, (Oxford: Clarendon Press, 1927), 2:36-43. Considered by many the authority on Clovis, Gregory lived from A.D. 538 to 594.

and purple robe in the Church of St. Martin at Tours. . . ."[46]

In bestowal of an honorary title upon Clovis, the Roman emperor Anastasius publicly conferred recognition and approbation upon Clovis:

> "I have still to speak of Clovis's relation to the Roman Empire and the Roman Emperor. It is generally said that the advance of the Frankish power under Clovis is distinguished from the advance of the Teutonic power, such as the Visigothic and Burgundian, by the circumstance that there was no disguise about it; that, while those other Teutons were settling within the Empire, the Franks snatched provinces from the Empire and never professed to be inside it. Now there is a certain truth in this view: there is generally a difference between the process by which the Franks formed their kingdom in Gaul and the process by which the Visigoths and Burgundians formed theirs; but this difference has been exaggerated. In the first place, remember that the Salians, like the Visigoths and Burgundians, were originally settled as federate subjects in an imperial province, and remember that Childeric throughout his reign acted as a federate and supported the imperial administration. In the second place, if my interpretation of the letter of Remigius to Clovis is right, Clovis maintained and supported the Roman administration [252] in Belgica for a considerable time after he had overthrown Syagrius, and his attitude must have been that of the king of a federate people, not of an outsider. But the most important point is that his Gallic kingdom, when it was an accomplished fact, was recognised by the Emperor Anastasius as nominally within and not outside the Empire This fact has been questioned. It depends on a passage of Gregory of Tours which has been largely discussed. At the end of his account of the Visigothic War and Clovis's arrival at the city of Tours, Gregory goes on to say: *Igitur ab Anastasio imperatore codicillos de consolato accepit . . . et ab die tanquam consul aut augustus est vocitatus.* That is: the Emperor Anastasius conferred the consulship on Clovis and hence-forward he was styled *tanquam consul.* This statement has been rejected by some critics as a fable because the name of Clovis does not appear in the consular lists. This criticism misapprehends the meaning. Clovis is not made a *consul ordinaries*, one of the ordinary consuls of the year. He received

⁴⁶ Ibid., 89.

an honorary or titular consulship, an honour that was often conferred. The technical title of such an honorary consul was *ex consule*, and this is what is meant by Gregory's expression *tanquam consul*. The word *codicilli* for the deed by which the Emperor conferred the titular consulship is technical. There is therefore no reason to question the truth of Gregory's statement, while we recognise his inaccuracy in introducing the title *augustus*, which Clovis undoubtedly never assumed.

"The founder of the Frank monarchy died in 511, and for the last three years of his life he was by virtue of his consular title formally recognized by the [253] Empire. That title was doubtless a recognition of his championship of orthodoxy against the Arian Visigoths. Actually it made no change in the situation; but it is significant as illustrative of the relation of the Empire to the Germans who were dismembering it."[47]

The Catholic Encyclopedia likewise confirms Clovis's role in establishing a 'National' church among the Gallo—Romans in the new world:

"Beyond encouraging individual bishops to play a vital role in his kingdom, Clovis sought to use their collective presence as a force to shape a 'National' church that would serve under royal direction to institute a common religious life throughout his realm. . . . His entire religious policy played an important role in bringing the Christian establishment into support for the new regime. . . . At the same time Clovis played a significant role in establishing a political and religious order which provided a framework in which the Germanic and Roman worlds could join hands in shaping a new civilization in Western Europe."[48]

"The Church of France was distinguished for many ages by its zeal for the independence and purity of ecclesiastical elections. Under the first and second Frankish dynasties the Church was the main source and principle of civilization—the dominant power of society. All important acts of legislation emanated from its Councils. Its prelates were Ministers of State; its priests

---

[47] J. B. Bury, *The Invasion of Europe by the Barbarians* (New York, London: Norton, 1967), 251-3.
[48] *New Catholic Encyclopedia*, s.v. "Clovis" (Thomson-Gale, 2003), 4:809-11. In asso. with Catholic University, Washington, D.C.

were civil magistrates; justice was ordinarily dispensed through its tribunals. Church and State were in fact so intimately blended, as to be scarcely distinguishable the one from the other. During this period, the right of the Church to freedom of action in the choice of its chief pastors was fully admitted in theory; and elections to the episcopate were made, according to primitive usage, by the suffrages of the clergy and faithful laity of the diocese; subject always to the regulations of the canons, and to the approval of the sovereign. It is true that this practice was often interfered with, especially under the later Merovingian princes; but such cases were exceptions and abuses. Freedom of election was the universally acknowledged rule, and was more or less exactly followed until after the fall of the Carlovingian Empire."[49]

"Bishops were the ones who had helped the king of Franks to establish his power; it was through them and with them that he was governing. He knew it, and his deference to them was anterior to his conversion."[50]

"It was now not simply exaggerated politeness when one spoke of the bishops as lords of the cities[51] in which they had their seat. For the lord of a city is he who carries the concerns of the people. The high position of the bishops had its firmest grip through the dependency of the population. It was an inheritance from the last times of the Romans; this makes clear why it remained in place and increased. However, other relationships had effects as well: above all it must be considered that the bishops hailed from the cities' old, well-regarded, and rich families[52]

---

[49] W. Henley Jervis, *The Gallican Church: A History of the Church of France* (London: John Murray, Albemarle Street, 1872), 1:16.

[50] Kurth, Godefroid. Clovis, 3rd ed, 2 bks. (Brussels: Albert Dewit Library, 1923), 2:180.

[51] Dynamii ep. ad. Villic. Mett. ep. (Ep. Austr. 17 p. 130): Non credit coronae vestrae magnitude sufficere, quod in urbe cui praeestis non desinit universis immense largitas ministrare, nisi ut illos stipendiis donetis propriis qui moenibus inhabitant alienis; cf. Greg. Tur. H. Fr. VI, 46, Chilperich's statement: Periit honor noster et translates est ad episcopos civitatum.

[52] I bear in mind men such as Sidonius Appolinaris or Simplicius of Bourges; Gregor of Tours also mentions the formidable lineage of the bishops many times, as well as that of the priests; cf. for example H. Fr. IV, 12 V, 37, 45; VI, 7; X, 31; de glor. mart. 87; cf. Ven. Fort. Carm. I, 15.

[133] German ones in the episcopate[53]. . . . . The church was the only Institution [134] that had survived the great shift of all circumstances unchanged; the clergy was the only bearer of the old culture. Whoever wrote in the Sixth Century was certain to be a cleric or a monk. This not only constrained the speakers of Latin to the clergy; it was also of worth for the position to the Franks."[54]

Godefroid Kurth, the celebrated Catholic Belgian historian back in 1896, had the following to say about the role played by Clovis in establishing Christianity in the new world:

"Clovis is, in a sense, the creator of modern political society. He founded the oldest state, the one that directed the world's destinies during the centuries when the principle Western nations were created. His name is indissolubly linked to the memory of that society's origins, of which he opened the annals. So long as there is history, his place in it will be kept, not only among famous conquerors, but especially among the creators of nations and founders of civilization. There is his glory, which can be neither contested nor diminished. . . . [242] In the Frank kingdom there is a fusion so harmonious and so profound that every distinction

---

[53] Friedrich, KG. D. II p. 116 ff, has carefully gathered together the names from the signatures of the synods. When Löning, D. KR. II p. 303 expresses the speculation that the more humble church offices were still long occupied by the Romanics, these seems to me incorrect: among the names of priests, etc, which we know, there can be found relatively many German ones, cf. for example Rufi ep. ad Nicet. (c. a. 550 Ep. Austr. 21 p. 133): Sunnowech and Catellio. Gogi ep. ad Petr. Mett. episc. (Ep. Austr. 22 c. a. 568 p. 134). Here the following names are named: Johann, Theodulf, Flitomer, Mactaric, Avolus, Sinderich, Theodosius, Theodemund. An Urk. [?] of the Domnolus of Le Mans, 572, is signed by 19 clerics; they are named DInamius, Drauscio, Iniuriosus, Meterius, Populonius, Alloveus, Setrius, Leudoneus, Dauvaredus, Frigimodus, Ursicinus, Ceusus, Romolus, Daddus, Noxus, Sennovech, Theodulf, Affar, Dorus (Havet, Oeuvres I p. 420). One sees overall a mixture of names. Now, it is certain that some Romanics bore German names; but it is still difficult to assume that all of these German-named clerics are of Romanic descent. That the clauses on wergild [Wehrgeldsätze] the original text of the Ripuarian Law tit. 36, 5 for the lower clergy are based on the wergild of the Romans, while that for priests and bishops was based on the wergild of the Franks (Schröder, RG. p. 139 note 3, Brunner, RG. I p. 227 f. and 306), does not offer anything toward our question, since no one was priest who had not passed through the lower orders of the clergy.

[54] Albert Hauck, *Kirchengeschichte Deutschlands*, [*Church History of Germany*] Bd. I 3rd and 4th edition, 1904, 1:132-4.

between [243] the materials that compose the whole disappear in its absolute unity. For the others, Romans were on one side, barbarians on another; the latter oppressing the former, the former responding to tyranny by a deaf and implacable hate. For the Franks, there were neither Romans nor Barbarians; all had the name of Franks, all possessed the same rights, all banded together with a proud patriotism around the royal throne. For the others, a state of interior war was permanently in place, and the smallest conflict became a catastrophe without remedy; for the Franks, peace between the races was so strong, and their co-inhabitance so intimate, that even from the first generations they formed but a single nation.

This, not an ordinary situation, at once elevated the Frankish kingdom so high above all those of its time, permitting only it to stand up over centuries, while around it new nationalities crumbled even before being built. This situation reposed on two principles that were poorly understood everywhere outside of the Merovingian dynasty, which it made as its fundamental law of relations between the two races over which it reigned: the principle of religious unity and political equality.

This rare and double benefit was not the work of force. Founded on violence, the benefit would have been a scourge. Religious unity had been obtained by the victor's spontaneous conversion; political equality was the result of a pact that the conversion facilitated. The barbarian peoples, until then, were mixing into the Roman populations like a two-edged sword that destroys and murders all; the Franks entered there in some sort like a yeast that lifts off and activates all. The Franks became Romans through bap- [244] tism, and the Romans became Franks through participation in all the rights of the victors. They mutually lent their great qualities to one another. The Roman populations, through contact with the Barbarians, found again the nerve and vigor of a young nation; the barbarian peoples acquired strong discipline that makes saints and great men through contact with the civilized. One of the two races was regenerated and the other civilized, and it was this relation thus created between them that led up to this marvelous fusion with incredible promptness. Before the end of the sixth century, it was no longer possible in Gaul to recognize which race a man belonged to, so long as one did not know his family traditions! The Merovingian dynasty was accepted by all as the expression of the new nationality, as the image of the country. A true loyalty that was sometimes translated in a touching manner in writings of contemporaries was born of it.[55] And in the oldest sacramentaries of the Frankish Church we hear the voice of the Gaulish bishops demanding of God, with the consecrated words of the Catholic liturgy, to bless the Christian king of the Franks and his kingdom.[56] [245] To whom does the initiation of this generous and daring policy owe itself to, Clovis or to the episcopy? They both incontestably share the merit, but the honor of it returns first of all to the Gaulish episcopy and, in particular, as it seems, to the illustrious archbishop of the second Belgium.[57]

The bishops, according to the famous word of a Protestant writer, made France;[58] as it has come through the centuries, it is the work of their hands.[59] [251] . . . . It is proud to be the first of the Catholic peoples, and we have heard the ardent and juvenile expression of this sentment [252], translating itself for the first time in history on the first page of a barbarian code.

---

[55] Gregory of Tours, IV, 50; v. init.; VII, 27: ne quis extraneorum Francorum regnum audeat violare.

[56] Ut regni Francorum nomenis secura libertas in tua devotione semper exultet.— Et Francorum regni adesto principibus. Et Francorum regnum tibi subditum protege principatum.—Protege regnum Francorum nomenis ubique rectores, ut eorum votiva prosperitas pax tuorum possit essepopulorum.—Et Francorum regni nomenis virtute tuae compremas majestatem.—Hanc igitur oblationem servitutis nostrae quam tibi offerimus pro salute et incolomitate vel statu regni Francorum, etc. V. L. Delisle *Mémoire sur d'anciens sacramentaires français (Mém. De l'Académie des Inscriptions et Belles-Lettres,* 1886, pp. 71 and 72).

[57] Hauck, I p. 141

[58] From Gibbon, *Histoire de la décadence de l'Empire romain,* vol. VII, Ch 38, p 24, Paris 1812. However, it is not necessary, as a multitude of writers have done for a century (most recently Lecoy de La Marche, *La fondation de la France,* 1893, pp. 64 and 100, who makes out-of-touch reasonings on the origin of the word) to say that "the bishops made France as the bees make their hives." This expression is the product of the very involuntary collaboration between Gibbon and Joseph de Maistre, or rather is a product of the light reading that the latter was given. Here is how Gibbon expresses himself in speaking of the bishops: "the progress of superstition augmented their influence, and one can attribute in some sort the establishment of the Frankish monarchy to the alliance of 100 prelates who commanded in the independent or revolted cities of Gaul." And here is how J. De Maistre writes in his book, *Du Pape* (ed. Pélagaud 1870, p. 7): "The bishops, as Gibbon observes, *made the kingdom of France;* nothing is truer. The bishops constructed this monarchy as bees construct a hive." But see *Les Soirées de Saint-Petersbourg,* vol. II, p. 222 (Lyon edition): "Why was the most noble, the strongest, the most powerful of monarchies made, literally, by the bishops (an opinion of Gibbon) as a hive is made by bees?

[59] A pact between the Northern bishops (St. Remi) with Clovis.

Such is, such will be, over the course of centuries, the kingdom founded by the bishops and by Clovis. His glory is to have made of himself without hesitation the agent of Episcopal politics."[60]

Professor Michel Rouche finds himself in total agreement with Godefroid Kurth:

"Godefroid Kurth was therefore right in 1896 when he concluded that Clovis's action rested on a two-fold benefit, "the principle of religious unity and that of political equality" (*Clovis, op. cit.*, p. 572), for one did not go without the other. Romanity could only be Christian for the Roman law and Catholicism, both claiming universalism, mutually comforted each other. . . ."[61]

---

[60] Kurth, Godefroid. *Clovis*, 3rd ed, 2 bks. (Brussels: Albert Dewit Library, 1923), 2:241-252.

[61] Rouche, Michel. *Clovis*, (Fayard: France, 1996), 380.

4

A.D. 508 and the Legislation that "Set Up" the Beast Power

In order for the *"arms"* of a civil entity (in this case, Clovis) to *"stand"* or to have allied itself on behalf of another, (that of Catholicism) the legal process must be engaged. Therefore, legal documentation will reveal that just such legislation will be found in the books of the legal code of the day. This documentation will cement the accuracy of the scriptures and the union of church and state that *"they"* so cordially *"set up"* in the year A.D. 508.

In the late 560's or early 570's, when the Byzantine historian Agathias was writing the history of Justinian's wars, he chose to include in it an excursus on the Frankish kingdoms:

> ". . . The Franks are not nomads, as some of the barbarians certainly are, but actually follow a political system that is for the most part Roman, and the same laws as us. In other respects too—contracts, marriage and religion—they follow the same practice. For they are all in fact Christian, and completely orthodox. They have magistrates and priests in their towns and celebrate the festivals just as we do."[62]

---

[62] Agathias, *Historiarum Libri Quinque*, ed. R. Keydell (Berlin: n.p., 1967), 1:2; trans. Greek, cited in Averil Cameron, "Agathias on the early Merovingians," *Annali della Scuola Normale Superiore di Pisa* 37 (n.p., 1968), 95-140, at p. 105. See also Yitzhak Hen, *Culture & Religion in Merovingian Gaul, AD 481-751* (Leiden: Brill, 1995), introduction. Remember, Averil Cameron reminds us that Agathias is the one to rely on in Frankish matters. See Averil Cameron, *Agathias* (Oxford: n.p., 1970), 50-51, 54-5, 120-21; id., *Procopius and the Sixth Century* (London: n.p., 1985), 210-13; id., "Agathias on the early Merovingians," 136-139. See also H. Ditten, "Zu Prokops Nachrichten über die deutschen Stämme," *Byzantinoslavica* 36 (n.p., 1971), 1-24. Agathius lived from A.D. 536-582. See also, Frendo, Joseph, Trans; *Agathias The Histories*, (Berlin-New York, Walter De Gruyter, 1975), 10.

Since it is admitted that the Franks adhere to a similar political and legal system as that of the Romans, follow the same practice in religion and are completely orthodox, it behooves us to investigate their legal code. To do so, we must turn to the *Lex Romana Visigothorum* law code:

"Alaric II composed, in 506, the Lex Romana Visigothorum, commonly called "Breviaricum Alaricianum," for the benefit of the Roman residents in the kingdom of the Visigoths. It contains extracts from the Theodosian Code and the Novels annexed to it, from the two works of Gaius and Paulus, from the Gregorian and Hermagenian Codes, and from the Responses of Papinian. This code was in force in Spain till the middle of the seventh century. In Gaul the code of Alaric was also in force throughout those provinces, which the Franks conquered from the Visigoths. The Burgundians also formed a code, in 517, known as the Lex Romana Burgundiorum. This was the shortest and most insignificant of them all. It was in force until 536 when the kingdom of the Burgundians was conquered by the Franks, when it was superseded by the Breviarium."[63]

What is of interest, for our study's purpose, is why Alaric composed his code of law, and what the political and ecclesiastical conditions were at that time. Notice, too, that Alaric, an Arian Christian, undertook his compilation of law in part to "conciliate his Catholic subjects," and that bishops participated in its formulation and in its approval:

"The sources of Roman law, however, which included the Hermogenian, Gregorian and Theodosian codes, the Theodosian Novels and the writings of the jurists, and interpretations of law now unknown were too voluminous, their language was not sufficiently clear for popular use, and custom had also made changes in their interpretation. These facts and the opportunity to conciliate his Catholic subjects, who had suffered persecution under Euric, and who, it was feared, might support the Franks in the conflict with that nation which seemed imminent, led Alaric II to undertake a compilation of Roman law for use in purely Roman litigation. This was the *Lex Romana Visigothorum*, generally

---

[63] Andrew Stephenson, *History of Roman Law* (Boston: Little, Brown, and Company, 1912; reprint, Littleton, CO: Fred B. Rothman, 1992), 106-7.

known as the *Breviary of Alaric*. It is the work of a commission of provincial Roman lawyers and bishops. It was approved by a council of bishops and nobles and was then published in 506 with the command that in the future no other source of law should be used by Roman subjects. In its legislation and interpretations of law, which were derived from existing glosses, we have the Roman law of the fifth and early sixth centuries as it was applied in the courts. A review of its provisions relating to the church and clergy will illustrate their position in an age when the civilizations of German and Roman were blending and ecclesiastical aims were coming to dominate both. The political conditions under which the Breviary was compiled prevented any extensive reproduction of the imperial edicts against heresy. Only two of these in the Theodosian code were included, one in which Honorius ordered the 'one and true Catholic faith' to be observed in Africa, the other his confirmation of the legislation of Theodosius, while the Novels of Theodosius II and Valentinian III, enacted when heresy was no longer a political problem, were allowed to remain unaltered."[64]

"The glosses of the *Breviary* were formerly regarded as unimportant. But legal historians now recognize that they represent the custom of the later fifth and sixth centuries."[65]

In *The New Catholic Encyclopedia* under "Lex Romana Visigothorum," the great significance of this law code is recognized:

"LEX ROMANA VISIGOTHORUM, also called, since the 16th century, the *Brevairium Alarici*. It is a code of Roman law issued by the Westgothic King Alaric II in 506 for the Latin population living in his kingdom. A commission made up of legal specialists prepared a draft of the code, which was then examined and approved by an assembly of bishops and provincials. It was abolished in the Westgothic kingdom by King Recceswind in 654, but in southern France, even after the collapse of Westgothic rule, it served the Roman population and the Church into the 12th century, as one of the most important sources for the knowledge of Roman law. The *Lex Romana Visigothorum* contains extracts

---

[64]   William K. Boyd, *The Ecclesiastical Edicts of the Theodosian Code* (New York: Columbia University Press, 1905; reprint, Clark, New Jersey: Lawbook Exchange, 2005), 109-11.

[65]   Ibid., 110.

from the *Theodosian Code (438) and imperial constitutions of the successors of Theodosius to 463, worked-over material from the Institutes of Gaius, the Sentences of Paul, parts of the *Codex Gregorianus and Codex Hermogenianus*, and also a citation from Papinian. In addition, it contains interpretations that explain the meaning of the extracts or fit them into the altered conditions of its own time. While quite inferior to the codification of *Justinian (the *Corpus Iuris Civilis*, which appeared only 30 years later), the *Lex Romana Visigothorum* constitutes a significant contribution to late Roman legal science in the western half of the empire."[66]

In yet another source, the long-standing, far-reaching dominance of the *Lex Romana Visigothorum* is again validated:

"In 654 it was repealed by Recceswind, who enacted a new code which was to apply to Goths and Romans indifferently, and thereafter it was forgotten in Spain. In other countries, however, especially France, though it had no formal validity, it continued to be used, (See especially Wretschko's article printed in Mommsen's Theodosianus, I. cccvii sqq.) and was the chief document through which knowledge of Roman law was preserved in the West until, in the eleventh century. . . ."[67]

Thus far, we have established that the Breviary law code, an extensive and complex code of law established in 506, was an important development for the regulation of civil life for Gallo-Romans in Gaul as well as of the Franks. Its merits caused long and widespread use in maintaining social order and civil peace. It is also acknowledged from the academic community that Clovis adopted the *Lex Romana Visigothorum* law code immediately after the battle of the Visigoths at Vougle in A.D. 508:

"Clovis wanted a juridical pluralism by maintaining the palace and the central government well away from the Salic law, but by practicing unity in diversity, he also adopted, after Vouillé, Alaric's Breviary for all of his Gallo-Roman subjects, and we know that this text was also applied north of the Loire. The principle of development was the same (cf. chapter XI, p. 304). The

---

[66] *New Catholic Encyclopedia*, s.v. "Lex Romana Visigothorum" (Washington: Catholic University of America, 1967), 8:688.

[67] H. F. Jolowicz, *Historical Introduction to the Study of Roman Law* (London: Cambridge University Press, 1932), 482.

juriconsults who had written it had taken care to specify, in a warning preceding the body of law, that the prince (*princeps*) is bound by the laws that he promulgated."[68]

Even the records of the church council Clovis convened in AD 511 fully cement the fact that he used the *Lex Romana Visigothorum* law code:

> ". . . *Id constituimus observandum quod ecclesiastici canones decreverunt et lex romana constituit.* . . . "

In other words:

> ". . . . We have decided that which shall be observed is what the ecclesiastic canons have decreed and the Roman law [*Lex Romana Visigothorum*] has established."[69]

However, in our study, the Breviary has even greater significance because it contained certain constitutions from the preexisting Theodosian law code. Those constitutions, which all citizens under the Breviary law code were legally bound to obey, were religious in nature. The *Theodosian* law code, compiled in A.D. 438, contained three constitutions of particular importance:

"TITLE 11: RELIGION (DE RELIGIONE)

1. Emperors Arcadius and Honorius Augustuses to Apollodorus, Proconsul of Africa.

<u>Whenever there is an action involving matters of religion, the bishops must conduct such action.</u> But all other cases which belong to the judges ordinary and to the usage of the secular law must be heard in accordance with the laws.

Given on the thirteenth day before the kalends of September at Padua in the year of the consulship of the Most Noble Theodorus. –August 20, 399.

[Interpretation:] This law does not need any interpretation.

---

[68] Rouche, Michel. *Clovis*. Fayard, France, 1996, 335.

[69] *Canon I of Orleans I*, AD 511.

2. Emperors Arcadius, Honorius, and Theodosius Augustuses to Diotimus, Proconsul of Africa.

It is Our will that the edict regarding unity which Our Clemency dispatched throughout the districts of Africa shall be posted, throughout various regions, in order that <u>all men may know that the one and true Catholic faith in Almighty God, as confessed by right belief, shall be preserved.</u>

Given on the third day before the nones of March at Revenna in the year of the second consulship of Stilicho and the consulship of Anthemius.—March 5, 405.

3. Emperors Honorius and Theodosius Augustuses to Their dear friend, Marcellinus, Greetings.

We abolish the new superstition, and <u>We command that those regulations in regard to the Catholic law shall be preserved unimpaired and inviolate as they were formerly ordained by antiquity or established by the religious authority of Our Fathers or confirmed by Our Serenity.</u>

Given on the day before the ides of October at Revenna in the year of the consulship of the Most Noble Varanes. —October 14, 410."[70]

Clyde Pharr lists the *Breviary of Alaric* law codes in his footnotes for title 11 on pg. 476, 600. The following quote is taken directly from the *Lex Romana Visigothorum*. Also called the *Breviary of Alaric*, this is the most complete work of this law code to date which was issued in 506 in Latin. The original is supplied for those who would appreciate the documentation:

"TITULUS V. a) DE RELIGIONE. 1. b) Impp. Arcadius et Honorius AA. Apollodoro Proconsuli Africae. Quoties de religione agitur, episcopos convenit agitare; ceteras vero causas , quae ad ordinarios cognitores vel ad usum publici iuris pertinent, legibus oportet audiri. Dat. XIII. Kal. Sept. Patavio, Theodoro V. C. Cos. Haec Lex interpretatione non indiget. (2.) c) Imppp. Arca-

---

[70] Clyde Pharr, *The Theodosian Code and Novels and the Sirmondian Constitutions* (Clark, New Jersey: Lawbook Exchange, 2001), 476. Clyde Pharr lists the *Breviary of Alaric* law codes in his footnotes for title 11 on pg. 476. See also pg. 600

dius, Honorius et Theodosius AAA. Diotimo Proconsuli Africae. Edictum, quod de unitate per Africanas regiones clementia nostra direxit, per diversas provincias proponi volumus, ut omnibus innotescat, Dei omnipotentis unam et veram fidem catholicam, quam recta credulitas confitetur, esse retinendam. Dat. III. Non. Mart. Ravenna, Stilicone II. et Anthemio Coss. (3.) d) Impp. Honorius et Theodosius AA. Marcellino suo salutem. Ea, quae circa catholicam legem vel olim ordinavit antiquitas, vel parentum nostrorum auctoritas religiosa constituit, vet nostra serenitas roboravit, novella superstitione summota, integra et inviolata custodiri praecipimus. Dat. prid. Id. Oct. Ravenna, Varane V. C. Cos. Haec Lex interpretatione non indiget e). EXPLICIT CODICIS THEODOSIANI LIBER DECIMUS SEXTUS."[71]

For this same work in German, see Max Conrat (Cohn), *Breviarium Alaricianum* (1903, 1963). See also Theodor Mommsen, Theodosiani, for a good reference to the *Breviary* codes in Latin.

These three constitutions from the *Theodosian* law code were incorporated into the *Breviary* law code in 506. Their presence in the Breviary law code gives unmistakable prophetic significance to the following historical summation, as Schaferdiek rightly commented:

"The exclusivity of the bishops' jurisdiction in ecclesiastical affairs is legally fixed."[72]

"When Clovis ascended to the throne, [508] he saw the imperium in the West and with the church-rulership of Caesar no longer able to stand. . . . it was the law-book of Alaric for this population which also won validity now in France.[73]

---

[71] Gustavus Haenel, *Lex Romana Visigothorum*, XVI. 5.1-3. (Teubner: (Lipsiae) 1849, 1962), 252.

[72] Code *Theodosian*. XVI 11.1 = *Lex Romana Visigothorum*, XVI. 5.1.
Schaferdiek, Kurt von. *Die Kirche in den Reichen der Westgoten und Suewen bis zur Errichtung der westgotischen katholischen Staatskirche*. Berlin: Walter de Gruyter, 1967, 53. [The Church in the Empires of the Visigoths and the Suevi up to the Establishment of the Visigothic Catholic State Church].

[73] Schubert, Hans, *Staat und Kirche in den arianischen Königreichen und im Reiche Chlodwigs*. Bd. 26. (Munich: Druck and Verlag von R. Oldenbourg, 1912), 167-8. [*Nation and Church in the Arian Kingdoms and in Clovis' Kingdom*. (Munich Press and Publishing House of R. Oldenbourg, 1912), 167-8.]

It is sometimes just as important if not more so of what the Bible is not saying then what it is. For example, the scriptures do not deny nor do they affirm that the "daily" was usurped from Christ for the first time in A.D. 508. What the scriptures do affirm is that in AD 508, the "daily" or the ministry of Christ was then legally usurped through legislation and cast down from heaven, *jointly*, (Daniel 11:31) by Clovis (The State) and the Church (Catholicism) to the earth as had been foretold by the scriptures and faithfully acknowledged and recorded by the *Lex Romana Visigothorum*, and backed by Ellen White, as well as competent historians that have chronicled the steps taken by church and state in the formation of the beast power into the New World.

After Clovis received the titles and dignity of Roman Patricius and consul from the Greek Emperor Anastasius, the diadem and purple robe in the Church of St. Martin, and baptism at Rheims in 508, he was then on his way to Paris to his royal residence and capital. Henceforth, from his coronation in 508, it was the *Breviary* law code that was in place and implemented as the official law code in the provinces of the Gallo-Romans and also in those provinces that were conquered by the Franks. As already established by legal historians, that same law code remained in use until the twelfth century.

Thus, there is indisputable historical confirmation and legislative documentation that "the one and true Catholic faith" was indeed "set up" or established as prophesied. With "Catholic law" "commanded" to be "preserved unimpaired," and with the exclusivity of the bishops' jurisdiction in ecclesiastical affairs legally fixed, Clovis had become the first Catholic king of the ten symbolic horns of the Western Roman Empire dating from A.D. 476. His ascension to the throne in 508 brought in its train the first instituted "National" religion. All other faiths were outlawed. Then began the long chain reaction in prophetic history until every European nation accepted the one and true Catholic faith and was led to follow the example of the Franks in using the civil power to enforce the church's dogmas!

It is not without great significance that Gregory of Tours likens Clovis, the first King that ever embraced the Catholic Religion in the new world, to that of Constantine, the first Emperor that ever recognized the Catholic Religion in the old world:

> "Like a new Constantine, he moved forward to the water, to
> blot out the former leprosy, to wash away in this new stream the

foul stains borne from old days. . . . Of his army were baptized more than three thousand."[74]

However, a most significant point needs to be understood here. When Clovis adopted the *Lex Romana Visigothorum*, also called the *Breviary of Alaric* law code, for his Roman subjects, it was not established under the same premise as a Constantinian Christianity under the *Theodosian* law code of the pagan Roman Empire:

"Clovis bowed to laws developed by others and reinforced them through his own authority. He founded anew a State of law, even if he practiced unity in diversity and recognized the Church's sovereignty in the spiritual domain. In each text, he found the means to reinforce the autonomy of the State and the rights of each people all the while refusing a Constantinian Christianity. Obviously, religious unity was the most important for him: it allowed him in particular to make Arianism disappear, to condemn incestuous marriages, and to distinguish the non-religious from the priests."[75]

"When Clovis ascended to the throne, he saw the imperium in the West and with the church-rulership of Caesar no longer able to stand. He had to deal with the inheritances of the latter (with whom all circumstances were already altered, the old law was in opposition with the new, pushed through and modified), since 486 only with the powerful young states which had emerged through Germanic strength on the old cultural terrain of Southern Gaul, the creation [168] and it was the law-book of Alaric for this population which also won validity now in France.[76]

"The kingdom of the Franks is not a Constantinian Christianity. Clovis, by accepting this concept of unity in mutual independence and in respect of religious truths, lays down [341] the foundations of a society. He destroys the Roman and Germanic

---

[74] Gregory of Tours' *The History of the Franks*, trans. O. M. Dalton (Oxford: Clarendon Press, 1927), 2:22 (31), pgs. 69-70.

[75] Rouche, Michel. *Clovis*. Fayard, France, 1996, 346.

[76] Schubert, Hans, *Staat und Kirche in den arianischen Königreichen und im Reiche Chlodwigs*. Bd. 26. (Munich: Druck and Verlag von R. Oldenbourg, 1912), 167-8. [*Nation and Church in the Arian Kingdoms and in Clovis' Kingdom*. (Munich Press and Publishing House of R. Oldenbourg, 1912), 167-8.]

societies where the emperor was godlike and the king a priest."[77]

Godefroid Kurth acknowledges how Clovis used his "arms" to enforce and protect the dogmas of the Catholic Church:

"There it is, the position conquered by the king [Clovis] in the life of the Frank people. The one he holds in the Church is of a special nature; he exerts an influence equaled by anyone else. Undoubtedly, he is neither, like the emperor, above it to dominate it, nor outside of it to fight against it like the Arian kings did. He belongs to it both as a simple faithful man and as a sovereign; faithful, he obeys to its laws, he believes in its doctrine; king, and Catholic king, he listens to the advices of its prelates, he protects it with his forces, he has an action and an authority over which it does not fight. [174] An authentic episode will show us very closely this situation of the royalty faced with the Church, and the nature of its acknowledge influence. On Clovis' recommendation, Saint Remy of Reims had conferred the Holy Orders on a certain Claudius. This person was probably suspect already; after the king's death, he caused a great scandal. We see that among other things, fraudulently he had stripped a faithful man named Celsus of his possessions, and Saint Remy acknowledged himself the fact that he was guilty [175] of sacrilege. Nevertheless he intervened in favor of him and demanded him to be eligible for penitence, whereas he should have been excommunicated according to the terms of the council of Orleans. This leniency caused him bitter reproaches from three bishops, Leon of Sens, Heraclius of Paris and Theodore of Auxerre. As much as it is possible to make their attitude out, they made the bishop of Reims responsible of his protégé's misdemeanors; in particular they made it his duty to look for and compensate Claudius' creditors himself; finally, they reminded him that if this poor soul could have had discredited him on his robe, it was thanks to pusillanimous Remy, who had ordained him on the king's demand and contrary to the canons. In his response which has been preserved to us, the saint defends himself quite feebly on getting to the bottom of things; moreover he admits having deferred to Clovis' will and pursues energetically:"[78]

---

[77] Rouche, Michel. *Clovis.* Fayard, France, 1996, 339, 341.
[78] Kurth, Godefroid. *Clovis,* 3rd ed, 2 bks. (Brussels: Albert Dewit Library, 1923), 2:173-5

Kurth now quotes part of a letter from the Bishop St. Remi,[79] however, we include the entire primary document translated from the Latin:

Bishop Remegius to the truly holy and very blessed in Christ by the merits of our lords brothers Heraclius, Leo and Theodosius.

[410]

1. "Apostle Paul says in his letter: "Dearness never departs." Which, in order that you sent such letters to me, does not abate in your feelings. For on behalf of Claudius I have established a simple request, that you produce the one whom you write is not a presbyter, into the indignation of your heart by me. 2. I do not deny that that one has gravely committed an offense; but it was proper that you had announced for my age, even though not for merits, what, with a propitious divinity, is said: I preside for fifty and three years on the Episcopal seat, and no one has addressed me so brashly. You say: "Better that you have not been born." This had been opportune for me, lest I had heard the disgrace of the transgressor. 3. I made Claudius presbyter, not because I was corrupted by reward, but the testimony of the very excellent king, who was not only a preacher of the catholic faith, but also a defender. You write: "What you ordered, is not canonical." You are engaged in the highest priesthood; the presul of the regions, the guardian of the fatherland, the conqueror of races has enjoined. You have broken forth stirred up to deceive against me so much, in order that you have not announced to the author of your episcopate. 4. I have asked, that Claudius, perpetrator of a sacrilege, be preserved for penitence. For I have read, I do read, that the Ninivites avoided the annihilation predicted by the celestial denunciation through penitence, which John, precursor of the Lord, preached in the gospel, so that, the things of the people made the approaching kingdom of the heavens, and do not perish. In the Apocalypse it is written by the angels of the churches from the precept of the lord savior, that, the things which they had done less worthily, they corrected with the satisfaction of penitence. 5. Concerning the wrath I understand by the language of your sanctity, what lapse you do not lament {or: that you do not lament the lapse} after the ruin; but I see that you wish more, not to change and to live, when the Lord has said: "I do not wish the death of the dying, but that he change and live." This hastens me to fol-

---

79 (I) M.G.H., *Epistoloe Merovingici et Karolini oevi*, p. 114.

low, not to neglect but to keep this wish of the Lord, because he has placed me not for wrath, but for the care of humans, and to obey the piety, rather than the fury. **6.** You put in your letter, that a certain Celsus trusted to Claudius, who when he was abducted, and whether he lives or has died you do not know, and you instruct that I am the inquisitor of this one and you do not know, if he should be interrogated in the world or if in the underworld, and you wish that your own matters be restored by me, which I did not know had been suffered: you direct impossible things, in order that you continue impious things. [411]

You write that the numbers of years for me is a jubilee, laughing more, than rejoicing for the love, for which, when the bond of dearness has been broken insincerely, it is neither abstained by you nor brought. It unfolds {=is finished}."[80]

Clovis was only following the precedent set before him by the church:

"In order to restore peace after the resolution and to take all possibilities of spreading their crack-pot teaching from the heretics, the Pope suggested that Acacius should have become introduced and propose that the Emperor that anybody who was consecrated by a heretic should be dismissed from the community of people through a special imperial constitution.[81] With that the Pope wanted to prevent the danger of a contamination through the Emperor and to immunize the legal belief system. Here, it handled a very early practical application of the organic fundament in the external area of the church,[82] and it is one of

[80] Body of Christians, Latin Series, CXVII, Book of the Defender of Sparks, Letters of Desiderius of Cadurcense/Cahors, Austrasican and Other Letters, Brepols Editors of the Pontiff Pertaining to Print Of Turnholt, MCMLVII, The letters of Austrasica, By the care and interest of W. Gundlach, (Translated from the Latin). Corpvs Christianorvm, Series Latina CXVII, (Gundlach, W; Epistvlae Avstrasicae, Tvrnholti, 1957).

[81] JK 577: [JK = Phillip Jaffe ed. *Regesta Pontificum Romanorum*, [Records of the Roman Pontiffs] (Leipzig, 1885).] PS 121-122. V. GRUMEL: *Les regestes* Nr. 149 Consider also Avellana [Avellana = Guenther, Otto. Editor, Epistulae Imperatorum Pontificum Aliorum, Avellana Quae Dicitur Collectio, 2 pts. In Corpus Scriptorum Ecclesiasticorum Latinorum, vol. 35. Prague: F. Tempsky, 1895.] 369-398 Nr. 95; EVAGRIUS: *Hist. eccl.* 3 (PGr 86/2, 2609 ff.).

[82] To that, also consider 2 Cor. 11,29, where the organic belief in the graphic speech was stated. Simplicius wanted to summon the help of the Emperor "ut pro omnibus, quae regno eius Dominus tribuit, nec ulterius in orbe terrarum, quas subditas suo

the oldest testimonies for the idea, that heresy is an infected sickness, that makes it necessary, to isolate the germ-carriers.[83] About this, Simplicius clarified in this writing, that he would administer the ban to the originators of the denounced heresy and would shut them out of the community of the Christians.[84] One would be tempted to speak of a anticipation of observation and banning here. Simplicius saw the leadership ground of the Emperor in his charge of care, because God would have awarded him leadership, in order to take the men of legal belief into his care. The intention of imperial leadership is protection of the Christian faith."[85]

"One expects, that he would obey the godly decrees as the Christian leader.[86] The Emperor would know without a doubt that the highest position would be entrusted to him in the area of the mortal matters provided that, when it involved godly matters, he would listen to the specific administrator.[87] And the Emperor was immediately charged that is would be his charge to learn, not just to teach- it turned the phrase, which had become the ground floor of papal argumentation, and he should therefore subordinate his leadership will of priests in godly matters, in that he obeyed the guidelines laid down by the church. The Emperor would not be allowed to self-importantly ignore churchly orders, because "God wanted your Majesty of the church to subject your neck in pious devotion."[88]

(Cont.)

cognoscit imperio, ecclesiae Dei ab haereticorum *contagione* et privatate violentu, sed doctrinae diabolicae etiam a conventu hominum segregandi iubeantur excludi" (PS 121 Z. 12-17)

[83] Exactly as the middle-age papacy prescribed" PG 300 f.; PGP 79 f. Consider also JK 579: the innocent ability of the "perniciosa contagia" was protected (Avellana 141 Z. 16-17 Nr. 62).

[84] PS 122 Z. 1 ff.

[85] JK 576: Avellana 137 Z. 10-15 Nr. 60. [Pope Simplicius letter to the Emperor Zeno, dated April 6, 477.] Ullman, Walter von. *Päpste und Papsttum* [*Popes and Papacy*]: *Gelasius I. (492–496)*. Bd. 18. Stuttgart: Anton Hiersemann, 1981, 124.

[86] JK 601: "Puto autem quod pietas tua, quae etiam suis mavult vinci legibus quam reniti, coelestibus debeat parere decretis" (PS 82 Z. 12 f. Nr. 33)

[87] "Ita humanarum sibi rerum fastigium noverit esse commissum, *ut* tamen ea, quae divina sunt, per dispensatores divinitus adtributos pericipienda non ambigat" (PS 82 Z. 14 f. Nr. 33).

[88] Ullman, Walter von. *Päpste und Papsttum* [*Popes and Papacy*]: *Gelasius I. (492–496)*. Bd. 18. Stuttgart: Anton Hiersemann, 1981, 146.

"But the writing to the Emperor made something else clear. It repeated the thesis, that the Christian religion is not a natural religion, that the Christian belief content may not be recorded with natural means, even because he is not of natural origin, but was given by God himself, wherefore only the "dispensatories", as the writing called the administrators, could give guidelines; they alone are authorized to spread information about the Christian norms and axioms, to clarify and determine what is Christian and what the Christian norm doesn't correspond to by virtue of their education and their special standing. In the opposition pair of *discere-docere* it was manifested the knowledge and awareness element which was essential for the Christianity in sharply contoured form. Christian norms must-as the beliefs stated therein made clear-be learned by those who were authorized; they could not be "naturally" understood."[89]

"The fear of God and protection of the Catholic community will be the only valid motives;[90] there will be no stronger incentive than the maintenance of the true faith."[91]

"In order to most powerfully emphasize the care of the Emperor. The concepts of *defensor fidei, custos fidei, divinae cultor religionis* and of *imitator Christi*[92] [defendor of the faith, guardian/protector of the faith, worshipper/supporter of the divine religion—imitator of Christ] don't require commentary."[93]

The following letter was written by Pope Fellix III (II) (A.D.

---

[89] Exactly this consideration makes it understandable, why LEO the Great had forbidden the preaching of laymen: JK 495. The ban also counted for monks. H. KOCH: *Gelasius im Dienst* 48 A. 1 refers to Seneca as the root of the diastasis *discere-docere* (Ep. 6,62 and Ep. 7,8). Ullman, Walter von. *Päpste und Papsttum* [Popes and Papacy]: *Gelasius I. (492–496)*. Bd. 18. Stuttgart: Anton Hiersemann, 1981, 148.

[90] JK 611: PS 42 Z. 23-24.

[91] JK 611: "Nulla tamen maior est necessitas quam divino cultui et religioni, unde omnia prosperantur . . . et cuncta adversa removentur" (PS 40 Z. 23 ff. Nr. 11.). Ullman, Walter von. *Päpste und Papsttum* [Popes and Papacy]: *Gelasius I. (492–496)*. Bd. 18. Stuttgart: Anton Hiersemann, 1981, 170.

[92] The legitimate expression by [Pope] SIMPLICIUS: JK 576: Avellana 137 Z. 8 f. Nr. 60; further [Pope] FELIX III.: JK 595: "fidei custos et defensor orthdoxae" (PS 74 Z. 6. Nr. 22). [Pope] BONIFACE I. cited Pg. 54 A. 66 and [Pope] LEO th. GR.: JK 546: Avellana 117 Z. 5 f. Nr. 51.

[93] Ullman, Walter von. *Päpste und Papsttum* [*Popes and Papacy*]: *Gelasius I. (492–496)*. Bd. 18. Stuttgart: Anton Hiersemann, 1981, 195.

483–492) in March 483 to the Emperor Zeno:

> "Since the universal Church rejoiced that peace was returned
> to it, after the heretics, who endeavored to support themselves
> through you, have been constrained, and the rule of your piety
> has received also the victory concerning its enemies; and through
> the whole world there was a prayer of everyone for the safety of
> your serenity to the Lord/master of the priests, that your piety *the
> protector and defender of the orthodox faith*, reign under the propi-
> tiation of the eternal king. . . ."[94]

To see the entire translated Latin letter and many more from
the Popes demanding from the emperor the protection of the faith
between the years A.D. 476 and 508, see my website at www.the-
sourcehh.org. Gelasius has been proven by historians to be the pen
and influence behind Pope Simplicius as well as behind Pope Felix
III. The significance of this is that Gelasius was setting the ground
work for a paradigm shift in church and state relationships in the
new world. Gelasius was to become Pope Gelasius I in 492. Pope
Gelasius I had promoted the clear separation between kingship
and priesthood but demanded the protection of the faith from the
state with the force of its arms.[95] This paradigm shift has been recognized by historians as well as legal historians. Since this is a
critical point, we shall include the comments of Walter von Ullman, as well:

> "This first letter of Felix is the start of the crowning end of
> the leonian [Pope Leo the Great] program through Gelasius and
> a landmark in the development of the papacy from late-antiquity
> to the middle age. Therefore in the letter the patrinological thesis
> stood in the foreground, which closely stamped all of the writings
> of Felix and Gelasius. Petrus spoke similarly through the Pope to
> the Emperor as his most distinguished son[96]- the rebirths ideal
> had ensured its place in the official speech and as far as the let-
> ter went into the ecclesiastic thesis that held together the church
> as a complete *Corporation*. The standpoint held by the successor

---

[94] Thiel, Andreas, ed. *Epistolae Romanorum pontificum genuinae*, bk. 1. Brunsbergae
In Aedibus Eduardi Peter, 1868, 240.

[95] Ibid., Ep. 12, 349-358.

[96] "Rursus ergo apostolic Petri veneranda confessio maternis te vocibus ut suorum
praecipuum filiorum compellere non desinens confidential tuae pietatis exclamat .
. ." (PS 64 Z. 7-8).

of Petrus would be the only standing[97], because through him, the "representative" of Petrus[98] installed by God himself, would speak. For the benefit passed down to him through God, the Emperor should not turn out to be unthankful,[99] because the true faith would have effected the rebirth of his imperial worth.[100] Therefore he should direct his leadership, that his subjects could take part in the full effect of the true rebirth."[101]

The author uses capital C throughout his discourse for Corporation in the legal sense which is significant as the church pushes onward with her political agenda. Our understanding of this paradigm shift is made plain with the following quote. In A.D. 494, Pope Gelasius I wrote to Emperor Anastasius declaring the theory of the two swords, or two powers, governing the world:

"'There are two . . . by which the world is chiefly ruled: the sacred authority (auctoritas) of bishops and the royal power (potestas). Of those the responsibility of bishops is more weighty insofar as they will answer also for the kings of men themselves at divine judgment.' The popes did not claim to wield the temporal sword but to direct its proper use. . . . Gelasius conceived church governance as analogous to that exercised by temporal rulers. This juridical understanding of the papacy guided papal theory and practice in subsequent centuries. The two swords theory maintained that secular leaders were subject to the pope's spiritual authority."[102]

Pope Gelasius I was working hard to move the papacy away from a Constantinian Christianity under the *Theodosian* law code

---

[97] "Nonne mea fidea est, quam solam esse veram et nulla adversitate superandam Dominus ipse monstravit, qui ecclesiae suae in mea confessione fundandae portas inferi numquam praevalituras esse promisit" (PS 64 Z. 16 f.).

[98] ". . . tam per eius *qualemcumque vicarium* quam *praesentis apostoli* velut auctoritate commonitus" (PS 64 Z. 22-23).

[99] "*Non ingrates* existere videaris conlate *felicitates auctori*" (PS 64 Z. 25 Nr. 20).

[100] "Haec (scil. fides) te *renatum* ad *regiam* sustulit *dignitatem*" (PS 64 Z. 19).

[101] "PS 68 Z. 26-27 Nr. 20." Ullman, Walter von. *Päpste und Papsttum [Popes and Papacy]: Gelasius I. (492–496).* Bd. 18. Stuttgart: Anton Hiersemann, 1981, 137.

[102] J. Michael Miller, *The Shepherd and the Rock: Origins, Development, and Mission of the Papacy* (Huntington, IN: Our Sunday Visitor Publishing, 1995), 94-5. Imprimatur. For the entire translated letter from the Latin see **APPENDIX IV**, pg. 123.

of the pagan Roman Empire in order to further distance the civil power from any internal interference in church procedures and dogmas. Continuing on, Karl Voigt addresses the intermingling of Caesar in the affairs of the church as he outlines the course taken by Pope Gelasius I:

> "The next Pope, *Gelasius I*, [A.D. 492-496] occupied himself in an even more thoroughgoing manner with these questions.[103] He had already, in fact, authored the writing of Felix III to Caesar Zeno as the former's chancellor. Already in the year 488, still before his elevation to the Papal see, he explained in a letter to the Oriental bishops: Caesar is the son of the church, *not its head*,[104]in religious things it was his duty to *learn* and not to *teach*; he obtained his power from God for the administration of *the state*, the direction of the *church* on the other hand should be granted according to God's will to the *priests* and *not the secular powers*.[105] Here again, the idea of the *separation* of the spheres of activity of the two powers is clearly expressed; here again, as earlier by Hosius of Corduba and Ambrosius of Mailand and then by Felix III in his letter authored by Gelasius to Caesar Zeno, it is entirely recognized that to Caesar is granted in *secular* matters a high authority conferred on him by God. But the direction of the church is not his affair, and it is the sole responsibility of the *priesthood*. Even more important that this letter is a *tractate* in which Pope Gelasius went more comprehensively into the question of the rights of the secular ruler in the ecclesiastical area.[106]The *old-testament king-priesthood*, as already mentioned, offered an important example for the unification of secular and spiritual powers in one hand; Gelasius nevertheless rejected completely such a state of things for *Christian* times. *Before* the appearance of Christ, one and the same person had been king and priest, as Melchisedek, even the heathen Caesars had been simultaneously pontifices maximi, and *Christus* was true king and priest. But then Christus separated the offices and the spheres of activity of the two powers on account of human weakness in such a way that the Christian Caesars needed the bishops for eternal life and bishops used Caesarian commands in secular affairs, so that the priesthood could remain far away from secular [100] affairs, and so that

---

[103] On Gelasius I cf. *Caspar*, Papsttum II p. 33 ff., 63 ff., 749 ff., 753 ff.

[104] Cf. the parallel expression of Ambrosius of Mailand above p. 91.

[105] J.-K. 611, S. Gelasii pape epist 1 c. 10 Thiel loc. Cit. I p. 292 ff.

[106] Tractatus IV c. 11, *Thiel* loc. Cit. I p. 567 ff

a person saturated in worldly things would not have the directing hand in matter of religion.[107] These explanations are particularly important because according to them the separation of the two power is traceable to *Christ himself,* and thus is to be regarded as *desired by God*—a teaching which appears that much more meaningful when we take account of the fact that only a few decades before this the *general Council of Chalcedon* had described the Caesar as "priest and Caesar" and as "teacher of the faith." Like this tractate,[108] a *letter* which Pope Gelasius directed to the East-Roman Caesar *Anastasius* in the year 494,[109] also had long-term influence and was often quoted. There Gelasius differentiates *two powers from which the world is ruled most highly*, the holy authority of the bishops (auctoritas sacrata pontificum) and the kingly power (regalis potestas). Between them, the priestly power is that much the more weighty[110] since the priests have to give account even over the kings in the divine court. Even the Caesar bows his neck before them, he must subordinate himself to them in matters of religion, but *not rule* over them. If the priesthood recognized that the *imperium*, the secular ruler ship, was conferred on *Caesar* by God, and if they in accordance with this obeyed his laws in matters of secular order, how much more zealously should Caesar thus prove obedience to those to whom administration of ecclesiastical means of mercy was given.[111] In the sense of that older teaching on the *separation of the two powers*, it is also here recognized [101] without reserve that the *secular power* has been conferred on *Caesar* by God and that the *priesthood*, too, owes *him* obedience in *earthly* matters. In questions of *religion*, however, the Caesar is *not* to *rule*, but to *obey* the priesthood. Thus each of the two powers is to have its separate sphere of activity, inside which the highest authority is granted to it.

But this does not mean that Pope Gelasius also *valued* these

---

[107] *Caspar* (Papsttum II p. 68) points out that the *opposition* and mutual *delimitations* of the functions of the two powers which are to be found in the tractate stood in a certain condtradiction to the ideas of *Augustine*, whose ideas were, so Caspar directed solely to the *common* task of regnum and sacerdotium.

[108] The writing of protest of the princes of the party of Philipp of Schwaben of the year 1202 against the interference of the legates of Innoncenz III in the German dispute over the crown, MG. Constit. II p. 6 Z. 28 ff., offers a noteworthy example of later citation of the tractate.

[109] J.-K. 632, Epist. 12 c. 2, *Thiel* loc. Cit. I p. 350 ff.

[110] "In quibus tanto gravius est pondus sacerdotum."

[111] Cf. on this letter the explanations of *Caspar*, Papsttum II p. 64 ff.

two powers as equal. It is certainly not without meaning that he said in that tractate that Christ separated the two powers from each other such that *the Caesars need* (indigerent) the bishops for eternal life, the *bishops*, on the other hand, use (uterentur) Caesarian orders in secular matters; and it should also be noticed that the Pope, in his letter to Caesar, described only the authority of the *bishops*, *but not the kingly power as "sanctified."* Gelasius actually spoke entirely explicitly in his letter to Caesar of the greater *"weightiness"* of the bearers of the priestly power, bearers who were to give God an account even of the kings.[112]

It was mentioned earlier that *Ambrosius of Mailand*, when he entered the debate in favor of the *separation* of the two powers, only rejected a *rule* of Caesar over the church and fought against his authoritative interference in questions of faith, on the other hand, however, he counted amongst Caesar's duties *care* of Caesar for the pure faith. A picture entirely in keeping with this is offered to us in Felix III and Gelasius I. They turned only against the *rule* of Caesar over the church; that Caesar should interfere for the *protection* of the church and the true [102] Faith—this they not only approved of,[113] but in fact they themselves emphatically demanded it,[114] indeed Gelasius I had expressed in that letter to Caesar Anastasius where he treated of the *separation* of the two powers, that it was the *duty of conscience* of the Caesar to lead the people to the true reverence for God. Thus even these Popes claimed the *help* of Caesar for the fight against heresy, *but which was the true faith was to be decided by the church and not Caesar.* Pope Gelasius expresses in the sharpest way that Caesar had mixed himself up in questions of faith with his Henotikon: A Caesar is not a sanctified bishop. *Caesar should protect and promote*

---

[112] The words: "In quibus gravius est pondus sacerdotum" have, however, been understood recently to have been supposed to be speaking of the *burden* which the priests had to *carry* (cf. *Carlyle and Carlyle*, Political Theory I p. 191 and 256, *Kissling*, Sacerdotium und Imperium p. 125 ff.). This is clearly a misunderstanding (cf. here *Caspar*, Papsttum II p. 69 ff.). The correct sense is given by *Jonas of Orléans* in the 9th century in his writing De Institutione regia c. 1: "tantoque est *prestantior* sacerdotalist (persona)" (Migne p. l. 106, 285, new printing in *Jean Reviron*, Les idées politico-religieuses d'un évêque du Ixe siècle. Jonas d'Orléans et son "De institutione regia" [1930] p. 134).

[113] Pope Felix occasionally described Caesar as "fidei custos et defensor orthodoxae," Ep. 4 c. 1, Thiel loc. Cit. I p. 240

[114] elicis II. Papae epist. 1 c. 2, 3, 13; ep. 15; Gelasii papae epist. 12 c. 10, Thiel loc. Cit. I p. 223 ff., 231 ff., 270 ff., 357 ff.

the church, but not desire to rule over it."[115]

"His [Clovis] three juridical actions—the Salic Law, the acceptance of Alaric's Breviary and the Council of Orleans—made him the guarantor of normative law without having participated in their elaboration. The Salic, Roman and Canon law founded political equality between the Germanic ethnicities and the *provinciales*, between the secular and the clergy. Once again, following Augustus, he founded the State of law."[116]

A.D. 495 Pope Gelasius I was the first pope at a Roman synod to be saluted as "Vicar of Christ."[117]

A.D. 501 (Pope Symmachus, A.D. 498-514) The church council in Rome pronounced sentence on October 23, 501, that no human court could judge the pope; God alone could do that. Thus, the pope was officially exalted above every other man:

"Thus it was that men acknowledged that they had no power to judge the Pope. St. Avitus, Bishop of Vienne, had declared before the opening of the council: To question the authority of the Pope of Rome is to overthrow not one bishop alone, but the whole Episcopate."[118]

Now, as promised, we return to our Biblical italicized clause that will be seen to perfectly align itself historically with the account of Daniel:

Daniel 11:31. "Shall *place* [set up] the *abomination* that *maketh desolate.*"

---

[115] Voigt, Karl. *Staat und Kirche: Von Konstantin dem Grossen Bis Zum Ende der Karolingerzeit.* Aalen. [*State and Church from Constantine the Great to the End of the Carolingian Period.*] New printing of Stuttgart ed., 1936. N.p.: Scientia Verlag Aalen, 1965, 99-102.

[116] Rouche, Michel. *Clovis.* (Fayard, France. 1996), 380.

[117] J. Michael Miller, *The Shepherd and the Rock: Origins, Development, and Mission of the Papacy* (Huntington, IN: Our Sunday Visitor Publishing, 1995), 101. Imprimatur.

[118] Fernand Hayward, *A History of The Popes* (New York: Dutton, 1931), 76. Trans. from the French by monks of St. Augustine's Abbey, Ramsgate. See also Archibald Bower, *The History of the Popes* (London: 1750), 2:261-2

In developing the identity of the "abomination," Daniel 11:31 describes its distinctive action: ". . . that maketh desolate." When church and state amalgamate, the fruit of that union will always be one of force. To confirm this, all one has to do is read the four verses after Daniel 11:31. All too well, history confirms that Rome physically desolated Christ's true church for nearly 1260 long years. By the acts of Clovis and Catholicism, the union of church and state had been conceived in AD 508:

> "The mingling of church craft and statecraft is represented by the iron and the clay. This union is weakening all the power of the churches. This investing the church with the power of the state will bring evil results. Men have almost passed the point of God's forbearance. They have invested their strength in politics, and have united with the papacy. But the time will come when God will punish those who have made void His law, and their evil work will recoil upon themselves."[119]

Once again, the scriptures and Ellen White rightly direct us to the foundational issue, the uniting of church and state after the passing of AD 476. The bride of Christ (the church) cannot unite with the state in any degree, for to do so is to practice idolatry and commit spiritual adultery. Thus, the church separates herself from Christ.

The facts have revealed that the "abomination" or (sin) that "desolates" was "set up" and established (Daniel 12:11). What had taken place was the amalgamation or union of church and state. The *two swords* theory proposed by Pope Gelasius I was to become accepted church and state policy, which, in turn, brought *literal desolation* to the Christian church. Simultaneously, the "daily" was "taken away" when the false gospel of the papal mediatorial system was established as the "one and true Catholic faith" which, in turn, brought *spiritual desolation* to the Christian church as verified from the *Lex Romana Visigothorum* law code. It is important to note that those from whom understanding of Christ's heavenly mediation was "taken away" were the true people of God, spiritual Israel, as we have here before demonstrated. When the false mediatorial system of the *"daily"* was imposed, free exercise of non–Catholic faiths was proscribed by law, and compulsion of Sunday worship was next to be instituted.

---

[119] Ellen White, *Manuscript 63, 1899; Manuscript Releases*, (Washington DC: Review and Herald, 1981), 1:12–13.

Under the spiritual care of the flock by Saint Caesarius of Arles
we submit a few exerts from one of his sermons as the church progressed into the new world:

Sermon 55

SAINT CAESARIUS OF ARLES

A SERMON IN REPROOF OF THOSE WHO COMMIT MANY SINS THROUGH DRUNKENNESS ON FEAST DAYS AND ACCEPT BRIBES IN HEARING CASES AT THE EXPENSE OF THE INNOCENT

"It is a source of great joy to me, dearly beloved, and I thank
God that you come to church with pious devotion on the holy
feasts. Although we rejoice at your devotion through God's good-
ness, there are many more whose ruin causes us sorrow. I am
speaking of those who desire to quarrel rather than to pray when
they come to church. When they ought to be receiving the divine
lessons in church with attentive ears and entire devotion, they
strive to plead cases outside and to assail one another with different tricks. Sometimes, what is worse, they are inflamed with
excessive wrath, quarrel bitterly, and hurl disgraceful insults and
accusations at each other; at times, they even fight each other
with fists and boots. It would be better for such people not to
come to church than to provoke the divine wrath against themselves by such evils. Although they come to church with but slight
offenses, they return from it with many sins. . . . There are some
people who come to the birthday festivals of the martyrs for this
sole purpose, that they may destroy themselves and ruin others
by intoxication, dancing, singing shameful songs, leading the
choral dance, and pantomiming in a devilish fashion. While they
should be doing [272] the work of Christ they are attempting to
fulfill the service of the Devil. Not love of God but love of dissipa-
tion brings such people to the feast, because they do not prepare
themselves to give an example of good works or for the remedy
of faith, but for the poisonous snare of the Devil. If anyone wants
to look for and imitate these men, they condemn themselves to
eternal punishment. . . . [273] When you come to church, do not
busy yourself with things in which you may acquire more sins. Do
not be occupied with disputes but with prayer, so that you may

not offend God by quarreling but may obtain His grace by prayer. Do not drink in measure without measure; do not efface your names from heaven by drinking under pretexts. What is worse, there are many people who not only get drunk themselves but also beg others to drink more than is proper; moreover (so much the worse!), even some of the clergy do this. O unhappy soul, it is not enough for you that you yourself perish; in addition, you also destroy others. It is not enough for you that you sink down in the sewer of drunkenness; you drag still others along with you. It does not suffice for a miserable drunken man to plunge himself into the slough of intoxication, without attempting to involve others with him. Do not commit this evil, brethren, do not! Listen to the Apostle when he says: "Nor will drunkards possess the kingdom of God," (1Cor. 6:10) and again: "do not be drunk with wine, for in that is debauchery." (Eph. 5:18) . . . . Do not busy yourself with idle gossip in church, and do not engage in useless conversation. Indeed, there are many, especially some women, who chatter idly in church so much that they neither hear the divine lessons themselves nor allow others to do so. Women who do this will have to render an evil account to the Lord both for themselves and others. . . .

Perhaps when we preach these truths some people will get angry at us and say: The very ones who preach this fail to observe it; even bishops, priests, and deacons do many such things. Indeed, brethren, this sometimes is true. So much the worse, even clerics who are accustomed to get drunk do not blush to corrupt just cases, plead them on feasts, quarrel, and engage in business transactions. However, are they all to be condemned because a few wicked ones are found?. .[120]

As error and superstition grew dominant, confusion increased in God's faithful waiting ones. Over time, they became so completely oblivious to the ongoing work in the heavenly sanctuary that by 1844 God's people actually believed the sanctuary to be cleansed was the earth. They simply had no awareness of Jesus' priestly ministration in the heavenly sanctuary until specific light was given to reestablish that understanding. To say, then, as we have beforehand shown, that the "daily," meaning Christ's first-apartment mediation, was not intentionally removed, legally taken away or obscured from human mindfulness, is a denial of some of

---

[120] Mueller, Sis. Mary Magdeleine, trans. *Saint Caesarius of Arles, Sermons, The Fathers of the Church.* New York: Fathers of the Church, 1956, 1: 271-274.

the most obvious facts of history and of the plain writings of Ellen White.[121]

The "one and true Catholic faith" having been legislatively established, then, it was methodically enforced by the state as the law of the land. All other faiths were prohibited. Thus, Satan succeeded in turning the people away from Christ (heavenward) to man (earthward), nay, more, to the prince of darkness himself, which indeed brought desolation to millions of true Christians. Now it can be seen that the one was being taken away at the same time that the other one was being set up. Both find their prophetic commencement in AD 508 (Daniel 11:31; 12:11 and 8:11). The warning that Paul had given the church in II Thessalonians 2:3–12 regarding the rise of the mystery of iniquity (the Antichrist) then began to take on real meaning. And in reference to spiritual desolation, Ellen White adds this particular:

> "This degrading confession of man to man is the secret spring from which has flowed much of the evil that is defiling the world and fitting it for the final destruction."[122]

---

[121] Ellen White, *The Great Controversy*, (Nampa, Idaho: Pacific Press, 1911), 55.

[122] Ibid., 567.

5

Religious Liberty—The Best Kept Secret
of the Dark Ages

The issue of religious liberty, two completely different ideologies or governments warring against each other, will be illustrated to be one of the main themes and premises of the prophetic periods of Daniel, thus fully establishing the above written directive of the Bible and Ellen White:

> "The doctrine of religious freedom was termed heresy, and its upholders were hated and proscribed."[123]

Some have erroneously concluded that the Visigoths were pagans[124] and that, therefore, the conflict in the West was over paganism. In fact, though, the Visigoths were Arian Christians:

> "The Goths were a people of Germanic stock who erected powerful Christian kingdoms upon the ruins of the Roman Empire in the West. . . . Their spiritual life was perhaps higher than that of their opponents, and their moral standards were admittedly superior. They were more tolerant and their theology was simple and based on the Scriptures. . . . After the fall of the Vandal and Ostrogothic kingdoms and the conversion of the Suevi and the Burgundians the Visigoths were the only Germanic people of Arian faith."[125]

> "To these last year's also belong the few contemporary pieces of evidence on Clovis' church policy. . . . The earliest piece

---

[123] Ellen White, *The Great Controversy*, (Nampa, Idaho: Pacific Press, 1911), 45.

[124] *The American Heritage College Dictionary*, 3rd ed., 1997, s.v. "pagan." "One who is not a Christian . . . , One who has no religion . . . , Professing no religion; heathen."

[125] *The New Schaff-Herzog Encyclopedia of Religious Knowledge*, s.v. "Goths" (New York, London: Funk and Wagnalls, 1909), 5:32-34.

of Merovingian ecclesiastical legislation was in many ways the
manifestation of the ideals of Remigius; in a letter written after
Vouille [Vougle], Clovis announced to his bishops that en route for
the battle he had promulgated an edict protecting widows, clerics
and those whom the church wished to defend."[126]

"It is evident, from the language of Gregory of Tours, that this
conflict between the Franks and Visigoths was regarded by the
orthodox party of his own preceding ages as a religious war, on
which, humanly speaking, the prevalence of the Catholic or the
Arian creed in Western Europe depended."[127]

"Clovis fought his last campaign, against the Visigoths in 507,
[508] as a Catholic."[128]

"Chlodowech [Clovis] already had not held back on gifts to
the church.[129] It is not improbable that he had granted the bishops the necessary possessions to improve poorer churches' fa-
cilities.[130] After the Goth War he conferred the former Arian chapels upon the Catholic Church, doubtless along with the Arian
church's possessions.[131] He also began the freeing of individual
churches and ecclesiastical persons from the burdens of state.[132]
Chrodechilde [Clovis' wife] did not remain in his shadow; Gregory of Tours is full of her praise: she richly gave churches, mon-

---

[126] Ian N. Wood, *Revue Belge de Philologie Et D'Histoire*, (Brussels: n.p., 1985),
63:264. See also *Chlodowici Regis ad episcopos epistula, Capitularia Merowingica*,
ed. A. Boretius, *Monumenta Germaniae Historica, Capitularia Regum Francorum, I*
(Hannover, 1883), 1. For the entire translated letter from the Latin see **APPENDIX
V**, pg. 135.

[127] Walter C. Perry, *The Franks* (London: Longman, Brown, Green, Longmans, and
Roberts, 1857), 85. Perry quotes from Gregory of Tours' *The History of the Franks*,
trans. O. M. Dalton (Oxford: Clarendon Press, 1927), 2:36-43. The authority on
Clovis, Gregory lived from A.D. 538 to 594.

[128] J. M. Wallace-Hadrill, *The Long Haired Kings* (New York: Barnes and Noble,
1962), 173

[129] Cf. Chapter 1 p. 120 note 1

[130] This conjecture is guided by the way in which the first Synod of Orléans can. 5
speaks of the king's gifts, still to be made: *De oblationibus vel agris, quos domnus
noster rex ecclesiis suo munere conferre dignatus est vel adhuc non habentibus deo
sibi inspirante contulerit.*

[131] Con. Aurel. I (a. 511) can. 10.

[132] Cf. Con. Aurel. I (a. 511) can. 5, where the subject is gifts: *ipsorum agrorum vel
clericorum immunitate concessa.*

asteries, and other holy places; one could have held her not for a queen but for a maiden of God."[133]Appendix[134]

A most significant point to be grasped here is the confiscation of Arian church property for bestowal upon the Catholic Church sometime after the decisive battle of Vougle in 508. Remember that Clovis then reigned in the West. In A.D. 538, under Justinian, that procedure was repeated. And it is once more to be repeated in the soon-coming crisis:

"As far as Merovingian Gaul is concerned, there is no evidence to suggest that any of the pagan religions persisted beyond the fifth century, and there is no pagan religion with a 'complex set of beliefs and practices reflecting man's attitude to the supernatural' which can be identified or reconstructed from the information provided by the sources. All one can say is that the condemned practices were negligible fragments, which did not form any coherent system of beliefs and practices, and which had long since lost their original meaning and implications. Thus, there is no justification for talking in terms of living paganism in Gaul during the Merovingian period. Christianity crushed all sorts of religious systems which existed in Gaul even before the Frankish occupation. Those bits and pieces which did survive, were disconnected from their original system, and therefore do not represent any non-Christian religious or cult. They all survived as fragments of ancient traditions within a Christian framework, and they represent not more than a stage of pluralism which characterized the transition from paganism to Christianity."[135]

"Then, from the *22nd of June, 508* (*Variae*, I, 42), Theodoric, liberated from imperial attacks on the Italian coasts, thanks to the retreat of the fleet that believed to have attained its goal—that is to help Alaric II—hurried to rally his troops. Lead by Duke Ibba, they entered Provence. These events verified one more time the principle of *lex gothica*, this law that confounded ethnic belonging

---

[133] Hist. Franc. III, 18; cf. IV 1.
   Albert Hauck, *Kirchengeschichte Deutschlands*, [*Church History of Germany*] Bd. I 3rd and 4th edition, 1904, 1:136.
[134] For some highlights into The Church's Business or Financial Status in the Sixth Century see **APPENDIX VI**, pg. 137.
[135] Yitzhak Hen, *Culture & Religion in Merovingian Gaul, AD 481-751* (Leiden: Brill, 1995), 160.

and Arian belief. As Gregory of Tours said: "they call, in effect, the men of our religion Romans" (G.M., 24 and 78-79).) This confusion between Roman political status and Catholic faith shows to what extent the conflict was insoluble. *It could only be separated through the disappearance of one of the two religions, the one that mixed the State and the Church.*"[136]

Professor Rouche just placed his finger on the central contentious issue between the Catholic Church and the Arian Christians: *Religious Liberty.* The religion that did not have the "arms" of Clovis backing it was destined to be nothing but a memory of history. The government of the Catholic Church, as we have witnessed, was established on the principle of force. The government of the Arian Christians in religious matters was established on the Biblical principle of freedom of choice, religious liberty (albeit in its primitive form). Procopius will supply us with further details:

> ". . . . There were many Gothic nations in earlier times, just as also at the present, but the greatest and most important of all are the Goths, Vandals, Visigoths and Gepaedes. In ancient times, however, they were named Sauromatae and Melanchlaeni;[137] and there were some too who called the nations Getic. All these, while they are distinguished from one another by their names, as has been said, do not differ in anything else at all. For they all have white bodies and fair hair, and are tall and handsome to look upon, and they use the same laws and practice a common religion. For they are all of the Arian faith, and have one language called Gothic; and, as it seems to me, they all came originally from one tribe, and were distinguished later by the names of those who led each group."[138]

While there was a difference between the Goths and the Ostrogoths, it must be understood that when Procopius is referring to the Goths it is in reference to the Ostrogoths. This is confirmed in his books, *History of the Wars.* However, Procopius informed us of a very important point that must not be overlooked when he wrote of these Arian kingdoms:

---

[136] Rouche, Michel. *Clovis.* Fayard, France, 1996, 322.

[137] "Black—Coats"

[138] Procopius. *History of the Wars.* Translated by H. B. Dewing. Bks. 1–8. In Loeb Classical Library, edited by Jeffrey Henderson. Cambridge, MA: Harvard Univ. Press, 2000–2001, III. ii. 1-8.

"They use the same laws and practice a common religion. For
they are all of the Arian faith." For they "do not differ in anything
else at all."[139]

From the pen of Procopius himself, we have the actual viewpoint of an eyewitness then living as to who was considered to be
the chief armaments of opposition to the Catholic faith because
they were of the Arian faith. As Procopius has rightly informed us,
the Visigoths were one of the main Arian kingdoms in opposition
to the principles or government of the Catholic Church. Gregory
of Tours confirms that the Visigoths embraced the principles of
religious liberty. The Visigoth Agilan once admonished Gregory of
Tours declaring:

> "You must not blaspheme against a faith which you yourself
> do not accept. You notice that we who do not believe the things
> which you believe nevertheless do not blaspheme against them. It
> is no crime for one set of people to believe in one doctrine and an-
> other set of people to believe in another. . . ." "Legem, quam non
> colis, blaspheme noli; nos vero quae creditis etsi non credimus,
> non tamen blasphemamus, quia non deputur crimini, si et illa et
> illa colantur. Sic enim vulgate sermon dicimus, non esse noxium,
> si inter gentilium aras st Dei ecclesiam quis transiens utraque
> veneriyur."[140]

The Catholic Church now had a powerful "heretical" Arian
race largely in control of all of Gaul and Italy with a mutual ideology diametrically opposed to the government of the papacy. As
rightly stated by Rouche:

> "It could only be separated through the disappearance of
> one of the two religions, the one that mixed the State and the
> Church."[141]

Unfortunately, it was already decided for the Visigoths by the
decisive battle of Vougle in 508 as Clovis defeated Alaric II and then
reigned in the West. With Clovis' Merovingian dynasty coming into
power and his ascension to the Catholic Faith, Theodore the Great,

---

[139] Ibid., III. ii. 1-8.

[140] Thorpe, L. Trans. Gregory of Tours—*The History of the Franks* (Harmonds-worth,
1974), 309-10.

[141] Rouche, Michel. *Clovis*. Fayard, France, 1996, 322

the Arian King of Italy, decreed between the years 507-511 a most remarkable decree. This decree was honored by the Arians but was diametrically opposed to the principles and government of the Catholic Church:

The Letters of Cassiodorus

507 A.D.—511 A.D
Book II—27.

King Theodoric to all the Jews living in Genoa

"The Jews are permitted to roof in the old walls of their synagogue, but they are not to enlarge it beyond its old borders, nor to add any kind of ornament, under pain of the Kings sharp displeasure; and this leave it granted on the understanding that it does not conflict with the thirty years 'Statute of Limitations.'

'Why do ye desire what ye ought to shun? In truth we give the permission which you craved, but we suitably blame the desire on your wandering minds. *We cannot order a religion, because no one is forced to believe against his will.*"[142]

While the Arian Christians of the West and East were not at all free from some entanglements of church and state as we know and understand today, nevertheless, they never crossed the red line by resorting to force in religious matters against the will of an individual whether he be of the Arian or Catholic faith. This could hardly be said of the Catholic Church. It is here, in the issue of religious liberty, that the war between two completely different ideologies climaxes in 538. This has been the best kept secret of the Dark Ages. Theodore Mommsen dates Theodore the Great's Book II, 27, law code between 507-511 and no one disputes the dating of his letters of Cassiodorus. When Clovis overthrew the Visigoths at Vougle in A.D. 508, religious intolerance reared her ugly head. This came about slowly at first, but, nevertheless, methodically. To say that religious persecution was fully employed when Clovis, the first Catholic King in the New World, took the crown in A.D. 508 would be a mistake. Catholicism in Gaul was

---

[142] Cassiodorus, Magnus Aurelius, Hodgkin, Thomas, *The Letters of Cassiodorus.* London: Henry Frowde, 1886, 185-6.

in a minority at that time as Gaul was surrounded by Arian Kings, but by 538 that all changed. On the other hand, to say that religious bigotry did not lift her ugly head when the church had the civil and judicial system behind her would be just as inaccurate, especially after the Council of Orleans I in A.D. 511 called for by Clovis:

> If the decision of the 1st Council of Orléans of the year 511 only intended that the public performance of the cult should be made impossible for the Arians, then there must have been state *punishment-regulations*, too. . . ."[143]

"A certain limit was given to any action of the state against *unorthodox Christians* (heretics) from the beginning by the fact that the *Arians*, who had come under Frankish rule through the conquering of Gaulish districts, were too numerous for one to be able to force them to *convert* to Catholicism.[144] Only the freedom of the *cult* was taken from them very early on. Already the 1st Council of Orleans of the year 511, which, as has been noted, consulted on issues suggest by Clovis, decided that the formerly Arian churches of the Goths should be re-sanctified and taken into use for Catholic worship.[145] According to this, therefore, clearly the Arian Goths were to have their churches forcibly taken from them *in general*. A letter of the Burgundian bishop Avitus of Vienna shows that at this point in the Frankish Empire there actually occurred a violent repression of the Arian worship. In this letter, the bishop expresses himself against taking the *objects of the churches* [*Kirchengeräte*] of the otherwise-believing (i.e. the Arians) for the favor of the Catholic cult in Burgundy as in the Frankish Empire (in superioris Galliae partibus).[146] If the decision of the 1st Council of Orleans of the year 511 only intended that the public performance of the cult should be made impossible for the Arians, then there must have been state *punishment- regulations*, too, in the Merovingian Empire against heretics. The 3rd Council of Orleans of the year 538 threatened a one-year-long excommunication for

---

[143] Voigt, Karl. *Staat und Kirche: Von Konstantin dem Grossen bis zum Ende der Karolingerzeit*, Aalen. [State and Church from Constantine the Great to the End of the Carolingian Period.] New printing of Stuttgart ed., 1936. Aalen, Scientia Verlag, 1965, 259.

[144] The conversion of the Visigoths to Catholicism under king Rek-kared took place only towards the end of the 6th century.

[145] I. Conc. Aurel. A. 511 c. 10, Concil I p. 5

[146] MG. Auct. Antiq. VI 2 p. 35 ff.

the *secular judge* and the Count who did not take action against a priest of a sect who had performed *re-baptism* on a Catholic, and who omitted forcing him to appear before the *legal court of the king*.[147] The punishing action of the state remained; it appears, in very narrow borders."[148]

"The first and foundational examples were the Catholic regional synod in the Arian western Gothic state of Alarich II's under the administration of Bishop Caesarius of Arles at Agde in the year 506 shortly before the collapse of the empire; the Catholic Frankish imperial council of Chlodwig at Orléans in the year 511; and the Burgundian national synod, immediately following the Catholic conversion of King Sigismund at Epao [5] in the year 517 under the administration of Bishop Avitus of Vienne.[149] It is instructive to compare these examples to see how each, within their respective constellations of church-politic, came to deal with the confrontation between Catholicism and Arianism, between the old constitution of the church and the regional church.

The Council of Agde was a proclamation of tolerance of West Gothic Arianism for the Roman Catholic subjects, to whom a codification of their law had been presented a few months prior in the Lex Romana. In the opening section the synodical acts emphasized the authority of the king, who granted the Catholic bishops the authorization to convene the synodical assembly, and in the conclusion he was thanked for that following thanks to God. At the top of the resolutions, demonstratively emphasizing Catholic continuity, the doctrine was stated that the canons and statutes of the fathers should be read aloud.[150] Thereby the Arian problem was implicitly side-stepped. Notably, the conversion of Jews and convivium with them was brought up, yet not a word about the Arians.[151] In Epao, on the other hand, this very topic was at

---

[147] III. Conc. Aurel. A. 538 c. 34, Concil. I p. 83, cf. Schubert, *Staat und Kirche*, p. 31 n. 1.

[148] Voigt, Karl. *Staat und Kirche: Von Konstantin dem Grossen bis zum Ende der Karolingerzeit*, Aalen. [*State and Church from Constantine the Great to the End of the Carolingian Period.*] New printing of Stuttgart ed., 1936. Aalen, Scientia Verlag, 1965, 259.

[149] Agde: Mansi, Coll. Conc. VIII, p. 319 ff. Orléans: MG Conc. I, p. 1 ff. Epao: MG. Auct. Ant. VI, 2, p. 165 f.; Conc. I, p. 15 ff.

[150] A decretal statement of Innocent I (JK. 293 c. I, no. 2, 4) was also included verbatim in the canon (c. 9).

[151] An indirect, indeed acknowledging reference to them is argued by Hauck, *Kirchengeschichte Deutschlands* 3.4 I, p. 117 note 1 (corroborating von Schubert,

the center of interest. Not only with Jews but also with heretics, convivium was prohibited,[152] and for lapsi, the baptized Catholics who "crossed into damnable heresy," a period of penance limited to two years per the old canon was prescribed. Also forbidden was the further use of Arian churches, with the exception of those that had formerly been Catholic."[153]

Since the Council of Nicea in A.D. 325, condemned Arianism as heresy, the general tone and attitude of the Catholic Church toward Arianism is now to be illustrated:

> "In order to be able to evaluate the situation, one should realize that Arian churches were spread all over Italy and had also settled into Rome. One knew of Arian churches, which similarly found residence near the papal churches, for example every church that was still mentioned by Gregory the Great.[154] Another Arian church was named after the holy Agatha.[155] More Arian

---

(Cont.)

Geschichte der christlichen Kirche im Frühmittelalter. 1921, p. 25) in c. 42: *Ac ne id fortasse videatur omissum, quod maxime fidem catholicae religionis infestat, quod aliquanti clerici sive laici student auguriis* etc. However, *maxime* here undoubtedly does not mean "mostly," "especially," but rather "at the most." A praise "even indirectly" of the Arians from the mouth of the Catholic synod would be unthinkable.

[152] c. 15 Epaon, cf. with c. 40 Agath. (The canons 60 and 67 of Agde, which dealt with heretics, are later additions; cf. Hefele, *Conciliengeschichte.* II, p 650; French translation Leclercq II, p. 980).

[153] c. 32. In a separate opinion (ep. 7, I. c. p. 35 ff.) Avitus had already previously treated this question in depth. Here, the Catholic disdain of the heretics, otherwise carefully hidden from the landed proprietary power of the kingdom, expressed itself freely. The worldly wisdom of Avitus was also evidenced by his advice, not to turn the heretics into martyrs through absorbing them into the Arian churches, and not to provoke other Arian kings to retaliatory measures. Thus reads his summarizing judgment: *Dices forsitan haereticos, si eis potestas datur, altaria nostra temerare. Verum est, nec refello. Saeviunt quidem, cum possent, foedis unguibus alienarum aedium pervasores. Sed vim intendere, loca pervadere, altaria commutare non pertinent ad columbam...Quocirca non quid statuam, sed quid optem, breviter indicabo. Haeretici cultus loca pervadi nollem, cuperem praetermitti in morem ergastulorum, quae usu careant. Semper optandum est, non ut mutata transeant, sed infrequentata torpescant. Salubri populorum correctione desertis maneat aeterna viduitas, nec unquam recipiatur a nostris, quod conversionis studio repudiator a propriis.*Erich Caspar, *Geschicthe des Papsttums,* [*History of the Papacy*] 1933, 2:4-5.

[154] Gregory the. Great: JE 1223, Reg 3,1 9: "*Iuxta domum Merulanam regione tertia*" (MG Epp. I 177 Z. 11 ff.) He let them be hallowed in a Catholic Church.

[155] He also let this hallow: JE 1291, Reg. 4 19: MG Epp. I 253-254 (Feb-Mar 594).

houses of God were understandably directed out of Ravenna, under those others which were devoted to the holy Martin.[156] Theodoric himself directed one of the holy Martin consecrated Arian
churches near his residence in Ravenna, while he let another, the
Basilica Herculis, be reinstated.[157] Near that there was yet another church of Andrew and, as far as it is known, a church of
George.[158] It is visible that every Arian church had to be entrusted to another Arian church, which itself stood under an Arian
bishop. The picture filled itself in, if one considers the fact that
in many localities, one catholic and one Arian bishop officiated.
[220]

In Rome itself there was an Arian bishop.[159] As massive as
the distance between the new ruler of Italy and the old inhabitants was, it came well out, that the Arian religious service would
be held in the language of the people. The Bible was read in the
gothic language, and the entire cult served the same language of
the people, a fully non-understandable means of communication
for those born into it.[160] As the situation looked completely different in the West, foremost in Italy. There Theodoric led the Arians,
who brought about little, if only an understanding for the Roman
church as the head of Christianity.[161] He didn't walk in step with
it, because there was no touching point between him and it. The
Roman church offered to him, the leader, no areas of attack, because it didn't exist as a leadership institution in the realm of the
Arianism. On the other hand, and that is the even more important

---

(Cont.)

Until then it was the center of the Roman gothic community.

[156] G. Pfeilschifter: *Der Ostgotenkönig* 50; C. Cecchelli: *L'Arianismo* 743-774

[157] See Agnellus: *Liber pontificalis ecclesiae Ravennatis* 334 Z. 22 ff.; here also the
report about the St. Martin church "quam Theodoricus rex fundavit, quae vocatur
caelum aureum . . . nulla ecclesia vel domus similes in laquearibus vel travibus ista .
. . in tribunali vero, si diligenter enquisieritis, super fenestras invenietis ex lapidibus
exaratum ita: Theodoricus rex hanc ecclesiam a fundamentis in nominee domini
nostri Iesu Christi fecit" (334-335).

[158] Agnellus: *Lib. pont. eccl. Ravennatis* 334 and 356-357. About the finds in Ravenna, consider V. Bierbrauer: *Die odtgotischen Grabfund* 298 ff.

[159] Consider somewhat Theoderich to a Faustus; *Cassiodorus: Variae* 1,26 (CC 96
34 Z. 1 ff.) (= MG AA. XII 28 Z. 35 f.), where he speaks of weiland Bishop Unscila.
Also about that Pfeilschifter: *Ostgotenkönig* 51.

[160] All handed down gothic Bible translations come from Gothic Italy: Pfeilschifter
53. About architecture and sculpture, consider S. FUCHS: *Kunst* 10-45; about
Gothic altertümer, N. Aberg: *Die Goten* 2-30.

[161] Put forth correctly by Pfeilschifter: *Ostgotenkönig* 252.

point- there was barely a cause for the papacy to step into contact with the Arians. Just because they were condemned at the latest at Nicea, the Arians remained shut out from the community of believers. They stood outside of the ecclesiological company."[162]

"Theodoric at his time-for the contemporary consideration, certainly highly notable- let the Catholic officials rein their offices, just because it didn't connect anything to him. Theodoric was through and through pragmatic, who let the inner peace of his newly directed kingdom be very laid out and not through him. . . ."[163]

"It may seem like a paradox that in the realm of a Catholic community disquiet ruled, and there where Catholic and heretical communities opposed, peace ruled. This appearance was clarified with a tip on the wholeness fundament of the contemporary Catholic Christianity which claimed the right to permeate the whole (private and public) life. It was exactly this attempt to apply the wholeness fundament practically and to set it into reality which made the conflict with the imperial government unavoidable, because they were supported by the fundament, namely of historical and constitutional legal origin, which allowed no room for the translation of papal represented theses. For a comparison with the situation in the Gothic leadership realm lacked any foundation. . . ."[164]

"Gelasius saw a greater danger for the salvation of the Catholic Christians in Arianism than in the invasion of the Barbarian. He expressed himself in this way in his writing to the bishops of Picenum, a region of the Adriatic Sea, close to the Ancona of today, in which he bitterly complained about the harrying of the Barbarians, but did not eschew warning of the devilish enticement to heresy, which would be much more dangerous than the bodily injuries brought on by the cruelty of the Barbarians.[165] [224]

---

[162] Ullman, Walter von. *Päpste und Papsttum* [*Popes and Papacy*]: *Gelasius I. (492– 496)*. Bd. 18. Stuttgart: Anton Hiersemann, 1981, 219-220.

[163] Ibid., 221.

[164] Ibid., 222.

[165] JK 621: "Barbaricis hactenus dolebamus incursibus maxime vicinas urbi provincias et bellorum saeva tempestate vastari, sed quantum inter ipsa recentium calamitatum ferventia pericula comperimus, perniciosorem diablous Christianorum mentibus labem quam corporibus hostilis feritas irrogavit, quod malum

It is certainly no coincidence that Gelasius turns so sharply
against Arianism in this writing in consideration of the baptismal rebirths ideal and emphasized under reference to John 3:5.
This shows how the entrance into the church as the community
of believers through baptism was always current to him.[166]   In
the previously mentioned writing to the Dardanian bishops he
made unambiguously clear that the Nicean condemnations decree over Arianism would effect members of the strange teaching
much later."[167]

"In a letter to an Mrican bishop, the pope could point out that
although the Catholic Church in Mrica was suffering from the
"saeventium barbarorum feralia iura," the situation in Constantinople was just as bad: "Have you not noticed that in the East, as
in Africa. The Antichrist has been striving to conquer Jesus?"[168]

"For example, in the midst of the "tempest of continuing
wars" tearing apart Italy in 493, the pope wrote to the Dardanian
bishops to warn them about monophysitism, which he compares,
as an evil, to Arianism."[169]

"He [Pope Gelasius I] wrote five books against Nestorius and
Eutyches; he wrote also hymns after the manner of the blessed

---

(Cont.)

principaliter illarum regionum respicit sacerdotes . . ." (Avellana 357 Z. 4 ff. Nr. 94).
About that also Phielschifter: Ostgotenkönig 52, Ensslin: Theoderic 104. The
essay by S. Prete: La lettere di Gelasio I ai vescovi was not accessible to me.

[166]   JK 621 (under reference of John 6:54 and 3:5): Avellana 359 Z. 27 ff.; 362 z. 1
ff.; 363 Z. 23 ff. Nr. 94.

[167]   K 664: "Sic propter blasphemias Arrii forma fidei communionisque catholicae
Nicaeno prolata conventu Arrianos omnes vel quisquis in hanc pestem sive sensu
seu communione deciderit sine retractione concludit" (Avellana 371 Z. 13-17 Nr.
95).

Ullman, Walter von. Päpste und Papsttum [Popes and Papacy]: Gelasius I. (492–496).
Bd. 18. Stuttgart: Anton Hiersemann, 1981, 223-4.

[168]   13Gelasius. JK 628 =ep. "Cum tuae dilectionis" (Thiel 9. pp. 339-41) §3. p. 340.
Amory, Patrick. People and Identity in Ostrogothic Italy, 489–554.
Cambridge: Cambridge Univ. Press, 2003, 199.

[169]   14 Gelasius. JK 623 = ep. "Ubi primum respirare" (Thiel 7. pp. 335-7):
"continuorum tempestas bellorum ... vel in illis provinciis vel in istis." §I. p. 335;
Arianism. §§2-3. pp. 336-7.

Amory, Patrick. People and Identity in Ostrogothic Italy, 489–554. Cambridge:
Cambridge Univ. Press, 2003, 199.

Ambrose; likewise *two books against Arius*; he wrote also prefaces to the sacraments and prayers in careful language and many eloquent epistles regarding the faith."[170]

"Moreover, Theodoric's mother Ereleuva was Catholic, and Gelasius enlisted her support in his petitions to the king."[171]

In quoting from Amory and Ullmann on Arianism, Amory takes issue with Ullmann in that he adduces to an alleged cultural divide between pope and king. There was indeed a cultural divide between the pope and the king [Theodoric], but Ullmann paints a picture of next-to-nothing contact with Pope Gelasius I and that it was anything but friendly on the part of the pope. Amory portrays Theodoric as a strange friend of Pope Gelasius I. While Ullmann goes perhaps a touch too far to the right, Amory definitely goes too far to the left. The truth lies between them both, but much closer to Ullmann. The fact of the matter is that the papacy was and is tolerant where she is helpless:

"Clovis bowed to laws developed by others and reinforced them through his own authority. He founded anew a State of law, even if he practiced unity in diversity and recognized the Church's sovereignty in the spiritual domain. In each text, he found the

---

[170] The hymns of Gelasius have all been lost, as also his refutations of Arianism. Jaffe list among his writings one treatise on the dual nature of Christ "against Eutyches and Nestorius." *Regista*, p. 89, 670. The prefaces and prayers were evidently parts of a liturgy. In the ninth century the *Liber Sacramentorum* or office of Gelasius was distinguished from that of St. Gregory. Duchesne, op. cit., p. 257, n. 14. Jaffe enumerates over one hundred letters of Gelasius dealing with matters of doctrine, ecclesiastical government, morality and the temporal needs of his flock. *Op. cit.*, pp. 83-95, 619-743. One of the most striking was written in 494 to the Emperor Anistasius, setting forth the superiority of the priestly to the civil power. "There are two powers which for most part control this world, the sacred authority of priest and the might of kings. Of these two the office of priest is greater, inasmuch as they must give account to the Lord even for the kings before the divine judgment. . . . You know, therefore, that you are dependent upon their decision and that they will not submit to your will." Jaffe, *op. cit.*, p. 85, 632. Ayer, Source Book, p. 531." Loomis, Louise Ropes, trans. *Book of the Popes (Liber Pontificalis)*, vol. 1. New York: Columbia University Press, 1916, 113.

[171] 26 Gelasius, JK 683 = *ep.* "Qui pro victu" (Thiel, p. 502); JK 721 = *ep.* "Felicem et Perrum" (Ewald 46, pp. 521-2). Various other members of Theoderic's family were probably Catholic: see ch. 7, below, pp. 268-9. Amory, Patrick. *People and Identity in Ostrogothic Italy, 489–554.* Cambridge: Cambridge Univ. Press, 2003, 200.

means to reinforce the autonomy of the State and the rights of each people all the while refusing a Constantinian Christianity. *Obviously, religious unity was the most important for him: it allowed him in particular to make Arianism disappear,* to condemn incestuous marriages, and to distinguish the non-religious from the priests."[172]

"The conciliar canons [Council of Orleans I, A.D. 511] show the application of these principles. The tenth, in particular, permits the Arian clergy of Aquitaine who have converted to Catholicism to be integrated in the ministries that the bishop would grant him "by laying of the hands." The Arian churches will be consecrated according to Catholic rite. Thus, heresy effectively disappeared."[173]

[165] "In the period of Arian kingship, the circumstance of the Catholic church (as generally of the Catholic-Roman part of the population in Visigothic kingdom) was almost entirely based upon Roman Caesarian laws, and the *Lex Romana Visigothorum* of Alaric II was a new codification of the Roman law. But also in the laws of the Visigoth kings which concern the circumstances of the Arian church, the Roman influence cannot be missed. *Under the Catholic kings, the Arian church completely disappeared very quickly.* For the circumstance of the Catholic church, the *Lex Romana Visigothorum* remained immediately decisive, ... [239] . . . . The church of the Frankish kingdom was, further, in a very definite way a state church, for it was subject to royal church-rule."[174]

"The Visigoths were Christians, though Arians, since the time of Ulfilas,[175] and the Burgundians did not attempt to change or alter in any sense the religious situation of Gaul. Although Gregory of Tours 'portrayed the Vandals and Goths primarily as Arian

---

[172] Rouche, Michel. *Clovis*. Fayard, France, 1996, 346.

[173] Ibid., 341

[174] Voigt, Karl. *Staat und Kirche: Staat und Kirche: Von Konstantin dem Grossen bis zum Ende der Karolingerzeit*, Aalen. [State and Church from Constantine the Great to the End of the Carolingian Period.] New printing of Stuttgart ed., 1936. Aalen, Scientia Verlag, 1965, 165, 239.

[175] "See; E.A. Thompson, *The Visigoths in the time of Ulfila* (Oxford, 1966), pp. 78-131; P. Heather & J. Matthews eds. & trs., *The Goths in the Fourth Century* (Liverpool, 1991), pp. 133-53.

heretics who took up the persecution of the church',[176] the reality was probably different. No act of religious intolerance is known to us as committed by Arians against Catholics in Gaul.[177] That is not to say that Arian kings did not dispose Catholic bishops from time to time; after all, religious allegiance was part of politics in early medieval Europe. But that is rather different to destroying churches or interfering with the Christianization process. . . . It seems that such a tolerance characterized the Arians in Gaul. Furthermore, if one does not accept the hypothesis of Arian toleration, it should be noted that the supposed Arian violence was directed against Catholicism and not against Christianity."[178]

In the *Patrologia Latina*,[179] we have the Commentary on Revelation written by Saint Caesarius of Arles.[180] This is an extremely revealing document that was originally credited to St. Augustine, but it has been proven by G. Morin[181] and acknowledged and confirmed by Bertrand Fauvarque[182] that it was written by Saint Caesarius of Arles instead. Saint Caesarius of Arles declared in no uncertain terms that Arianism was the most dreaded foe of the Catholic Church:

> "And all the earth wondered at and followed the beast, and they worshiped the dragon which gave power to the beast": the heretics have power without condition, *but especially the Arians*.

---

[176] W. Goffart, '*The themes of "The Barbarian Invasion" in late antique and modern historiography*', in: E.K. Chrysos & A. Schwarcz eds., *Das Reich und die Barbaren* (Vienna, 1989), pp. 87-107, at p. 92. See also Sidonius on Euric's attitude towards Catholics: *Sidonius, Epistula*VII: 6:6. This deprecation, however, may also be attributed to the fact that Euric had had Sidonius arrested for his opposition.

[177] See: K. Schaferdiek, *Die Kirche in den Reichen der Wisigoten und Suewen bis zur Errichtung der westgotischen katolischen Staatskirche* (Berlin 1967), pp.18-31.

[178] Hen, Yitzhak. *Culture and Religion in Merovingian Gaul A.D. 481–751*. Leiden: E. J. Brill, 1995, 13.

[179] Patrologia Latina, *Sancti Aurelii Augustini, Expositio in Apocalypsim B. Joannis,* [*Exposition of the Apocalypse of Saint John*] Saint Caesarius of Arles, 1841, 35: 2417-2452.

[180] Saint Caesarius of Arles, 470/71, died at Arles, 27 August, 543.

[181] G. Morin, "*The Homiletic Commentary on Saint Césaire on the Apocalypse,*" *Benedictine Review*, 45, 1933, pp. 43 ss.

[182] Rouche, Michel, ed. *Clovis, Histoire et Mémoire* (Actes du Colloque international d'historie de Reims), 2 vols. Paris: Univ. of Paris-Sorbonne Press, 1997, 2:280. Bertrand Fauvarque, *Clovis' Baptism The beginning of the saint's millennium*, Paris: Univ. of Paris-Sorbonne Press, 1997, 2:280.

"And they worshiped the beast, saying, who is like the beast? or who will be able to fight with it?" Therefore because the heretics delude themselves with this, that no one believes more than those, and that no one conquers the nation of those, which bases its reputation on the name of the beast: to which it was given by the devil himself, and was permitted by God, to speak great things and blasphemies; just as the Apostle says: "It is necessary that there are heresies, so that those who have been proven, may be manifest in you" I Corinthians 11:19. "And there was given to him the power to make forty-two months": the time of the very recent persecution we understand in those forty-two months. "And then he opened his mouth into blasphemy against God": here it is clear that those who have withdrawn from the Catholic Church are signified;"[183]

To better understand the mind set, theological position and the propaganda or smear campaign that was used by the papacy during this critical period of the early sixth century against those who held to a government that supported the principle of freedom of choice in religious matters, better understood as *religious liberty*, we have translated the entire commentary of Revelation by Saint Caesarius of Arles from the Latin for the benefit of the reader.[184] Because the Arians have been grossly misrepresented and falsely accused throughout much of history, we also submit the following extract from Ferdinand Gregorovius, the world-renowned historian on the government of the Arians under the rule of Theodoric the Great, so the reader may have an unbiased view and be able to compare the spirit and mind set of the Arian Christians with that of the papacy. The early reign of Theodoric the Great is recognized by historians as the "golden age for the church."[185] Labeled as *barbarians* but painted with a completely different hue to the intended meaning of the day,[186] the Arian Christians will finally be seen in

---

[183] Patrologia Latina, *Sancti Aurelii Augustini, Expositio in Apocalypsim B. Joannis*, Saint Caesarius of Arles, 1841, 35: Homily X, 2436.

[184] For the entire translated commentary of Revelation by Saint Caesarius of Arles from the Latin see **APPENDIX VII**, pg. 143.

[185] Amory, Patrick. *People and Identity in Ostrogothic Italy, 489–554*. Cambridge: Cambridge Univ. Press, 2003, 203.

[186] "Barbarian"-"A word probably formed by imitation of the unintelligible sounds of foreign speech, and hence in the mouth of a Greek it meant anything that was not Gr, language, people or customs. With the spread of Gr language and culture, it came to be used generally for all that was non-Gr. Philo and Jos sometimes called

their true colors: respectable, intelligent, masters of architecture, God-fearing and law-abiding citizens:

> "Theodoric, a foreigner like Odoacer, had already acquired the respect if not the affection of the Romans; *his Justice, and yet more his acquiescence in all existing forms of government had endeared him to the people.* Long usage, moreover, had accustomed Italy to German rule and taught Italians to regard it as an inevitable necessity.
>
> The Gothic King did not meddle with any of the existing institutions of the Roman Republic, but rather sought to flatter the people by awarding them a pompous recognition. The political and civil character of Roman administration remained unaltered; the conditions both of public and private life as entirely Roman as in the times of Theodosius or Honorius. Theodoric himself adopted the gentile [288] name of Flavius. The Senate he treated with peculiar distinction, although the illustrious Fathers no longer retained any share in the administration of the State, and were now only regarded as the centre of such dignities as entitled their occupants to a seat in the Curia. The Petronii, Probi, Fausti and Paulini, all members of the great family of the Anicii, were those who still held the highest offices in the State. In political affairs Senators were sent as ambassadors to the Court of

---

(Cont.)

their own nation 'barbarians,' and so did Roman writers up to the Augustan age, when they adopted Gr culture, and reckoned themselves with the Greeks as the only cultured people in the world. Therefore Greek and barbarian meant the whole human race (Rom. 1:14). In Col. 3:11, 'barbarian, Scythian' is not a classification or antithesis but a 'climax' (Abbott)—'barbarians, even Scythians, the lowest type of barbarians.' In Christ, all racial distinc-tions, even the most pronounced, disappear. In 1 Cor. 14:11, Paul uses the term in its more primitive sense of one speaking a foreign, and therefore, an unintelligible language: 'If then I know not the meaning of the voice, I shall be to him that speaketh a barbarian, and he that speaketh will be a barbarian unto me.' The speaking with tongues would not be a means of communication. The excited inarticulate ejaculations of the Corinthian revivalists were worse than useless unless someone had the gift of articulating in intelligible language the force of feeling that produced them *(danantis tes phones,* lit. 'the power of the sound'). In Acts 28:2,4 (in AV of verse 2 'barbarous people' = barbarians) the writer, perhaps from the Gr-Roman standpoint, calls the inhabitants of Melita barbarians, as being descendants of the old Phoen settlers, or possibly in the more general sense of 'strangers.' For the later sense of 'brutal,' 'cruel,' 'savage,' see 2 Macc. 2:21; 4:25; 15:2." *The International Standard Bible Encyclopedia* (Chicago: Howard-Severance, 1915), 1:402-403

Constantinople, while in the city itself they exercised a share in
the criminal jurisdiction, retained all matters connected with the
public well-being under their protection, and, lastly, possessed an
influential voice in the papal elections and in ecclesiastical affairs. The collected letters of Cassiodorus contain seventeen Rescripts of Theodoric to the Patres Conscripti, in which the King,
in the official style of the Empire, expresses his high esteem for
the Senate and his intention to uphold and increase. its dignity.[187]
The Council of the Fathers appears in these Rescripts as the most
dignified ruin of the city, and the reverence of the barbarian King
was shown no less in his anxiety to preserve the [289] ancient institution than in his care for the Theatre of Pompey or the Circus
Maximus. In appointing men of merit from among his retainers,
or from the provinces, to the Patriciate, Consulate, or to other
high offices, Theodoric politely recommended these candidates
to the Senate, begging it to receive them as colleagues. From the
titles of his officials—Magister Officiorum (Chancellor), Count of
the Household troops, Prefect of the City, Quaestor Count of the
Patrimony (the private domain), Magister Scrinii (Director of the
Chancery of State), Comes Sacrarum Largitionum (Minister of
the Treasury and Commerce)-and still more from the two books
of Formulas of nomination left us by Cassiodorus, we perceive
how firmly Theodoric held to all the appointments of Constantine
and his successors, and even sought to revive them in the public
esteem. Roman legislation suffered no change.[188] The safety of his
position as a foreigner in Italy required that the military dominion of the Gothic intruders should be concealed under the titles of

---

[187] See the first rescript to the Senate in which he notifies the appointment of
Cassiodorus to the Patriciate,-*Var.*, lib. i. ep. 4 and 13: *quicquid enim humani
generisnfloris est, habere curiam decet: et sicut arx decus est urbium, ita illa
ornamentum est ordinum caeterorum*, and iii. ep 6. In the *Paneg.* of Ennodius we
find: *coronam curaie inumero . flore velasti.* Theodoric writes to the Senate: *Domitori
orbis, praesuli et reparatori libertatis, Senatui; urbis Romae Flavius Theodoricus rex.*
So in the *Praeceptune-contra illos sacerdotes, qui substantiam Ecclesiae-vendere aut
donare praesumunt.* A. Thiel, *Ep. R. P.,* i. 695.

[188] The well-known edict of Theodoric (issued in Rome in the year 5oo contains
only 144 short paragraphs, all taken from the Imperial codes, and referring more
particularly to landed proprietors, slaves, and women. The only innovation was the
appointment of the Gothic Count endowed with judicial power (Cassiodor., viii.
3). With regard to the offices of State under Theodoric, see Manso, *Cesch. des Ost-
Gothischen Reichs,* Breslau, 1824, p. 92, &c., and Appendix, p. 342; and F. Dahn,
Die Könige der Germanen, Abtheil. iii. And iv., which treats of the *Edictum Tkeodoici*
and *Athalarici regis.*

the Republic, and that for the Romans Roman laws should be preserved. The position, however, of a German nation isolated amid
Latin's, and governed [290] by Roman institutions, brought with it
its inevitable downfall; the instability of the political constitution
and the lifelessness of political forms, which, resting on artificial
support, endured like the ruins of antiquity, made the civil re-
organization of Italy impossible, and served only to further the
rising power of the Church, which waxed powerful as the State
decayed. Theodoric came to Rome in the year 500.[189] The foreign
King who now ruled over Italy showed himself for the first time
to the Romans in the capital, not only in the hope of gaining the
good will of the people, but also in that of quieting party strife,
which still raged over the papal election. His entry was celebrated
with the honours due to an Emperor, and by Roman flatterers
he was saluted as another Trajan. Outside the city, either at the
bridge of the Anio or at the foot of Monte Mario, he was received
by the Senate and people, and by the Pope at the head of the clergy. The Arian King, from motives of policy, forthwith proceeded to
the basilica of S. Peter, knelt in prayer, "with great reverence and
like a Catholic," at the grave of the Apostle, and then advanced
in triumphal pomp across Hadrian's bridge into the city. Following the precedent set by Theodoric, his German successors, bearing in later times the Imperial title, on their solemn entry into
Rome, always proceeded direct to S. Peters and it is interesting
to [291] observe that this ritual of Imperial reception, which survived throughout the entire Middle Ages, was established three
hundred years before the days of Charles the Great.

The Gothic King made his dwelling in the now deserted Imperial palace on the Palatine, and gladdened the hearts of the
Romans by appearing in the Curia, noble Boethius delivered the
customary panegyric. The King then proceeded to the" Senatus,"
the building erected by Domitian beside the Arch of Severus and
near the Janus Geminus, and delivered a public address. The
spot where he stood, called "ad Palmam" or "Palma Aurea," must
have been a platform belonging to the "Senatus."[190] Theodoric, a

---

[189] *Hoc anno dn. rex Theodoricus Romam cunctor. votis expetitus advenit et senatum
suum mira affabilitate tractans Romanae plebis donavit annonas,atque admiirandis
moeniis deputata per singulos annos maxima pecuniae quantitate subvenit.* Cassiodorus' *Chronicle*, ed. by Th. Mommsen, vol. iii. of the *Abhandlungen der Sachs.
Gesellsch. der Wissensch*

[190] *Anon. Valeslii: venit ad Sentatum et ad Palmam populo alloquutus.* Fulgentius or
his biographer ("Vita B. Fulgentii," c. 13, t. ix. Max. *Bibl. Veter. Patr.*, Lugduni, 1677):
in loco qui Palma aurea dicitur, memorato Theodorico rege concionem faciente. In

rude unlettered warrior, had never even learned to write, and his address in the corrupt Latin, acquired in the camp rather than amongst rhetoricians, must naturally have been brief. It may, perhaps, have been spoken through the mouth of a secretary.[191] [292] He explained to the Romans that he would conscientiously uphold all existing institutions of the Emperors and in testimony of his sincerity had his promises engraved on tables of bronze.

Amid the applauding crowd of degenerate Romans who, at the foot of the plundered Capitol, beside the mutilated statues of their ancestors and the Rostra, listened to the official speech of a barbarian King, and where togas mingled with the cowls of monks and priests, was an African Abbot, Fulgentius, a fugitive who, escaping from Vandal persecution, had come from Sicily to Rome. Our informant, his old biographer, tells us that Senate and people being alike moved to transports of rejoicing by the presence of the King, even the pious Fulgentius was unable to resist the prevailing enthusiasm. "When he" (these are the words of the biographer) regarded the noble bearing and distinguished splendour of the Roman Curia, ranged according to order of pre-cedence, and heard the shouting applause of a free people, the splendour and pomp of this world became suddenly revealed to him. The poor fugitive, shocked at himself, turned his glance from the magnificence of Rome towards Heaven, and astonished the surrounding crowd with the sudden ejaculation: "How beautiful must be the heavenly Jerusalem when [293] earthly Rome shines in such splendour."[192] The naive outburst of enthusiasm on the part of an African abbot testifies to the overpowering impression

---

(Cont.)

Cassiodorus, *Var.*, iv. 30, it is expressly called *Curiae porticus, quae juxta domum Palmatam posita.* We must not, however, confuse this building with the *porticus palmaria* in S. Peter's. *Lib. Pont.*, "Vita Honorii": *in Porticu b. Petri Apos., quae adpellatur Palmata* (at *Palmaria*). In the life of Sixtus III., on the other hand, *Domum Palmati intra urbem.* Preller, p. 143, quotes a passage from *Acta SS. Mai.*, t. vii. p. 12: *juxta arcum triumphi ad Palmam.* The *arcus triumphi* can be none other than the Arch of Severus.

[191] Theodoric had spent ten years in Byzantium, where Latin still remained the official language. The Gothic tongue survived in the Gothic race, but has left no monument of its existence behind in Italy, partly from the fact that but few Goths were able to write, and also because Latin was the language of the Church, the State and the Law. Edicts of Gothic kings to subjects of their own race were drawn up in Latin.

[192] *Vita B. Fulgentii*, and Baron. *ad Ann.* 500, *quam speciosa potest esse Hierusalen coelestis, si sic fulget Roma terrestris.*

which the venerable city, already falling into ruin, but still essentially the Rome of antiquity, yet possessed over the minds of men. The invaluable collection of the rescripts of Theodoric,-which we owe to the pen of Cassiodorus, however, gives fuller information of the condition of Rome at this period, as well as of the active care of the Gothic King for the preservation of a city over which he was more worthy to rule than many Emperors had been before him. These edicts, in the turgid language of the minister, are a mixture of official pomposity and pedantic loquacity; while the admiration of the monuments of antiquity, and the effort to conceal the barbarian descent of the ruler under learned dissertations upon the origin and aim of individual buildings, and finally, the repeated allusions to antiquity, betray but too plainly that the period of barbarism had set in. To the passionate enthusiasm of the historian for his ancestral city is united the bitter grief of the Roman, who, watching the splendours of Antiquity hopelessly falling to decay, bids them a last farewell. Watching as he did the age of barbarism irresistibly draw near,[193] [294] Cassiodorus, by the exercise of his abilities succeeded in delaying its approach so long as he remained Theodoric's councillor. These two men, the Roman and the German, the last Senator and the first Gothic King of Italy, the representative of ancient civilization and the intelligent northern barbarian, present in their coalition an interesting sight, and one which not only serves to illumine the first of many centuries of union between Italy and Germany, but also to typify the whole of Germanic-Roman civilization.[194] . . . . [312] With no less solicitude did Theodoric, as far as his limited means allowed, care for the welfare of the people. We must guard ourselves, however, against describing by too exalted praise his reign as an absolutely golden age; it was golden only in comparison to the misery of the

---

[193] The term "barbarian" was generally used at this period without any sense of disparagement. Among the rescripts of Theodoric are some addressed simply to Romans and" barbarians" *(i·.e.,* non-Romans). It is frequently used in documents of the sixth century, and after the fall of the Goths we frequently find the expression *barbaricum tempus* naively employed as signifying war in opposition to peace (pax). Marini, *Papiri Dipl. Annot.,7,* p. 285, and Ducange's Glossary. In the same way, in the language of civil law, the words *Sors barbarica* signify the third part of the landed property which fell to the Goths. We find the term *"campus barbaricus"* still surviving in the eighth century.

[194] As Theodoric stood towards the Latin world of his time, so Peter the Great stood towards the German world of a later age. Since, however, the character of the rude Czar cannot be compared with that of the noble Goth, the parallel only holds good so far as culture, generally speaking, is concerned.

immediate past. The exhaustion was great, and the wounds were many. [313] The accustomed distributions of oil and meat were renewed, and the officials annually measured out to the hungry city mob the wholly insignificant sum of 120,000 modii of corn, yielded by granaries filled with the harvests of Calabria and Apulia.[195] The poor in the hospitals of S. Peter, as expressly noticed by Procopius, received also a special annual distribution of 3000 medimni of corn.[196] The Prefecture of the Annona, for the provision of the public necessities, was again raised to an honourable office. At least the minister of Theodoric flattered the official by the recollection of his great forerunner Pompey, and by pointing out to him the distinction he enjoyed in driving in the carriage of the City Prefect before the eyes of the people, and in occupying a place beside the Prefect at the Circus. But the formulae of appointment are not altogether to be trusted, and Boethius says, "In former days, when anyone had care of the welfare of the people, he was highly respected, but what is more despicable than the present Prefecture of the Annona?" Shortly before, he had also remarked, "the Prefecture of the city was once a great power, now it is only an empty name and a heavy burthen of the Senatorial census."[197] [314] Care was taken to see that the Magazines on the Aventine and the Pig-market (Forum suarium) in the region Via Lata were well supplied, a special tribune having from of old been appointed for the purpose. The bread was good and of full weight, the price so cheap that in the time of Theodoric sixty modii of wheat were bought for one solidus, and thirty amphorae of wine for the same sum.[198] "The public wealth grew," says Ennodius, in his panegyric on the noble King, "through the gains of private individuals, and since the court is without covetousness, the sources of prosperity flow in every direction.'" If this eulogy be somewhat exaggerated, since no sudden transformation could

---

[195] *Anon. Val.*, 67. Gibbon, reckoning the measure of 120,000 modii, as equal to 4000 bushels, infers that a great reduction had taken place in the population. As sixty modii were reckoned per head, Theodoric's- distributions could not have sufficed for more than 2000 men. Lud. Friedlander, *Sittengeschichte Rom's*, i. 22.

[196] Procop., *Histor. Arcana*, 26:

[197] The formulae of the *Praef. Annon. Var.*, vi. 18. Passage in Boethius, *De Consolat.*, iii. prosa 4.

[198] *Anon Val.* A solidus was the 1/72 part of a pound of gold. The· *LiberJunioris Phil.,in* Angelo Mai, t. iii., Class. Auctor. e Vatican. Cod. Nr. 30, celebrated in the fourth century the wines of Bruttium, Picenum, Sabina, Tibur, and Tuscany; the ham and lard of Lucania: *Lucania regio optima, et omnibus bonis habundans lardum multum aliis provinciis mittit.*

have taken place in the character of Roman officials, nor Goths all at once have renounced their avarice, it is nevertheless true that Rome returned, after her terrible sufferings, to a condition of peace and security. The Senators enjoyed again, as in the days of Augustus and Titus, their now dilapidated villas on the Gulf of Baiae, in the Sabine Mountains, or in Lucania on the Adriatic,[199] [315] and the diminished population, no longer dreading barbarian pillage, well nourished and amused with games, protected by Roman laws and in the enjoyment of a certain degree of national independence, saw no irony in their ancient city adopting, for the last time, the title Felix.[200]

If this condition of peaceful welfare (and there is no old author, whether Latin or Geek, whether friendly or hostile, who does not extol the rule of Theodoric) was disturbed in the city, such disturbance did not occur through any fault of the enlightened government, but through that of ecclesiastical fanaticism. Theodoric, an Arian in faith, had throughout his reign treated the Roman Church with perfect respect, so that not even his bitterest enemy could accuse him of ever having forced a Catholic to change his faith, or of having persecuted a bishop. On his entrance into Rome he "prayed like a Catholic" at the grave of the Apostle, and among the offerings. [316] Which the rulers of the time brought to S. Peter's, two silver candlesticks of seventy pounds weight were given by the Arian King. The discovery of some tiles in the church

---

[199] The villas of the nobility of the time may have presented as ruinous an aspect as many of the country houses of the Roman nobility of present days. Cassiodorus describes some districts in his native province: the Market of Leucothea in Lucania *(Var.,* viii. 33), Baiae (ix. 6), Mons Lactarius (xi. 10), and Squillace (xii. 15). He tells us how the people of Lucania, Apulia, Bruttium, and Calabria flocked to hear mass at the Fountain of Leucothea, as they throng to Nola at the present day; and we read how the priests already understood the art of deceiving the crowd by wonders worked by the miraculous water. The blood of S. Januarius was as yet undiscovered.
[200] *Felix Rama: Var.,* vi. 18; Fabretti, *Inscr.,* c. vii. p. 521; *Regn. D. N. Theodorico Felix Roma.* Herr Henzen has allowed me to share the materials collected by him for his *Corpus Inscr. Latin.,* with reference to the stamps of Theodoric. Of these there are twelve in all, six of which bear the words *Felix Roma,* five *Bono Romae* (see his work, Nr. 149-160). Stamps of the time of Athalaric are rare. Nr. J61 is distinguished by its inscription of *Roma Fida.* Stamps with *Regn. Dn. Athalaric. . . . Felix Roma* have been discovered in the Columbaria within the Porta Maggiore. Gori in Buonarolti, 1872, p. 133. There are also autonomous Roman copper coins belonging to the Gothic time; the obverse bears with the helmeted head of Rome, the inscription INVICTA ROMA, the reverse the she-wolf or an eagle. J. Friedlander, *Die Münzen der Ostgothen,* p. 56, f., and Plate iii.

of S. Martina in the Forum, and even on the roof of the buildings adjacent to S. Peter's, with the stamp, "Regnante *Theodorico
Domino Nostro, Felix Roma*," has given rise to the opinion that the
King had provided for the roofing of these churches. Such a supposition, however, is erroneous. The church of S. Martina was not
built at this time,[201]and we therefore incline to the belief that the
tiles had been brought from elsewhere and at a later date, or were
a product of the public manufactory. Theodoric's tolerance was
in advance of his century, and his Chancellor Cassiodorus almost
exhibits the traits of a minister of the later period of philosophic
humanism. Even the contempt for the Jews, which the Romans,
whether pagan or Christian had inherited, was kept in check, and
the edicts of the King show perfect toleration, mingled with com-
passionate disdain, towards the religion of Moses."[202]

We also include a selection of letters and edicts from Theodoric's "Letters of Cassiodorus" as these primary sources will benefit
the reader's overall picture, as well.[203] Little can be found in re-
gards to the Arians however, especially their Biblical beliefs. For
example, in all my years of perusing the primary sources, I have
never found from their own and limited sources the said or repeated claim that the Arians believed that Christ was a created being. Remember, there was a smear campaign against these people
as the commentary of Saint Caesarius of Arles testifies. They were
made to be looked upon in the most despicable light amongst the
populace. I would counsel that anything said against them must
be taken with caution until proven differently from the primary

---

[201] See the representations of the stamps in Bonanni, *Templi Vatican. Hist.*, p. 54.
Similar tiles were found in the Temple of Faustina, on the Via Labicana, on the roof
of S. Peter's, on that of S. Stefano degli Ungari, in the ruins of the Secretarium of
the Senate, in S. Gregorio, in an ancient aqueduct beside the College German.,
in S. Giov. e Paolo, on the roofs of S. Paul, S. Costanza, S. Martina, S. Giorgio in
Velabro; on the roof of the chapel of John VII. in S. Peter's; on the Palatine, where
Theodoric seems to have instituted restorations.

[202] "To the Jews in Genoa he writes: *religionem imperare non possumus, quia nemo
cogitur-ut credat invitus. Var., ii,27. Var.*, v. 37: *concedimus-sed quid, Judaee, supplicans
temporalem quietem quaeris, si aeternam requiem invenire non possis?*" Ferdinand Gregorovius, Translated from the Fourth German Edition, Mrs. Gustavus W.
Hamilton, *History Of The City of Rome In The Middle Ages*, (London, George Bell &
Sons, 1900, First Published, 1894. Second Edition, Revised, 1900), 1:287-294, 312-
316.

[203] For a selection of letters and edicts from Theodoric the Great, King of the
Ostrogoths see **APPENDIX VIII**, pg. 208.

sources. The sources, however, are few and far between because as Catholicism progressed into the provinces of the new world, heresy was outlawed, and anything that was not supportive of the Catholic faith was legally confined to the flames:

> "In his time [Pope Gelasius I, 492–496] Manicheans were discovered in the city of Rome, whom he transported into exile and whose books he burned with fire before the doors of the basilica of the holy Mary."[204]

> "After all this the blessed Symmachus [Pope Symmachus, 498–514] found Manicheans in the city of Rome and burned with fire all their images and books before the doors of the basilica of Constantine and condemned them to exile."[205]

> "The history of God's people during the ages of darkness that followed upon Rome's supremacy is written in heaven, but they have little place in human records. Few traces of their existence can be found, except in the accusations of their persecutors. It was the policy of Rome to obliterate every trace of dissent from her doctrines or decrees. Everything heretical, whether persons or writings, she sought to destroy. Expressions of doubt, or questions as to the authority of papal dogmas, were enough to forfeit the life of rich or poor, high or low. Rome endeavored also to destroy every record of her cruelty toward dissenters. Papal councils decreed that books and writings containing such records should be committed to the flames. Before the invention of printing, books were few in number, and in a form not favorable for preservation; therefore there was little to prevent the Romanists from carrying out their purpose.

---

[204] "There is no other reference in contemporary historians to the episode here narrated. If Duchesne's theory as to the date of the composition of the first part of the Lib. Pont. Be correct, the author may either have witnessed the burning of the Manichean books or have heard of it from witnesses. Supra, Introduction, p. XI." Loomis, Louise Ropes, trans. *Book of the Popes (Liber Pontificalis)*, vol. 1. New York: Columbia University Press, 1916, 111.

[205] This event must have taken place after the emperor Anastasius accused Symmachus himself of being a Manichean, probably during the latter half of his pontificate. Symmachus wrote an Apologeticus in his own defence. Duchesne, op. cit., p. 265, n. 14. Jaffe, Regesta, p. 99, 761."
Loomis, Louise Ropes, trans. *Book of the Popes (Liber Pontificalis)*, vol. 1. New York: Columbia University Press, 1916, 119-120.]

No church within the limits of Romish jurisdiction was long
left undisturbed in the enjoyment of *freedom of conscience*. No
sooner had the papacy obtained power than she stretched out her
arms to crush all that refused to acknowledge her sway, and one
after another the churches submitted to her dominion."[206]

We will now demonstrate how Clovis wanted to cement his position in the Church with the seat of Saint Peter:

"After having layed down new foundations of understanding
between the State and the Church, Clovis wanted to complete
his assumption of position in the Church by forming links with
the seat of Saint Peter. The official chronicle of the Popes, the
Liber pontificalis, notes that "a gift to the very happy Peter, the
apostle, a votive crown decorated with precious stones, given by
the king of the Franks, Clovis, a Christian" arrived in Rome. Symmachus (498-514), finally restored, and his successor, Hormisdas
(514-523) worked to set up, after the torment and slow disappearance of the two schisms, the pontifical institution. With this gift,
symbol of the recognition of papal supremacy, the unity of Christian was reforming itself. For Clovis, who was then constructing
a basilica in Paris dedicated to Saint Peter, this recognition went
without saying. His votive crown was going to be suspended,
from then on, above the altar of Saint Peter of the Vatican. This
veritable liturgical votive offering carried maybe the name of
Clovis in letters each separately attached to the diadem by little
rings: C.L.O.D.V.V.E.U.M., to [344] the style of the Visigothic votive crowns. We saw (chapter XI, p. 301) how [Pope] Symmachus
[A.D. 498-514] had thanked God for the conversion of Clovis by
dedicating a church to Saint Martin, the final author of his conversion, a short time after having re-established his prerogatives.
Between 507 and 511, Clovis responded to his initiative by this
gift, a new indication of his personal faith (*cf.* document XIV, p.
492)."[207]

The *Liber Pontificalis*, which is the earliest historical text of the
papacy, adds this little gem of history to our understanding:

"At that time there came a golden crown, (a diadem) set with
precious stones, from the king of the Franks, Cloduveus, for a gift

---

[206] Ellen White, *The Great Controversy*, (Nampa, Idaho: Pacific Press, 1911), 61-2.
[207] Rouche, Michel. *Clovis*. Fayard, 1996, 343-4.

to blessed Peter, the apostle."[208]

The footnote in *Liber Pontificalis* serves to clarify the just-quoted text:

> "Clovis died in 511, [27th of November] three years before the accession of Hormisdas. It is possible, however, that there had been a delay in the transportation of his votive crown to Rome."[209]

Pope Hormisdas (514-523) received this golden crown at the beginning of his reign in 514. However, the recognized source of the golden crown for the pope is Clovis. The making and transporting of such a crown would require time, being no minor undertaking. Although Clovis died unexpectedly in 511 at the age of forty-five, it would be only logical that he had intended the crown for his fellow political partner, Pope Symmachus, whose reign was from 498-514. The irony of it all is this: In 508 it was the French who gave the golden crown to the pope, literally, although somewhat delayed, and in 1798 it was the French that took back the golden crown, literally, as well:

> "The Vatican palace was entirely stripped, in the most extensive signification. There was not left the least possible thing that could be taken away, from the most trifling culinary utensil, to the most valuable furniture of the state chambers; and to make sure that nothing was overlooked, the walls and partitions were broken through in one or more places in each apartment, to be satisfied that nothing was concealed, and that no room had been missed for want of finding the door. The palaces at Monte Cavallo, Terracina, and Castel Gandolfo, I was told, underwent the same reverse of fortune; but of the Vatican I can speak with more confidence, as I was myself in that palace the whole time of its being plundered."[210]

The 1290-year prophecy of Daniel merits recognition of fulfillment. That prophecy of Daniel terminated in 1798 (see my *AD 1798 1843 Source Book*). In A.D. 508, with Clovis, the union of church

---

[208] Louise Ropes Loomis, *The Book of the Popes (Liber Pontificalis)* (New York: Columbia University Press, 1916), 130-1.

[209] Ibid., 131.

[210] Richard Duppa, *A Brief Account of the Subversion of the Papal Government 1798*, 2nd ed. (London: n.p., 1799), 63-4.

and state was "set up"; the marriage was consummated. In 1798, the union of church and state was torn down; the marriage was annulled—exactly 1290 years later. It now behooves us to determine whether the 1335-year prophecy of Daniel merits recognition of fulfillment:

> Daniel 12:12 "Blessed *is* he that waiteth, and cometh to the thousand three hundred and five and thirty days."

> Daniel 12:13 "But go thou thy way till the end *be*: for thou shalt rest, and stand in thy lot at the end of the days."

"Blessed is he that waiteth." Daniel states that the "wait" extends another forty-five years beyond the 1290 years, to reach a total of 1335 years. It forcefully implies that they both have the common starting point of A.D. 508. Ellen White quotes the 1290 and 1335-year prophecies. It is critical to understand whether she located those prophecies in the past or in the future:

> "'. . . Many shall be purified, and made white, and tried; but the wicked shall do wickedly: and none of the wicked shall understand; but the wise shall understand. And from the time that the daily sacrifice shall be taken away, and the abomination that maketh desolate set up, there shall be a thousand two hundred and ninety days. Blessed is he that waiteth, and cometh to the thousand three hundred and five and thirty days. But go thou thy way till the end be: for thou shalt rest, and stand in thy lot at the end of the days.' It was the Lion of the tribe of Judah who unsealed the book and gave to John the revelation of what should be in these last days.
> "Daniel stood in his lot to bear his testimony *which was sealed until the time of the end, when the first angel's message should be proclaimed to our world.*[211] These matters are of infinite impor-

---

[211] "The prophecy of the first angel's message, brought to view in Revelation 14, found its fulfillment in the Advent movement of 1840-1844." Ellen G. White, *Spirit of Prophecy* (Oakland: Pacific Press, 1884), 4:222. Keep in mind that all of the Advent believers acknowledged and used the Karaite Jewish calendar when calculating the end-time prophecies, because it was the Jewish time reckoning that applied to these prophecies. The Gregorian calendar, whose use was decreed by Pope Gregory in A.D. 1582 when he changed times, was not used in their prophetic calculations. The Karaite calendar year of 1843 extended from spring 1843 to spring 1844 and overlapped the Gregorian calendar.

tance in these last days; but while 'many shall be purified, and made white, and tried,' 'the wicked shall do wickedly: and none of the wicked shall understand.' How true this is! Sin is the transgression of the law of God; and those who will not accept the light in regard to the law of God will not understand the proclamation of the first, second, and third angel's messages. The book of Daniel is unsealed in the revelation to John, and carries us forward to the last scenes of this earth's history."[212]

Her statement "How true this is!" could not have been made unless the 1290 and 1335 time prophecies had already had their application. In no uncertain terms, she emphatically states that the 1335-year prophetic period has ended:

> "One week ago, last Sabbath, we had a very interesting meeting. Brother Hewit from Dead River was there. He came with a message to the effect that the destruction of the wicked and the sleep of the dead was an abomination within a shut door that a woman Jezebel, a prophetess had brought in and he believed that I was that woman, Jezebel. We told him of some of his errors in the past, *that the 1335 days were ended* and numerous errors of his. It had but little effect. His darkness was felt upon the meeting and it dragged."[213]

Since the 1335-day/year prophecy was ended, so then, naturally was the 1290-day/year prophecy ended as well, as we have just witnessed. For an exposition of the 1335-day/year prophecy, see my *A.D. 1798 1843 Source Book*.

While the church sought to destroy all traces of so-called heresy that would fully mirror her past, there has been preserved ample evidence for the sincere searcher of truth to evaluate the facts and make an intelligent decision either for or against the truth:

> "The evidence from Merovingian Gaul-law codes, edicts, church councils, sermons, saints' lives, penitentials, history and archeology- all point to the same conclusion: Merovingian society and Merovingian culture were nothing but Christian. Pagan survivals and superstitions, whenever and wherever they can be

---

[212] Ellen White, *Testimonies to Ministers and Gospel Workers* (Nampa, ID: Pacific Press, 1962), 114-15.
[213] Ellen White, *Manuscript Releases*, (Silver Spring, Maryland: E.G. White Estate, 1993), 16:208.

documented, were small in number and culturally insignificant. Furthermore, when there is some evidence of customs which are classified by the Christian authorities as pagan or superstitious, we have no indication that it retained the religious significance attributed to these customs and associated with them in a period long before the one with which we are concerned."[214]

CONCLUSION

Clovis adopted the Lex Romana Visigothorum law code immediately after the battle of the Visigoths at Vougle in A.D. 508:

> "Clovis wanted a juridical pluralism by maintaining the palace and the central government well away from the Salic law, but by practicing unity in diversity, he also adopted, after Vouillé, Alaric's Breviary for all of his Gallo-Roman subjects, and we know that this text was also applied north of the Loire. The principle of development was the same (*cf.* chapter XI, p. 304). The juriconsults who had written it had taken care to specify, in a warning preceding the body of law, that the prince (*princeps*) is bound by the laws that he promulgated."[215]

> "When Clovis ascended to the throne, [508] he saw the imperium in the West and with the church-rulership of Caesar no longer able to stand. . . . it was the law-book of Alaric for this population which also won validity now in France.[216]

> "The exclusivity of the bishops' jurisdiction in ecclesiastical affairs is legally fixed."[217]

---

[214] Hen, Yitzhak. *Culture and Religion in Merovingian Gaul A.D. 481-751.* Leiden: E. J. Brill, 1995, 205.

[215] Rouche, Michel. *Clovis.* Fayard, France, 1996, 335.

[216] Schubert, Hans, *Staat und Kirche in den arianischen Königreichen und im Reiche Chlodwigs.* Bd. 26. (Munich: Druck and Verlag von R. Oldenbourg, 1912), 167-8. [*Nation and Church in the Arian Kingdoms and in Clovis' Kingdom.* (Munich Press and Publishing House of R. Oldenbourg, 1912), 167-8.]

[217] Code *Theodosian.* XVI 11.1 = *Lex Romana Visigothorum,* XVI. 5.1. Schaferdiek, Kurt von. Die Kirche in den Reichen der Westgoten und Suewen bis zur Errichtung der westgotischen katholischen Staatskirche. Berlin: Walter de Gruyter, 1967, 53. [The Church in the Empires of the Visigoths and the Suebi up to the Establishment of the Visigothic Catholic State Church].

No longer was the code of Alaric II a compilation of Roman law for use in purely Roman litigation for his Roman subjects, but rather, after Alaric's defeat and death at the hands of Clovis, its validity then took on the legal jurisdiction throughout all of Gaul against the Arians, as well. From that historic event in AD 508, the ministry of Christ was then legally usurped through legislation and cast down from heaven, *jointly,* (Daniel 11:31) by Clovis (The State) and the Church (Catholicism) to the earth as had been fore-told by the scriptures and faithfully acknowledged and recorded by the Lex Romana Visigothorum, and backed by Ellen White, as well as competent historians that have chronicled the steps taken by church and state in the formation of the beast power into the New World.

After Clovis received the titles and dignity of Roman Patricius and consul from the Greek Emperor Anastasius, the diadem and purple robe in the Church of St. Martin, and baptism at Rheims in 508, he was then on his way to Paris to his royal residence and capital. Henceforth, from his coronation in 508, it was the *Breviary* law code that was in place and implemented as the official law code in the provinces of the Gallo-Romans and also in those prov-inces that were conquered by the Franks. As already established by legal historians, The *Breviary* law code, also called the *Lex Romana Visigothorum*, remained in use until the twelfth century.

By the acts of Clovis and Catholicism, the union of church and state was conceived in AD 508:

> "The mingling of church craft and statecraft is represented by the iron and the clay. This union is weakening all the power of the churches. This investing the church with the power of the state will bring evil results. Men have almost passed the point of God's forbearance. They have invested their strength in politics, and have united with the papacy. But the time will come when God will punish those who have made void His law, and their evil work will recoil upon themselves."[218]

Once again, the scriptures and Ellen White rightly directed us to the foundational issue, the uniting of church and state in the year A.D. 508. The facts have revealed that the "abomination" or (sin) that "desolates" was "set up" and established (Daniel 12:11). What had taken place was the amalgamation or union of church

---

[218] Ellen White, *Manuscript 63, 1899;* Manuscript Releases, (Washington DC: Review and Herald, 1981), *1:12–13.*

and state. The *two swords* theory proposed by Pope Gelasius I was to become accepted church and state policy which, in turn, brought *literal desolation* to the Christian church. Simultaneously, the "daily" was "taken away" when the false gospel of the papal mediatorial system was legally established as the "one and true Catholic faith" which, in turn, brought *spiritual desolation* to the Christian church as verified from the *Lex Romana Visigothorum* law code. Thus, two different ideologies were confronted and at war over the Biblical mandate of religious liberty:

> "It is evident, from the language of Gregory of Tours, that this conflict between the Franks and Visigoths was regarded by the orthodox party of his own preceding ages as a religious war, on which, humanly speaking, the prevalence of the Catholic or the Arian creed in Western Europe depended."[219]

Let it be remembered: "Force is the last resort of every false religion."[220] As Procopius has rightly informed us, the Visigoths were one of the main Arian kingdoms in opposition to the principles or government of the Catholic Church. Gregory of Tours confirmed that the Visigoths embraced the principles of religious liberty, as well. The Visigoth Agilan once admonished Gregory of Tours declaring:

> "You must not blaspheme against a faith which you yourself do not accept. You notice that we who do not believe the things which you believe nevertheless do not blaspheme against them. It is no crime for one set of people to believe in one doctrine and another set of people to believe in another. . . ." "Legem, quam non colis, blaspheme noli; nos vero quae creditis etsi non credimus, non tamen blasphemamus, quia non deputur crimini, si et illa et illa colantur. Sic enim vulgate sermon dicimus, non esse noxium, si inter gentilium aras st Dei ecclesiam quis transiens utraque veneriyur."[221]

---

[219] Walter C. Perry, *The Franks* (London: Longman, Brown, Green, Longmans, and Roberts, 1857), 85. Perry quotes from Gregory of Tours' *The History of the Franks*, trans. O. M. Dalton (Oxford: Clarendon Press, 1927), 2:36-43. The authority on Clovis, Gregory lived from A.D. 538 to 594.

[220] Nichol, F. D. *The Seventh-day Adventist Bible Commentary*, (Review and Herald Publishing Association, 1980), 7:976.

[221] Thorpe, L. Trans. Gregory of Tours - *The History of the Franks* (Harmondsworth, 1974), 309-10.

With Clovis' Merovingian dynasty coming into power and his ascension to the Catholic Faith, Theodore the Great, the Arian King of the Ostrogoths in Italy, decreed between the years 507-511 a most remarkable decree. This decree was honored by the Arians but was diametrically opposed to the principles and government of the Catholic Church:

> *We cannot order a religion, because no one is forced to believe against his will."*[222]

This legal position held by the Arians that "no one is forced to believe against his will" enraged the papacy and the propaganda or smear campaign against the Arians by the papacy commenced during this critical period of the early sixth century against those who held to a government that supported the principle of freedom of choice in religious matters, better labeled today as religious liberty. This has been shown to have been the best kept secret of the Dark Ages. The Arian Christians were seen in their true colors: respectable, intelligent, masters of architecture, God-fearing and law-abiding citizens, demonized by religious bigots. While the Arian Christians of the West and East were not at all free from some entanglements of church and state as we know and understand today, nevertheless, they never crossed the red line by resorting to force in religious matters against the will of an individual whether he be of the Arian or Catholic faith. This could hardly be said of the Catholic Church. It is here, in the issue of religious liberty that the war between two completely different ideologies or governments climaxes in the year A.D. 538. But we now know of a surety that AD 508 was when the church officially divorced Christ and committed spiritual idolatry by marrying the State in the New World. In the same year (508) church and state jointly (Daniel 11:31) usurped the prerogatives of Christ by "taking away" of the "daily" or the priestly intersession from Jesus through legislation and cast it down to the earth. In his institution of a church-state alliance, Catholic Clovis caused a false mediation to be "set up" before mankind in place of the true "daily" ministration of Christ as all other faiths were outlawed and the papal government was then legally established in the New World. Thus, there is indisputable historical confirmation and legislative documentation that "the one and true Catholic faith" was indeed "set up" or established as prophesied.

---

[222] Cassiodorus, Magnus Aurelius, Hodgkin, Thomas, *The Letters of Cassiodorus*. London: Henry Frowde, 1886, 185-6.

With "Catholic law" "commanded" to be "preserved unimpaired," and with the exclusivity of the bishops' jurisdiction in ecclesiastical affairs legally fixed, Clovis had become the first Catholic king of the ten symbolic horns of the Western Roman Empire in A.D. 508. His ascension to the throne in 508 brought in its train the first instituted "National" religion in the new world. All other faiths were outlawed. Then began the long chain reaction in prophetic history until every European nation accepted the one and true Catholic faith and was led to follow the example of the Franks in using the civil power to enforce the church's dogmas!

Appendix I

Letter of Avit of Vienne to Clovis
"Avit, bishop, to King Clovis"

"The partisans of schisms appear to veil and obscure your perspicacity by the number and variety of judgments and opinions void of the truth called Christian. While we had deferred to eternity and were awaiting from the future judgment that it would be said what there was of right in that which each one felt, here is that among men there shone today a ray of enlightening truth. Divine providence has finally found a judge for our era. The choice that you make by yourself is a sentence that is valid for all. Your faith is our victory. Certain people in this same debate, while they could have been moved towards the desire for sound belief, either by the exhortation of bishops or by the suggestion of certain people in their entourage, oppose the custom of their people and the rite observed by their father, so much that they prefer in an unwholesome manner pusillanimity to salvation, while they conserve a futile reverence towards their fathers by remaining in incredulity. They admit in a certain way that they do not know that which they choose. How it goes away, after such a miraculous event, the unwholesome timidity of such an excuse! You, with a whole genealogy of ancient origin, you contented yourself with the only nobleness and you have wanted to raise up from yourself for your descendants all that can ornate this high rank with generosity. You have founders, men of good, you have wanted to make better ones come forth. You are higher than your great-grandfathers, in that you reign in the century; you are a founder for your lineage when you will reign in the sky.

Greece can also rejoice for having chosen a prince that is one of us; but from now on it is not the only one to deserve the gift of such a favor. Its clarity also illuminates your empire and in the West the splendor of a glory that is not new flashes on a king that is not new. It is indeed appropriate that the nativity of our Lord inaugurated this glory, so that the day when the regenerative water would prepare you for salvation was also the day that the world received he that was born for its redemption, the master of heaven. This is why the day that we celebrate the birth of the Lord, that it is also yours; that's to say that the day when you were born to Christ is also the day that Christ is born to the world, the day that you consecrated your soul to God, your life to your contemporaries, your renown to posterity.

What can be said now about the very glorious solemnity of your regeneration? If I could not participate physically among the ministers, at least I did not miss out on being in communion, all with your joy, since the divine piety also accorded to our regions this fact worthy of recognition that before your baptism a messenger came to us from your very sublime humility saying that you made the profession of catechumen. Thus, after that which you had said, waiting for the sacred night we were already assured of you. We discussed and meditated with ourselves to know what this event would be like, while the multiple hand of the assembled bishops, moved by zeal for the divine service, reanimated the limbs of the king by the waves of life, while his formidable head was inclined before the people in front of the servants of God, while the hair kept under the helmet of iron covered the salutary helmet of divine oil, while stripped for a time of the breastplate, his unblemished limbs shone with the same whiteness as his baptismal robe. May the softness of this clothing, oh the most flourishing of kings, as you believe it, I say, procures for you more force than the rigidity of arms; and all that the favor of fate accorded to you until then, may it be from then on sanctity that augments it.

I would want to add to all your praises some exhortations, if anything was lacking in your wisdom or your religion. Will we go preach the faith to the Christian convert par excellence, this faith that before this accomplishment you saw without preacher? Or the humility that for a longtime you have shown with devotion, while you did not owe it to us before your profession of faith? Or the mercy that a recently captive people, delivered by you, made known to the world by their cries of joy, to God by their tears. There is one thing in the world that we would want it to amplify: to know that God makes his, through you, all your people and that people further away, not yet corrupted, in their natural ignorance, by the seed of bad dogmas, receive from you the seed of faith, taken by the good treasure of your heart. Do not be ashamed, nor pains in constructing, by sending embassies on the subject, the kingdom of God, he who did everything to edify yours. In as far as these exterior pagan peoples will be ready to serve you, under the commandment of religion, then we will perceive that this has another property. We will discern them more by belonging to a people than to a prince."[222]

Commentary:

". . . . This brings him logically to the baptism. . . . . Insist on the choice of the day that the ceremony took place: Christmas. Avit was right, for this was exceptional. For a long time, the baptism of adults took place once a year, the night of Easter. For Clovis, an exceptionwas made: his baptism took place on Chirstmas night (l. 52). Why? First because of the meaning of the baptism: the water, symbol of life and birth in Christian faith, is the sign of another birth, to divine and eternal life. The baptism is an anticipation of the resurrection and this is why the night of Easter was used to signify this rebirth, this second birth, definitive, into eternal life. Chirstmas day, anniversary of the birth of Christ, was chosen at the beginning of the IV century to erase the holiday of the deified emperor that Aurelian had created. He had fixed the 25th of December as the Natalis Invicti, birth of the unconquerable sun (that's to say the emperor). The Church, in placing Christ in place of the emperor, thus signifies who is the real "master of the sky" (l. 51). It is not the sun, a pagan god. The parallel between Christ and Clovis insists then on the identity of their birth, one to the world, the other to faith. . . ."[223]

---

[222] Alcimi Ecdicii Aviti . . . M.G.H. AA., t. VI, 2, Berlin, 1883, ed. R. Peiper, 46 (41), pp. 75-76.
[223] Rouche, Michel. *Clovis*. Fayard, 1996, 406-7

Appendix II

Dating the baptism of Clovis :
the bishop of Vienne vs the bishop of Tours."

Danuta Shanzer

[30] . . . . "I come to Clovis' baptism from translating the Letters of Avitus of Vienne. The much-discussed Epistle 46 is the only surviving contemporary evidence for the event, yet scholarly confusion about it is still rife in the literature. Many who use it have not constituted a text, or considered what criteria should be adduced to choose between variants. Some have failed, for example, to distinguish manuscripts from editions.[224] Some show random eclecticism in choosing readings,[225] yet extreme conservatism in textual reasoning, preferring invariably to bend interpretations or translations to fit what they think the text ought to say, rather than to admit that the text is either corrupt or demands some other translation or interpretation. As an unfortunate result of a scientifically tidy way of thinking of problems as having 'dossiers' that contain limited numbers of documents related to a case, scholars fail to look beyond their documents. To understand an individual letter written by Avitus, one must read Avitus' other letters; to interpret a chancery letter of Cassiodorus, one must study epistolary conventions. 'In the case of a key historical witness that has been investigated and discussed for a long time, a new approach is hindered, not just by the problems inherent in the text itself, but perhaps even more by the accumulated weight of the scholarship on the subject, whose traditional approaches to problems and entrenched positions on controversies develop a life of their own and a tendancy towards self-justification. This is especially true of Avitus's letter to Clovis, for [31] virtually every sentence in it has already been turned upside-down and side-ways and made the basis for the most radi-

---

[224] E.g. Spencer, 'Dating the Baptism', p. 109, n. 64. For further examples see below, n. 59

[225] For more on this topic, see Staubach, below, n. 59.

114

cally different hypotheses.[226] Staubach has an important point: the
weight of the scholarship on this problem threatens to compromise
any discussion of the key primary texts. Scholars who have worked
on the date of the baptism have all too often come to the texts with
a point of view to defend, be it a late dating, an early dating, a need
to justify Gregory of Tours, a desire to expose him, or simply the
urge to agree or disagree with their predecessors. Most who have
worked on Clovis' baptism have been historians, usually early me-
dievalists, only occasionally later Romanists. As a philologist, I will
interpret a series of different loci vexati in the key texts, three from
Avitus (Ep. 46) and one from Gregory of Tours. I will question the
texts on four key problems in the baptism-controversy. First, what
was Clovis' religion prior to his baptism? Second, is there an allusion to an honorary consulate held by Clovis in Ep. 46? Third, who
is the populus captivus alluded to by Avitus in Ep. 46? Fourth, how
accurate is Gregory's chronology, and did he know when Clovis'
decisive battle against the Alamanni took place? Critical reading of
the texts in question can indeed provide answers to these questions,
or at any rate definitely exclude certain erroneous interpretations.
. . . [55] My re-examination of these four problematic passages has
led to the following conclusions. First, that Clovis was not a pagan,
but an Arian catechumen, or at least closely influenced by Arians at
the time of his conversion. This is obviously something that French
historians might prefer not to highlight: an Arianizing Clovis looks
just like the other barbarian kings. He ceases to be a pagan uni-
cum—the Frank who saw the light. Second, there is no allusion to
Clovis' honorary consulate in [56] Avitus, Ep.46, 75.17, so that that
passage does not provide a later terminus post quem of 508 for the
baptism. Third, the allusion to the freeing of a populus captivus is
most plausibly connected with Aquitainian prisoners from the war
of 507-8. It suggests a late date for the baptism: Christmas 508.

---

[226] N. Staubach, 'Germanisches Konigtum und lateinische Literatur [vom funften
bis zum siebten Jahrhundert]', Fruhmittelalterliche Studien "17(1983), pp. 1-54,
at p. 25: 'Bei einem historischen Schlusselzeugnis, das seit langem immer wieder
untersucht und diskutiert worden ist, wird ein neuer Zugang nicht nur durch die
Probleme des Textes selbst, sondern vielleicht starker noch durch das Geweicht
der Forschungsgeschichte behindert, deren traditionelle Fragestellungen und
verfestigte Kontroverspositionen eine Eigendy-namik und die Tendenz zur
Verselbstïndigung entwickeln. Dies gilt in besonderem Ma_e auch fur den Brief des
Avitus an Chlodwig, bei dem nahezu jeder Satz bereits hin- und hergewendet und
zur Grundlage fur die verschiedensten Hypothesen gemacht worden ist.' (English
translation mine).

Fourth, Gregory of Tours did not know when precisely Clovis had fought against the Alamanni and killed their king. 'L'histoire des lectures de Gre¨goire de Tours reste encore a ecrire.[227] Meanwhile the tradition of defending him persists. This has something to do with his style. He is long, selectively detailed, memorable, vivid, and, above all, there. Like Tacitus and Ammianus, he is a historian who impinges on his readers' imaginations and takes them over: one wants to believe the man—it seems so much easier that way. But to do so would often be a mistake. Time and time again, both his chronology and his facts have been seriously called into question. Gregory is lively and gripping.[228] He writes a curious sort of Vulgar Latin that lends him a certain folksy respectability or authenticity. This tempts scholars to see him as someone who is part of an oral tradition—one that can conveniently be traced to important actors in events of the beginning of the sixth century.[229] He writes 'bad' or 'naive' Latin. Therefore there is no art here. 'Therefore the man is telling the truth', goes the faulty syllogism.[230] Because he writes Vulgar Latin, classicists rarely study Gregory. This is a pity. In the nineteenth century German medieval historians could still recognize a glaring literary topos when they saw one and treat it accordingly. Yet many scholars still persist in labelling obvious literary inventions as 'oral folk tradition' or 'eye-witness accounts'.[231] According to Grell, French scholars treat the sources for the French monarchy with 'une curieuse absence de sense critique et une hypertrophie d'interpretation'.[232] She has put her finger on something very important about the way Gregory is han-

---

[227] Grell, 'Clovis', p. 177.

[228] Erich Auerbach, Mimesis[: the Representation of Reality in Western Literature] (Princeton, 1974), p. 87 draws our attention to horse-urine and on pp. 94-5 discusses the 'everyday reality' and 'reawakening sensory apprehension of things and events' in Gregory's work. He fails to discuss any of Gregory's sources or spools of material.

[229] For the trickledown of this idea see Auerbach, Mimesis pp. 85 and 95.

[230] I was delighted to see that Grell ('Clovis,' p. 180) shares my views precisely: 'les de¨fauts de Gregoire deviennent ses qualites . . . Les erudits supposent qu'en ces temps frustes et sauvages, les historiens ignoraient le mensonge et la dissimulation.'

[231] A textbook example is the treatment of Clotilde's sermon to Clovis in DLH 2.29. Gibbon saw the problem, see The Decline and Fall of the Roman Empire (New York, 1932), II.389 n.25. Yet Rouche, despite his better instincts, is still defending this preposterous literary pastiche, which clearly has a written source, as oral tradition. See Rouche, Clovis, pp.260-1.

[232] Grell, 'Clovis', p. 179.

dled. I would state my supposition even more provo- [57] catively: since Gregory is a 'foundation text', he is treated as if he were the Bible. One attempts to make sense of it. One explains away glaring discrepancies. One assumes that it is not subject to the constraints of transmission that other texts are, that is, that it does not have a textual criticism. It has a higher status. It 'trumps' other texts. One cannot add or subtract from it—after all Gregory had said so himself. (DLH, 10.18)[233] The date of Clovis' major victory against the Alamanni and his baptism is yet another case in point. Something had to 'give', and it turned out to be Gregory. This should be kept in mind, and we should be less willing to perform historiographical contortions merely to justify Gregory—even if he became 'pere de l'Histoire de France.[234] Only Louis Halphen dared to pose 'cette question sacrilege,' 'Gregoire merite-t-il vraiment creance?,' and reply in the negative.[235] The father of French history, whatever his intentions, became for Halphen the father of lies, and he concluded that 'Se figurer qu'il est possible d'evoquer a l'aide de Gregoire de Tours la societe franque au temps de Clovis est une dangereuse illusion.'[236] Few will go that far in throwing out the baby with the bathwater. But I suspect that Gregory is probably more reliable when overheard than when listened to—when he is inadvertently disclosing some significant realia than when he is preaching on the Franco-Visigothic war.[237] The contemporary epistolographic sources, Cassiodorus and Avitus, are more trustworthy, and should be accorded pride of place. To turn from Clovis to Avitus: I hope to have brought into relief the connections between various important issues in Ep. 46 and the bishop of Vienne's known career and interests—notably the ransoming of captives—and also to have made some conjectures, however tentative, about the origins of

---

[233] The parallel with Revelation XXII.18-19 is clear.

[234] Claude Fauchet, Oeuvres vol. 1, f. 147v (Paris, 1610). Fauchet's endorsement was qualified: what he actually said was `Toutesfois tel qu'il est, il le faut appeller Pere de nostre histoire.' No one however, cites Fauchet's complete sentence. Gregory became an authority. G. Monod, Eè tudes critiques sur les sources de l'histoire me˜rovingienne (Paris, 1872), p. 58, points out that Gregory was the first Latin historian of the Middle Ages to be printed in France (in 1522).

[235] L. Halphen, 'Gregoire de Tours: historien de Clovis', in Me˜langes d'histoire du moyen age offerts a M. Ferdinand Lot (Paris 1925), pp. 235-44 at p. 235. Krusch is ridiculed by Kurth (Eè tudes franques, II.240) for suggesting that Gregory invented the story of Clovis' baptism.

[236] Halphen, 'Gregoire de Tours', pp. 243-4.

[237] Ibid., pp. 238-40 points out Gregory's anti-Arianism

Clovis' and Avitus' correspondence.[238]

Professor Danuta Shanzer's full article, pgs. 29-57, Titled: *"Dating the baptism of Clovis: the bishop of Vienne vs the bishop of Tours."* may be purchased and highly recommended from Black-well Publishers, UK at:

http://www3.interscience.wiley.com/journal/119131132/issue

Used with permission.

---

[238] Although this piece is an offshoot of a collaborative project with Ian Wood to translate and annotate the Epistles of Avitus of Vienne, the opinions expressed represent my point of view about the texts others—as is the wont of philologists and historians—we do not. But I gratefully acknowledge my many e-mail discussions with my collaborator, his exceptional expertise in this area, and his kindness in allowing me to bounce ideas off him. I would also like to thank Professor Staubach and Professor Noble for their helpful criticism of a draft of this paper and Roger Tomlin for his generosity in tracking down material inValesius and in Fauchet for me.

Appendix III
Bibliographies

Godefroid Kurth, Ph.D. Bibliography: (May 11, 1847– January 4, 1916) was a celebrated Belgian historian. Kurth was born in Arlon and he became professor at the University of Liege and special Doctor in historical sciences in 1873, where he encountered difficulties because of his strongly-held Catholic views. In 1906 he left the university. He deceased in Asse. The funeral took place in greatest solemnity in the presence of the Cardinal Draper. Speeches were made by the burgomaster of Arlon, Mr. Reuter; professor Closson of the University of Liege, Mr. Emile Prum, former deputy of Clairvaux (Grand Duchy of Luxembourg).

Clovis, ED. Mame, Turns, 1896. 2nd edition V. Retaux, Paris, 1901. 3rd edition, A. Dewit, Brussels, 1923, 2 Vols. (Translated from the French).

Albert Hauck, Ph.D., Dr. Jur., Th.D., Bibliography: (1845-), German theologian and the famous church historian of Germany, was born at Hassertriidingen, M.-Franken, Dec. 9, 1845, and was educated at the gymnasium at Ansbach and later (1864-8) at the universities of Erlangen and Berlin. He took orders, and from 1875-8 was pastor at Frankenheim. In 1882 he became professor of theology at Erlangen, and in 1889 proceeded to Leipzig, where he was professor until 1898, and then for a year rector of the university. A contributor to, The Schaff-Herzog Encyclopædia of Religious Knowledge. After Plitt's death, G.L. Plitt (1836-1880) around 1877, Hauck began the publication of the third edition in 1896 of *Real-Encyklopädie für protestantische Theologie und Kirche* (completed in 22 vols., 1909). This encyclopedia presents in a condensed and modified form that great body of Protestant learning.

Kirchengeschichte Deutschlands, [Church History of Germany] 5 Vols. Leipzig: J. C. Hinrichs'sche Buchhandlung, 1914–1920.

(Trans-lated from the German).

Michel Rouche, born in Paris Ïon 30 May 1934 is a French historian Professor Emeritus of the University, a specialist in the history of Gaul between the Roman Empire and the Middle Ages He is married with four children.

Received a degree in history in 1959 he became Doctor of Letters in 1976. He taught at the University Charles de Gaulle – Lille III from 1969 to 1989 then at the University of Paris IV—Sorbonne as a University Professor. He was a lecturer at the Institut Catholique de Paris His research focuses on the end of the ancient and the establishment of kingdoms "barbarians" to the High Middle Ages including the Visigothic kingdom.

Professor Rouche is causing the international conference history in 1996 which was held in Reims to commemorate the baptism of Clovis. On this occasion, Pope John Paul II was able to meet and talk with historians, researchers, scientists gathered around the issue. The proceedings of the symposium in two volumes are published and are already date. Michel Rouche also participated in the drafting of the film and its Clovis time Jacques Barsac.

In addition, Catholic convinced, Michel Rouche runs the Institute for the Family, which is the Cathedral School an offshoot of the diocese of Paris. (Translated from the French).

Jean Heuclin, Professor, Catholic University of Lille

Laboratory rattachement

EA 4027 Center for Research and Studies "History and Society, University of Artois

Research Fields

The clergy during the Middle Ages.

Thesis: Research on L'eremita in northern Gaul, Lille, 1980

HDR: Search the clergy Merovingian and Carolingian Gaul in northern Paris IV Sorbonne, 1995

Highlights of research activities

Study of religious attitudes and medieval and Pastoral Liturgy. (Translated from the French).

Erich Caspar, (* November 14, 1879:–January 21, 1935) was a German historian and diplomat. Leben1902 he earned his doctorate in Berlin with a thesis on the diocese and church policy foundations Rogers I of Sicily, 1904, his book about Roger II, which still Regestenanhangs because of his works to the standard one. For Paul Fridolin Kehr and he *Italia Pontificia* south Italian archives. Erich Caspar was from 1909 to 1920 employees of the Monumenta Germaniae Historica *Epistolae* in the department for him Tangl Michael had proposed. From 1920 he taught as a lecturer, then as a professor inKonigsberg, Freiburg and Berlin. His research focuses on the history of southern Italy under the Normans and the papacy of the Middle Ages One notable are his edition of the Register of Gregory VII and his *History of the Papacy*. During his time in Königsberg, he published the Teutonic state 1928 he devoted his inaugural speech as rector this issue. (Translated from the German).

Knut Schaferdiek, Born 3-11-1930 in Cologne as the son of the writer Willi Schäferdiek (1903-1993) and his wife Ingeborg, born Krägeloh (1904-1966). 1951-1956 study of Protestant theology at the universities of Bonn and Göttingen. 1958 Dr. theol. Bonn. 1966 Habilitation (Church History) Bonn. 1970 Academic Council and a professor in Bonn. 1979 ordentl. Professor Bonn. Retired 1996. Married since 1962 with Helga, born Siermann.

Autobiography: Marginal hike: church history as autobiography, ed. Dietrich v. Meyer, Cologne, II 2002, 227-256. (Translated from the German).

Hans von Schubert, (1859-1931): Protestant theologian active in Anabaptist research as executive manager of the Verein für Reformationsgeschichte. He was a professor of church history at the universities of Strasbourg, Kiel, and Heidelberg, the author of numerous books, including *Kirchengeschichie Schleswig-Holsteins* I (1907), *Der Kommunismus der Wiedertäujer zu Münster und seine Quellen* (1919), and his biographical work, *Lazarus Spengler und die Reformation zu Nürnberg* I (Leipzig, 1934). (Translated from the German).

Appendix IV

Letter 12
Pope Gelasius I to Anastasius Augustus

A.D. 494
[Translated from the Latin]

With the excuse having been passed over, because it did not give letters to him through Faustus and Irenaeus (n. 1), it discussed about the dual powers, ecclesiastical and royal (n. 2 and 3), and beseeched the emperor that he not permit the church to be torn to pieces by his own division of Acacia (n. 4). Finally it separates the various different objections about the defense of the split (n. 5–12).

1. Your servants[239] of piety, my sons, the illustrious men[240] master Faustus and Irenaeus and their comrades, executing the public authority, [350] they said[241] they would turn back to the city to seek your clemency, for that reason I did not send you lines of my greeting. Not my purpose, I admit; but when some time ago the plain things about the Oriental parts or the sights dispersed to the whole world my freedom, having been denied for itself by your precepts, I believed in moderation by my letters, lest I appear trouble-

---

[239] a¹ c c these substituted in the custom of salutations *Gelasius spiscopus ad Anastasium Augustum*, except the faithful mss.

[240] F^d F^m *vir int.*, K³ *viri consularis*; certainly *Fausto consule* the year 490 is authenticated. Soon the same *publica legatione fungentes*, this is, on behalf of the civilian republic, not on account of the ecclesiastical business: by which sensation below n. 2 *religionis antistites* they were said to obey the imperial laws.

[241] O¹ O² c¹ *dicuntur*. And then the receiving not following thus, as if Gelasius not yet had saluted in letters the emperor, from which he was made pope. For this duty he himself declared he had performed already in letter 10 n. 2: but because it was offered by the opportunity of new authority, he had given no letters to that one himself.

some rather than attentive. Therefore see, it did not result from my dissembling, but it had been of meeting cautions, lest I inflict by spitting annoyance of spirit. But when I learned the benevolence of your serenity, with my humility invoked, by indicating I gently sought speech, now in truth I considered, the consideration[242] for myself not undeservedly, if I could be silent; because, glorious son, and thus[243], Roman born, I love Roman born, I honor, I esteem,[244] and thus a Christian[245] with him, who has the zeal of God, I desire to have following next knowledge of truth, and the servant of the throne of whatever kind of apostle, because[246] whenever for the full Catholic faith I shall have learned to fail, on behalf of my small measure I strive to fill with opportune suggestion. For indeed with the administration of the divine sermon having been attached to me, *alas it is for me, if I shall not have evangelized!* Because when the _____ of the elect, the blessed apostle Paul, might dread and proclaim, it must be more feared by me, to a very small extent, if by divine inspiration[247] and paternal devotion I shall have removed by conveying the service of proclaiming.

2. I beseech your kindness, lest you might judge pride of the duties of divine reason. It might be absent, I beg, from the Roman leader, so that he might judge by his innermost senses the true injury. Indeed there were two, Augustus Emperor, [351] by which this world is chiefly ruled: the sacred authority of the priests, and royal

---

[242] Thus mss. (even F^d F^m O^1 V^1) and d²; the other publications *imputandum.*

[243] Publications except d² *te sicut.* And then O^1 O^2 K^3 *Romae natus*, about the truth of which reading, if it stands, it must be thrown away to one vulgar opinion, supportedy by the authority of the library of the priest, by which Gelasius Afer was believed. However this opnion with that, that now Gelasius proclaimed himself *Romanum natum*, Baronius did not with difficulty _____ to the Panlian example, which when it had been created for Tarsus, nonetheless act. 22, 28 he boasted that he was *Romanum civem natum*. From this indeed this interpretation was mor probable, because at the same time as Anastasium, which was borned at Dyrrhacchii, Gelasius called *Romanum principem*.

[244] Thus D^1 D^2 D^9 d^1 d²; D^4 F^d F^m O^1 O^2 V^1 cc *suscipio.*

[245] Thus O^1 O^2 c; D^1 D^7 F^d F^m N^3 d² *cum eum*, D^6 *cum uno*. We preferred simply *eum*, as in D^9 second efforts. Although it was more modest, because Gelasius, making a sign that zeal following the knowledge of the emperor had failed, was entreated for this gift, as if not for him, but he might think himself to have failed. Wherefore the guesses of Harduinus were not necessary, by chance *pacem habere* must be read to the distinguishing margins. It was completed *zelum* rather before *habere.*

[246] a^1 cc *quodcumque plenae*, O^1 *quod quodcumque*, D F^d F^m O^1 V^1 N^3 d² *quod ubicunque.*

[247] Thus mss. D^1 N^3 d^1 d², *sc. evangelio* (from *evangelizavero*), F^d F^m *expirato*, O^1 O^2 c *inspiratum . . . transmissum*. And soon · D^7 D^9 *judicet.*

power. In which the authority of the priests is so much heavier, even as much as, on behalf of the kings of men[248] themselves, they are about to return reason in divine consideration. For Nostius, most gentle son, because it was permitted that you preside with dignity over the human race, however you, devoted, lower the necks of the divine matters with the patrons, and from these you wait[249] for the cause of your health, say with obtaining heavenly sacrifices and these that he agrees by distributing, you learn that you ought to be given the order of religion rather than presiding over it, and so[250] among these from those things I judge that you consider, that those things you wish to not be lead back to your will. For if[251] it might extend as much to the order of public discipline, learning the order brought in by your high disposition, the presiding priests of religion also serve your laws themselves, lest even in worldly affairs they seem to resist the excluded thoughts. By which, I beg[252] you, is it fitting to obey them, who were assigned to the asking be-

---

[248] In the place *hominum* Baron. substituted *Domino*, which then the editors of the assemblies grasped with no vote ms. But also in the Parisian council VI year 829 c. 3, because Capitular. Lib. 5. c. 319 was inserted, and in the house of Anselm. I, 85 (in Vat. 1364) the place itself was praised with the word *hominum*, which they claimed was also bound. Princes *reges hominum* and priesets *praesules divinarum rerum* were spoken, because those *humana administrant*, even these kings *divina dispensant*, as Symmachus, successor of Gelasius in letter 10 n. 8, addressing Anastasius himself, explained. With similar reason also Fulgentius presided over the truth also grat. II c. 22 he thus defined and distinguished that same power: *Quantum pertinet ad hujus temporis vitam, in Ecclesia nemo pontifice potior, et in saeculo Christiano imperatore nemo celsior invenitur.* See also Felicis II letter 8 n. 5 to Zenon.

[249] Thus most and preferable mss. (D⁵ O² c¹); N³ (in the first hand with Fᵈ Fᵐ *expectis*) O¹ *expectes*, editions (even d¹ d²) *expetis*. He looked here at that of pope Symmachus in letter 10 n. 8: *Tu imperator a pontifice baptismum accipis, sacramenta sumis, orationem poscis, benedictionem speras, poenitentiam rogas.* Soon · D⁹ Fᵈ Fᵐ *hincque* instead of *inque.*

[250] In common (excepting d¹ d²) *Nosti itaque.* The word *nosti* is absent from all mss. Then d¹ substitutes: *Itaque tua interest ex illorum te pendere*, with the other editors and all mss. resisting. Further *itaque* sounds the same, because *atque ita* or *adeoque.* (K³ simply *et inter haec.*) However before the words *pendere* and *velle*, it does not see *debere* to be understood.

[251] Only d¹ *sicut enim* with the mss. and editors resisting.

[252] K³ *quo oro te affectu eis convenit obedire.* In others (Fᵈ Fᵐ Q¹ V¹ V²): *quo oro* (V² *qua hora*) *te decet affectu eis convenit;* O¹ O² c *quo rogo te.* Then b and following conc. edit. Substituted *qui pro erogandis* badly. The same Gelasius letter 14 c. 8 *sacri corporis praerogationem* below the sight of the priests or training of the elders it denied the law of the deacon.

fore the venerable mysteries? Thus, therefore, a heavy crisis hangs over, not to have been silent on behalf of reverence for the Divine, which runs together with the priests; thus this, because it is absent, is no moderate danger, and those who, when they ought to obey, look down. And if , with all the priests in general pulling the divine straight, a string of the faithful comes together to be lowered, by how much more powerfully that agreement of the patron's seat must be applied, which is wished by all the priests and the greatest Divinity [352] to project, and the following piety celebrated perpetually in the general Church?

3.   When your piety evidently turned, by which it is never agreeable inwardly for anyone to be able to elevate themselves by human plan to that privilege or acknowledgment, which the voice of Christ showed to the world, which the Church worshipping always revealed and, having been devoted, had the first. They are able[253] to be attacked by human presumptions which were decided by divine judgment, however they are not able to be conquered by the power of anyone. And would that thus it might not be ruinous audacity against the shining, _____, that which was fixed in front by the authority of sacred religion itself, it is not able to be destroyed by any bravery! *For the support*[254] *stands to God!* Which, when religion is attacked by some, however greatly it is able to be prevailed on by newness, and this remains not more unconquered, by who is it estimated to be able to succumb? Therefore let them cease, I beg you, to surround headlong by your time through a certain occasion of church confusion, which they do not[255] permit: so that that also, which they seek badly, they in no way lay hold of, and they do not hold their own manner in the presence of God and men.

4.   Wherefore in the sight of God, purely and sincerely, I beg, I implore, and I encourage[256], that you do not receive my petition indignantly: I ask, I say, that you rather here me begging in this life, which, because it might be absent, you think finds fault in divine judgment. Nor is it concealed from me, Augustus emperor, what

---

[253] D^1 F^d F^m N^3 *non possunt.*

[254] Thus mss. and edition D^4 d^1 *Fundamentum.* Then many mss. (F^d F^m N^3 O^1 O^2 V^1 V^2) *cum aliquibus infesta religio,* and then D^1 N^3 *quantumque,*d^1 *quacunque.*

[255] Thus mss. also d^1 d^2. Other editions truly with F^d F^m *quae non licet.* And a little before O^1 *perturbationibus ecclesiastica.* The presiding priest of Constantinople, who sought the following seat, this was met by ambition.

[256] d^1 omits *exhortor.*

was the study of your piety in private life.[257] You chose always to be sharing in an eternal promise. Wherefore don't, I beg, become angry at me, if I prize you so much, as king, which you attained temporarily, I might wish you to have perpetually, and you who command for an age, you might be able to rule with Christ. Certainly by your laws, emperor, you are revealed to destroy nothing in the Roman name, you admit no[258] [353] damages to be carried in. And so it was true, excellent prince, who might desire the benefits of Christ not only presently but in the future, that with religion, that with truth, that with the sincerity of the catholic communion and faith you might not allow[259] with your time any loss to be carried in? By what trust, I ask you, are you about to seek his gifts, whose injuries you did not prohibit?

5. They might not be heavy, I ask you, which are said by eternity on account of your health. You collected the saying: *The wounds of a friend are better than the kisses of an enemy.* I seek your piety, so that by which condition they are spoken by me, they are made known to you by your senses. No-one deceives your piety. It is true, what the Scripture declares figuratively through the prophet: *One is my dove,[260] my perfection*: one is the Christian faith, which

---

[257] This was strengthened, which Cedrenus related, with Anastasius sitting in the Circus, the population cried out in one voice: *sicut vixisti, ita etiam impera domine! Quippe qui*, as the same Cedrenus follows, *ante galli cantum templum adire solebat ibique dum concio dimitteretur stabat deum precans, requens jejunabat et sua pauperibus et mendicis erogabat.* But while he put forth as a pretext that he siehd to renew nothing in the Ecclesiastical condition, he disturbed many churches with a witness, the same Evagrio 1. c., and plundered from his own patrons. However that lector Theodorus and Theophanes with mother Manichaea, however Victor handed over that one, having been born, to Ariana of Tununensis. For which reason the same lector Theodorus is the originator that had been to Euphemius of the suspected faithful and concerning his beginning Manichaeans and Arianans gave thanks, and Victor of Tununensis to him, comrades Theophanes and Marcellinus approved.

[258] O[1] O[2] c[1] *nullum admittis ingerere* (others cc *ingeri*) *detrimentum.* We follow F[d] F[m] d[1] d[2].

[259] We complete the small part denying, which was missing in common, from mss. Alludit to the study of that counterfeit peace, having been remembered from Evagrius place soon quickly, which Anastasius to the patrons, whoever he might free to be guarded, he wished to permit, so long as some took up the decrees of the Chalcedonian council, others rejected them, by Henoticus others clung to by their teeth. d[1] *quicquam inferri despendii.*

[260] F[d] F[m] N[3] cc went back for *una est.* And then O[1] *qua catholica.*

is catholic. However that is truly[261] Catholic, which is divided from all the faithless and by their successors with sincere, pure, unstained participation with communion. In general the separation was not divinely mandated, but blending was lamentable.[262]Nor is there already remaining any reason, if we wish to admit this in any contact, that[263] we might not extend the approach and entrance to all sects. *For who offends against one, is answerable to all;* and: *Who scorns the smallest, gradually falls.*

6. This is, which the apostolic seat greatly guarded against,[264] that because the elegant origin of the apostle is glorious confession, no crack of deformity, it was not defiled with straightforward contagion. For if, because God might turn away, because we did not trust him to be able to exist, might anything of such a kind appear, either[265] by which we might dare to resist error, or from which we might demand correction for our errors? Therefore if[266] your picture denied the population of the whole state to be able to be put together, which we are about to make with the total around the whole earth, if, because he might be absent, was he deceived by our collusion? If the whole world was reformed by the profane, [354] despised[267] tradition of your fathers, how would entire population of a state not be corrected, if the true proclamation succeeded? Therefore, glorious emperor, do I not wish[268] the peace of the churches, which, even if it might be able to appear at the cost of my blood, I embrace? But, I beg you, of such a kind ought that very peace to be, not any way but truly Christian, we might hold up with the mind. For how is it able to be true peace, from which undefiled love is missing. However love ought to be just as was clearly pre-

---

[261] 4 mss. *singulariter.* And then D^5 D^7 · d^1 *successorum sincera,* O^1 *successoribus communione,* D^1 F^d F^m N^3 d^2 *successoribus consortibus,* many other mss. (even O^2 V^1 V^2) thus editions conc. *successoribus atque consortibus.* From all these we dig up our reading.

[262] Thus F^d F^m N^3 O^1 O^2 V^1 V^2 c; d^2 *miranda.*

[263] Thus O^1 O^2 V^1 V^2 d^2 c; D^1 F^d F^m N^3 *nec;* d^1 *ut.* And then N^3 O^1 *decidet.*

[264] O^1 c^1 *praetacavit,* O^2 *taxavit,* c^7 c^9 c^{10} *cavet,* d^2 F^d F^m *praecavet.* And soon F^d F^m N^3 O^1 O^2 c d^2 *mundo,* where many mss. also d^1 *munda.* Then D^5 blots out *nulla rima pravitatis* and after a few has *fieri posse non credimus.*

[265] Thus D^1 F^d F^m N^3 d^2; O^1 O^2 *vel cuiquam,* c^1 *vel unicuique,* c^7 c^9 c^{10} *unde cuiquam.*

[266] Thus O^1 O^2c; d^1 *cur;* D^1 D^4 F^3 F^m N^3 d^2 ommit *si.* Then editions *posse pace componi* against faithful mss. F^d F^m *universi varicatione deceptus.*

[267] Scil. with the contemptible and common reverence of idols. d^1 *traditione contemta.* And then O^1 O^2 c^1 *praedication fidei.*

[268] $c^7$$c^9$$c^{10}$to the edge *non negligo,* D^7 · d^1 *pacem turbari,* against the faith of the many other mss.

dicted for us through the apostle, who said: *Love is from pure heart and good conscience is faithful, not false.* How, I ask you, was it *from a pure heart*, if it was infected by external contagion. How was it *from a good conscience*, if it had been mixed with the depraved and evil? How[269] *faithful not false*, if it remains combined with the faithless. Which though it was told to us often already, however it must be repeated incessantly, and not be silent for so long, as long as the name of peace is pleaded: that it might not be ours, that it might be thrown jealously, to make[270] peace, but we might teach ourselves to wish such a thing, such as to be only peace, and beyond which no peace is shown to exist.

7.   Certainly the Eutychianum decree, against which the precaution of the apostolic seat is vigilant, if it is believed that the wellness of the catholic faith is able to stand together in truth, it is expressed, it is asserted also however much it is added to by strength, so that not only through *seipsum*, which might be an enemy of the Christian faith, it is able to be revealed, but however much also as the lethal sects contain in their filth, it is able to be shown.[271] If however, as we believe more, it must be excluded from the judged catholic mind, I ask you, why not also from their contagion at the same time, which were approved to be polluted, you determine the refutation, when the apostle said: *Not only those who do that which must not be made, they seem answerable, but even those who agree with those doing?* Therefore thus it is not able by the taken up communication of perversity or equal perversity to be approved, thus it is not able to be refuted by the accomplice of perversity and the admitted follower of perversity.

8.   Certainly by your laws[272] the accomplices of crimes and the contractors of robberies are constrained by the equal punishment of justice, nor is one wanting [355] in villainy appraised, who, it is allowed did not himself do, however he retained the familiarity and agreement of those doing it. Therefore when the Calche-

---

[269]   Thus more powerful mss. and c d[2]; O[1] d[1] *quomodo.*

[270]   Only d[1] *velle pacem*, instead of the faithful mss. and the mind of Gelasius. Surely when it was not always ours, which we wish to make, however it was never not ours or not in our power, which it might be pleasing to wish, as Augustine often teaches. Then d[1] *propter quam*, c[7] c[9] c[9] c[10] *sed tamen velle doceamus . . . nulla esse monstratur.*

[271]   Only d[1] *monstretur . . . ut magis credimus*

[272]   This is with the imperial, where it seems to be noted, which Valentinian 1. 1 cod. Theod. IX, 29 consecrated: *Eos, qui secum alieni criminis reos occulendo sociarunt, par atque ipsos reos poena expectet*: nor that which the same emperor added with the following law: *Latrones quisquis sciens susceperit etc.*—there F[d] F[m] *constringit.*

donian council, on account of the Catholic faith and the truth of
the apostles and the communion of the celebrated, condemned the
Eutychen to removal[273] as the origin of furor, it was not enough,
unless that its equal might strike back also at the consort of the
Dioscuri and the others. Therefore in this way, just as in any sect,
either always done or not had to be doubtful, their successors Timotheus,[274] Peter, and the other Antiochan Peter, not individually on
account of everyone separate again with this plan, but with the rule
shattered, they once followed the led council. Therefore how does
it not appear clear, that all also are constrained in a similar way,
who[275] arose as their participants and accomplices, and all wholly
are separated from the Catholicism and the deserving apostolic
communion? This Acacia by any law we speak from our partner-
ship of expelling, who prefers to cross over into the fate of faithlessness, which he prefers in the communion[276] of Catholicism and
the apostles to stand together with sincerity, when the wild three
years, lest it might come in it, the matter is competently taught by
the letters of the apostolic seat. Afterwards truly it was made of
strange communion, not able to be cut short, except soon from the
society[277] of Catholics and apostles, so that not through him, if we
might even be idle for a little, we might seem to anyone to have
entered the contagion of faithlessness. But in truth does he even,

---

[273] Only d[1] *damnati.*

[274]   O[1] O[2] a[1] b c *Timotheum, Petrum atque Antiochenum Petrum non viritim propter
singulos quosque rursus facto concilio sed synodi semel acta* (O[1] O[2] *seme jacta*) *regula
consequenter elisit.* Many mss. *Timotheus Petrus atque alter Antiochenus Petrus non
viritim singulariter nominatim unusquisque pro partesua viritim propter singulos
quosque rursus facto concilio sed et synodi semel actae regulae* (Reg. with the
following cures *actis regulis*) *consequenter elisi*; they were corrected from F[d] F[m] N[3]
O[1] O[2], by which it favors D[9], where after *Antiochenus Petrus* by the second hand they
were cancelled *singulariter nominatim unusquisque pro parte sua*, and after *viritim*
they were cancelled *propter singulos quosque*, by the addition in the margine *in alio
non erat.* In truth those words *singulariter nominatim unusquisque pro parte sua* not
unless the scholion on behalf of the disentangled voice *viritim* seem to be apposition.
D[1] d[2] retain that, with the changed line: *non singular-iter...parte sua viritim propter
singulos.*

[275] Thus more powerful mss. d[1] d[2]; others *et qui.* Then only d[1] cancelled *merito.*

[276] D[5] d[1] *sincertatis communione.* Then in mss. also d[1] d[2] *triennio* or *triennium*, where
the editors *per triennium.* By which agreement it mist be considered this three year,
from the tract. I of Gelasius (gest. About nom. Acac. N. 8) we learn, where it was
had: *Per ferme triennium vel amplius sanctae memoriae papa Simplicius non desiit
scribendo ad Acacium etc.*

[277] Only d[1] adds *sedis.*

having been pushed, discharge punishment of such a kind, does he promise correction, does he correct error? Or[278] did that lenient treatment wish to be constrained, who even does not feel the harsh lash? In which, his faithlessness and delaying[279] condemnation, so much in the ecclesiastical recitation his name is not [356] able to be included, which the contagion of the outside communication ought not to be admitted. On which account either purity might be taught[280] by the heretic participation, of which he mingles himself with communion, or with the same he is not able to be un-repelled.

9. Thus[281] however they murmur of the oriental church, because the apostolic seat did not enroll that to them, as if either, concerning the legitimate receiving, it made more certain the apostolic seat to Peter, or the accomplices of this confused reception had not been already equal. Which[282] thus they were not able to teach to have been excused by the heretic depravity, thus in no way were the consorts able to excuse themselves of heresy. Anything[283] if perhaps they added to, which they brought back by the harmonious will of all to the apostolic seat about the undertaking of Peter through Acacia, through the same all thought to have been rewritten for themselves by equal change. Truly the authority of the apostolic seat which was displayed by all the ages of the universal Christian church, it was strengthened by both the lineage of the paternal canon and by the manifold tradition. But even[284] this, whether anyone might be strong to appropriate anything for themselves against the decision of the Nicaenean assembly, the college is able to be shown of one communion, not to be revealed by

---

[278] Thus $D^1 F^d F^m N^3 c^7 c^9 c^{10} d^2$. d^1 *an ille . . . voluit*, $K^3 O^1 O^2$ *valuerat*, a^1 *vateat*.

[279] $O^1 O^2 V^1 c^1$ *manente* (O^2 sec. cur. *moriente*). Then $D^7 a^3$ *ecclesiasticam recitationem* scripsisse vedntur; and soon $O^1 O^2$ *contagium communionis non debet*.

[280] Only d^1 *doceantur . . . sinceri . . . non posse repelli*, against the authority mss. D $F^d F^m O^1 O^2$.

[281] $D^4 O^1 O^2 c$ *si*. Then only d^1 *scripserit*. Concerning Peter Mongus scu Alexanderino after Gelasius spoke.

[282] d^1 *quam sicut non possunt dicere*; $D^1 F^d F^m N^4$ *quam si verum* (D^4 *si vere*) *possunt docere*; they are restored from $O^1 O^2 c^1 d^2$ (other editions *quem sicut vere non possunt*).

[283] Thus $D N^3 O^1 O^2 d^2$; others *quod*, $F^d F^m$ *qui*. And then $O^2 c$ *voce* (in place *volutante*), and then d^2 *voce*, where when $F^d F^m N^3 O^1 O^2 c^1 c^7 c^9 c^{10}$ *vice*. About the relation of Acacia we bring in this, having been remembered, in the knowledge of the letters not existing of Felix II n. IX. However those things having been rewritten in the name of the apostolic seat it is indicated the letter 6 of Felix, by which Acacius was first condemned.

[284] c^1 *licet hinc vel utrum sibi quisque*, $F^d F^m N^3 d^2$ *vel hinc vel utrum*, d^1 *vel huic*, $O^1 O^2$ we also follow the common ($c^7 c^9 c^{10}$). Then D^5 *unius communione*.

the mind of external society. In the presence of those, if anyone is assured, let him go out into the middle, and subdue and set up the apostolic seat from[285] both sides. Therefore the name was lifted from the middle, which[286] kept busy the discretion of the church and catholic communion from a distance, so that genuine peace of faith and communion [357] might be restored, and unity: and then anyone of us against veneration will rise up or depend on age to rise up, he will be sought competently and legitimately. And it will appear to him, anyone might guard with modest design the form and tradition of the majority, anyone[287] leaping above this irreverently, anyone might, with robbery, judge it able to be equal.

10. And the person of the Constantinoplian population is displayed[288] to me, through which it is said the name of scandal, that is of Acacius, is not able to be removed; I am silent, because even by the heretic, beaten Macedonius and the lately ejected Nestorius the

---

[285] O^2 and the editions except d^1 d^2 *de utraque parte* (O^1 *de utraque*). After Gelasius asserted the prerogative of his seat with the canon then by the authority of tradition, he called forward the Orientals and order them to be tested, whether they were well to refute and disprove their own assertion.

[286] d^1 *quod ecclesiarum et catholicae communionis descretionem proculcat, ut sincera pax communionis et fidei reparetur unitas*, corrupt. For what he wished for himself, because the name of Acacia *ecclesiarum et catholicae communionis descretionem proculcat*? Certainly when this being guilty was noted a certain *descretio*, Gelasius turned by the undeserved fault, because this was tread on. In other editions (even d^2) it was read *procul a catholica communione*. However in the older mss. (D^1 F^d F^m N^3 O^1 O^2 V^1) *procul a catholicae communionis*, which reading by restoring ac instead of *a* we thing more genuine. Soon O^1 *reparetur integritas et unitas*.

[287] Nor is this agreed, which in the presence of Quesn. *Quis supra haec irreverenter insiliat, quis rapinam rerum ecclesiasticarum posse fieri arbitretur*, with nothing supporting from our mss. d^2 following their own codes (even O^1 O^2 V^1) *insiliens, quis rapina posse fieri*; other editions *insiliens* (O^1 O^2 c^1 add. *quis*) *rapina* (c^1 *rapinam*) *aequalem posse fieri*. With these words Gelasius brought back excited jealousy for himself from the Oriental in the same: comfirming himself to adhere to the veneration of age and the religious tradition of the majority, in truth thus to bear the very things himself, as if the su-riors believed themselves to this. Gelasius seems to have said this same thing, because when himself and his predecessor reigning priests in Constantinople denied, the same which the leader wished yielded to himself from the Calchedonian council, from which the orientals snatched the occasion, so that they throw about that the Roman priests would bring themselves out above this plan. Because in truth the Constantinople affected the reigning priests against the Nicaenean canon following the seat, in turn by silence itself Gelasius reproached, which *rapina aequalem* judged himself to be able to be in the apostolic seat.

[288] F^d F^m O^1 V^2 *praeponitur*; conf. Gelas. Ep. 3 n. 15. And then K^3 *tota plebs*.

Constantinoplian plebs chose[289] to remain catholic, which of the majority of condemned leaders was restrained by affection. I am silent, because those who were baptized by the same condemned[290] leaders themselves, remaining in the Catholic faith, were agitated by no disturbance. I am silent, because on behalf of the sportive things the authority of your piety even now restrains[291] the tumultuous population; by the same many more, on behalf of the necessary health of your own minds, the multitude of Constantinoplian citizens yields to you all, if you princes lead it back to Catholicism and apostolic communion. For indeed, Augustus emperor, if you make public anything against the laws, which might be absent, anyone by chance [358] might attempt, you had not been able to suffer by any reason: to the pure and genuine devotion of Divinity[292] so that the plebs might be lead back, subdued, to you, do you not think yourself to be between your consciousness? Last, if the mind of one citizen population was not thought to be offended,[293] not divine, as the thing demanded, they were corrected: by so much more, lest the divine not be offended, we ought not at all to hurt the pious faith of the whole catholic name, nor are we able!

11. And however they demand themselves the same to be cured

---

[289] In the common this is added *potius*, which this voice as in n. 12 is silenced in mss. Nor was this strange to Gelasius; for also epist. 3 n. 13 we read *decet nos animas nostras ponere quam*, and num. 16: *vultis vobiscum medicos aegrotare quam*, particle *potius* both ways silence. The many of the same are keeping quiet and the example in the presence of Augustus.—Then Quesn. Following thus exhibits: *quam amore praesulum damnatorum ac defectione retineri*; whether by any authority, it escapes me. N³ d² *a defectione retineri*.

[290] Thus mss. O et c c. Other manuscripts *quibis*. Fewer truly d¹ d² *a quibis*, having been left out before *qui*. Gelasius teaches by the example of no greater time of the Constantinoplian plebs on behalf of Acacia the cause of tumult must be excited, when the collected baptism from himself, thus therefore it was done, that which Macedonius and Nestorius at that time baptized, he had settled.

[291] Anastasius to the lector Theososius lib. 2 pag. 566 by the evidence *venations amphitheatri sustulit*. This by chance the tumult of that population, which the same emperor now is said to have restrained, on that birth occasion.

[292] Mss. O c¹ *unitatis*.

[293] d¹ with D⁵ adds to this *debere* (because the word even above num. 2 we observed to be subticeri by Gelasius) and then the rest thus follows: *offendi, ne divinae auctoritates, ut res postulat, corrigantur* (to the edge *collidantur*) . . . *universi culotres piam*. And truly it is no speech from this divine authority, but from the sacred writings, which pertain to the divine mystery, each so that they might not be corrected by the cancelled name of Acacius, the matter of the church demanded. Fᵈ Fᵐ *divine ut res postulant . . . debeamus . . . possimus*.

by our will. Therefore they allow themselves to be able to be cured by the agreeing remedies: otherwise, what might be absent, in the destruction with their crossing we are able to be ruined with them, truly we are not able to save them themselves. Now by this something must be followed more, below divine justice I leave it behind to your consciousness: whether, thus we hope, at the same time we all might return to certain life or, thus those ones demand, we might tend towards certain death.

12. But hitherto they strained to call the apostolic seat, supplying healing to them, *proud and arrogant*. The quality of faintness often has this, so that they accuse[294] the doctors calling them back to health with suitable observations, how they might agree to entrust or reject their hurtful appetites to those themselves. If we are proud, who minister convenient remedies of the minds, what must they be called who spring back? If we are proud, who speak of obedience to the paternal institutions; those who oppose, by what name must they be called? If we are exalted, who wish the divine cult to be saved by the pure and undiminished course; those who also thing against Divinity, they say, what might they be called? Thus[295] also the rest of us, who are in error, they judge, because we will not consent to their frenzy. Where, however, the spirit truly consists of and strives for pride, truth itself shows.[296] [297]

---

[294] Editions also add to this *magis* (d^2 *magis quam ut*), and then d^2 *eos* after *congruis*, which is absent from the more honest mss.—then c c *quia animarum*.

[295] Thus c d^2 and better mss. (F^d F^m N^3); others also d^1 *Sic nos et ceteri.*

[296] D^1 N^3 thus include: *Explicit Papae Gelasii ad Anastasium Principem.*

[297] Thiel, Andreas, ed. *Epistolae Romanorum pontificum genuinae*, bk. 1. Brunsbergae In Aedibus Eduardi Peter , 1868, 349-358.

Appendix V

Letter from Clovis to the Bishops

****

King Clovis to the saint seigneurs and to the bishops very dignified by the apostolic see.

The news having been announced concerning that which was done and ordered to all our army, before we entered the homeland of the Goths, this could not have escaped Your Beatitude.

Firstly, we order, in that which concerns the service of all the churches, that nobody should try to take away in any way either saint nuns [saintes moniales in French] or the widows of which we know that they were dedicated to the service of the Lord; that it may be the same for the clerics and the children of the aforementioned, both of clerics and of widows of which we know that they reside with them in their homes; the same, for the slaves of churches for whom it will be proven by the oaths of bishops that they were taken from the churches, the order to follow is to exercise no harm or violence towards them. This is why we order, so that all this may be well known, that whoever among the aforementioned will have suffered the violence of captivity, either in the churches or outside of them, be totally and immediately given back. For the other lay prisoners that will have been taken outside of peace and that this be proven, we will not refuse letters written upon your decision for whom you will desire it. In effect, for those that will have been seized in our peace whether clerics or laymen, if you make it known to be true by letters signed with your seals, may they may be sent to us in any way and you will learn that the orders issued by us will confirm it. Thus our people demand that, for all those that you judge worthy of your letters, you will not hesitate to say under oath in the name of God and with your benediction that this thing is true that needed to be proved, since the variations and falsifications of many were discovered to the point that, as it is written: "the just perish with the impious."

Pray for me, saint seigneurs and very dignified fathers by the apostolic see.

[Here is the only authentic document that has come to us from Clovis from a manuscript of the monastery of Corbie dating from the VI-VII centuries.]

Appendix VI

The Church's Business or Financial
Status in the Sixth Century

[137] "The riches of the church grew so strikingly through the gifts of Chlodowech's [Clovis] sons that his grandson Chilperich declared, annoyed, that the state treasury was impoverished because all the riches had gone to the church."[298] . . . . [139] . . . . Around the year 567 Euphronius of Tours and his suffragans in Angers, Nantes, and Le Mans sent a pastoral letter to their congregation in reference to threatening attacks, in which they pressed for reform in customs with great emphasis. One of their main points was the payment of a tenth of all assets.[299] The piece of writing shows on the one side that the tithe was not common up to this point, but on the other side, it gives an example that the episcopate knew how to use the most imposing motives: it promised earthly profits and eternal reward. Not quite twenty years later the second Synod of Mâcon decreed, calling upon the Old Testament commandment and threat of excommunication that everyone must tithe:[300] a legal obligation was created out of moral duty, which would be enforced where necessary. How far the church pressed with this requirement cannot be determined; without a doubt it was not entirely in vain. If one summarizes these circumstances it becomes clear that the increase of the church's assets in the Sixth Century did not come to a standstill; one must rather think of an uninterrupted escalation. . . . the church anxiously took pains that nothing that had at one point belonged to the church ever left its possession: it declared its collected assets as inalienable and incapable of being lost,[301] it collected and preserved the documents,

---

[298] Greg. Tur. H. Fr. VI, 46.

[299] M.G. Con. I p. 136. Particularly telling is the demand that one should also pay a tenth of one's slaves, and that the poor, who had no slaves, should submit, for every son capable of work, a third of a solidus, *ut cum sic agitur, et praesentes irae remotio et mercies prificiat in futuro.*

[300] Can. 5.

[301] Conc. Arvern. (a. 535) can. 5 and 14. Aurel. III (a. 538) can. 13; 25 f. Aurel. IV (a. 541) can. 9, 11, 14, 19, 32. Aurel. V (a. 549) can. 13 ff. Paris III (556–558) can.

with which it could always prove the legitimacy of its possessions,[302] and it sought also to achieve a fitting [140] profit from its assets: the cleric who poorly managed the property entrusted to him was amerciable.[303] Initially, this all corresponded to the land property, which in all the general barter economy was the most important component of the church's assets. But in precisely this way did the church preserve a connection to the earlier cultural epoch that had passed it by: when necessary, it now became, as before in the Roman state, a manufacturer.[304] Also in this way it certainly increased its assets. It is understandable that the view may have been expressed that, gradually, a third or even more than half of all the land in the Frankish empire had become the property of the church.[305]. . . [141] . . . It is understandable that the Frankish episcopate strove to hold fast to the old church's tenets: at the first Synod of Orléans it proclaimed it as its right that all church property remain in the hands of the bishops.[306] . . . . [142] . . . . For, not only did the bishops' churches always

---

(Cont.)

1. Lugd. (a. 567) can. 2. Tur. II. (a. 567) can. 2. Tur. II (a. 567) can. 24 f. Matisc. I. (a. 583) can. 4. Rem. (a. 627–630) can. 13. Cf. Aurel. II (a. 533) can. 6. Lex Rib. tit. LVIII § 2 ff. Also Chlothocar's Praeceptio II. c. 13 protects the inalienability of the church's property. Cf. Löning, D. KR. II p. 286 ff.

[302] Con. Paris III (556–558) can. 1: Iniquum esse censemus, ut potius custodus cartarum, per quas aliquid ecclesiis a fidelibus personis legitur derelictrum, quam defensores rerum, creditarum, ut praeceptum est, iudicemur. Cf. the older decree Conc. Agath. (a. 506) can. 26. Ecclesiastical archives are mentioned several times: Test. Radeg. M. G. Dip. I, 10. Test. Bertechr. Cenn. ep. Pard. I, 203. Childebert's charter III, v. 695 M. G. Dip. I p. 60, No. 68.

[303] Conc. Arel. V (a. 554) can. 6. Cf. on Nicetias of Lyon, Greg. Tur. H. Fr. IV, 36: *Ecclesias erigere, domos componere, serere agros, vineas pastinare diligentissime studebat.* On the vicedominus, the administrator of the bishops' property, cf. Löning, D. KR. II p. 342 ff.

[304] In Strasbourg in 1767 a brick was found with the stamp *ARBOASTIS EPS FICET* (Kraus, Inschr. I p. 11 No. 16).

[305] Both estimates refer to a somewhat later time; the first in Roth, Beneficialwesen p. 248 referring to the end of the Seventh Century, the second in Kaufman, D. G. p. 264, to the time of Karl Martell. Löning, D. KR. II p. 654 raises, it seems to me, justified objections. On which types of money the bishops possessed—it emerges that the Bishop Faustianus of Dax, whose ordination the second Synod of Mâcon deemed invalid, received yearly reparations of 300 aurei from his ordainers [Ordinatoren], Greg. Tur. H. Fr. VIII, There were 84 aurei to the pound = 857 Marks; the reparations counted for more than 3000 Marks, cf. also p. 135 note 3 and 136 note 1.

[306] Conc. Aur. I. Can. 15: *De his quae parochiis in terris vineis, mancipiis atque peculiis quicunque fedeles obtulerint, antiquorum canonum statute serventur, ut*

remain the richest foundations, but the bishop also supervised the administration of the goods of the parochial churches[307] and had a stake in their income.[308] The power of the bishop over the diocese's clergy was almost unlimited. The clergy was dependent upon him in every way: through ordination he elevated laymen to the clerical standing; he helped clerics from one level to the next; he conferred specific offices[309] upon them and, in certain cases, could take them away again; without his consent, priests could not even be assigned to private chapels. He tended to all clerics' means of livelihood, as long as they did not blunder in their established offices; the entire disciplinary [143] power lay in his hands.[310] No cleric could extract himself from this dependency; for it was just as prohibited for him to leave the clerical standing[311] as it was to leave the diocese in which he had been ordained.[312] Complaints against bishops could only be

---

(Cont.)

omnia in episcope potestate consistant; de his tamen quae in altario accesserint, tertia fedeliter episcopis deferatur. Cf. Conc. Carp. (a. 527) p. 41.

[307] Conc. Aurel. III (a. 538) can. 26; Aurel. IV (a. 541) can. 11, alienation of property from parochial churches with the consent of the bishop; the latter was necessary also for exchange, see the formula of Marc. II, 23 ed. Zeumer p. 91. On the position of the bishop in relation to the property of monasteries, cf. chapter 4.

[308] See p. 141, note 4.

[309] In the Fifth Century it still happened that the presbytery was chosen by the congregation; Sid. Apoll. ep. IV, 24 tells of one of his friends, a certain Maximus: *Dixerunt, nuper impacto sacerdotio fungi, quo recusantem fatiose ligasset civicus amor.* In the Sixth Century no such case is known to me. Still, remnants of the old rights remained in the liturgical formulas. Before the consecration, the bishop had to introduce the priest, who had been selected by him or by the deacon, to the congregation and request their approval. The formula read: *Filium nostrum Illum cupio ad officium diaconatus . . . promovere. An eum dignum hoc officio censeatis, scire desidero; et si vestra apud meam concordat election, testimonium quod vultis vocibusadprobate.* Miss. Franc. in Duchesne Origines du culte chret. p. 355. At the ordination of priests the formula read: *Electionem vestram debetis voce publica profiteri,* p. 357. According to this, it was specifically recognized that every member of the congregation had the right of objection to the intended ordination, Conc. Elus. (a. 551) can. 5. That the bishop conferred offices in the parochial churches can be seen in Conc. Aurel. III (a. 538) can. 21, and that he supported the clerics, in Arvern. (a. 535) can. 11; Aurel. V (a. 549) can. 5; Arel. V (a. 554) can. 4, that he named archdeacons, in Agath. (a. 506) can. 23.

[310] How far this hand reached is attested by documents such as Conc. Aurel. II (a. 533) can. 9. Aurel. III (a. 538) can. 35. A constraint is imposed by Tur. II (a. 567) can. 7

[311] Conc. Chalced. can. 7; Turon (a. 461) can. 5.

[312] Conc. Chalced. can. 20. Epa. (a. 517) can. 5. Arvern. (a. 535) can. 11. Aurel. III

brought before the synod, before a court of bishops.[313] . . . .[144]. . . .
When one considers all this, it becomes clear what extensive power
the bishops had. . . . We know of more than thirty ecclesiastical assemblies that took place between the first Synod of Orléans in the
year of Chlodowech's [Clovis] death [511] and the Synod of Paris in
the year 614. They were of importance in every way for the life of the
church; in particular, however, they contributed to the strengthening
of the cohesiveness of the episcopate. In that the bishops consulted
with one another and made rulings, they not only appeared to be a
closed rank, but they became accustomed to consider themselves
such and to act accordingly.[314] [145] It was a question of greatest importance for the Frankish empire, as well as for the church, whether
the relationship of the church to the state would succeed in forming
itself such that neither the state nor the church would be hindered in
its development, and that the church would not suffer any damages
through subordination to the state.

The Frankish kings regarded the power of the church without distrust; it did not occur to them to want to lessen its prestige
or minimize its importance. They recognized the moral authority of the episcopate in the widest sense and allowed all honors,
over which the church had command, to accumulate. As to how
they enriched the church: they presented gifts to the bishops per-
sonally.[315] They loved to approach them in spiritual kinship, in that
they chose them to be godfathers of their children.[316] No one was
treated more respectfully at the court than the members of the
hierarchy;[317] they must have also gained influence in that they were
frequently trusted with the arrangement of political affairs.[318] This
went so far that King Guntchram appointed a bishop as arbitrator
in a conflict with his brother Sigibert.[319] Just as they judged over

---

(Cont.)

(a. 538) can. 16f. Aurel. V (a. 549) can. 5. Arel. V. (a. 554) can. 7.

[313] Conc. Aurel. III. (a. 538) can. 23

[314] That the bishops did not oversee this side of things can be seen in the writings of
Maximus of Rheims to Nicetius, ep. Aust. 11 p. 126. On the course of business at the
synods and the transcription of protocols, see Bretholz N. A. 18 p. 531 ff.

[315] For example Ven. Fort. Vit. Germ. 22 p. 16. Test Remig. Pard. I p. 82.

[316] Prätextatus of Rouen was godfather of Merovech, Chilperich's son, Greg. Tur.
H. Fr. V, 18. Agericus of Verdun was godfather of Childebert II, ib. IX, 8. Magnerich
of Trier was godfather of Theudebert II, ib. VIII, 37. Veranus of Cavaillon was
godfather of Theuderich II, ib. IX, 4.

[317] Cf. for example Greg. Tur. H. fr. III, 25; IV, 19; V, 18; VIII, 1; 9.

[318] Greg. Tur. H. Fr. IV, 47; VI, 3; 31; VII, 14; VIII, 30; IX, 18; 20.

[319] Ib. IV, 47: Guntchram calls the bishops to Paris, *ut inter utrusque*—Guntchram

secular leaders,[320] in criminal cases against bishops, the deciding word was left to members of the same rank. For the question of whether the accused was guilty or innocent was, according to rules, decided by a verdict from the synod;[321] only the punishment of the individual proven guilty by the synod was decided in the king's court.[322] And [146] not only in such temporary regulations did admiration reign in cases of the bearers of the ecclesiastical offices, this found its sharpest expression in legal determinations: the wergild for a murdered bishop was higher than for royal officials;[323] special supervision was provided over jurisdiction in the case of bishops,[324] if they took part in any court hearings, they always had the seat of honor;[325] they had protective power over all the freed

---

(Cont.)

and Sigibert—*quid veritas haberit, edicerent.*

[320] Ib. VIII, 30.

[321] Trial against Saffarich of Paris in the second Paris Synod 552 M. G. Conc. I p. 117. Charge against Praetextatus of Rouen 577 Greg. Tur. H. Fr. V, 19; against Salonius of Embrun and Sagittarius of Gap 567 and 579, ib. V, 20 and 27. Court over Gregor of Tours at Berny-Rivière 580, H. Fr. V, 49. Against Bertechramnus of Bordeaux and Palladius of Saintes 585, ib. VIII, 7 and 20; against Theodor of Marseille ib. VIII, 43; cf. Nißl, *Gerichtsstand des Klerus*, 1886, p. 48 ff. Brunner, D. RG. II p. 314 f.

[322] Cf. particularly Greg. Tur. H. Fr. X, 19, the actions against Egidius of Rheims: his dismissal, determined by the synod, was followed by exile to Strasbourg.

[323] According to the addenda to the lex. Salic. tit. 55, the wergild for a bishop is 900 solidi, while that of a count is 600, the same for the presbyter, that of the deacon 300 solidi. The lex Ripuar. tit. 36 assesses the wergild for the bishop at 900 solidi. According to the lex. Alam. tit. 11 the wergild for bishop and duke are the same. The Bavarian Law I, 10 has a unique clause: *Fiat tunica plumbea secundum statum eius (of the murdered bishop) et quod ipsa pensaverit auro tantum donet qui eum occidit; et si aurum non habet, donet alia pecunia, mancipia, terra, villas vel quicquid habet usque dum impleat debitum.*

[324] Chlothar. praecept. 6: *Si iudex alequem contra legem iniuste damnaverit, in nostri absentia ab episcopis castigetur, ut quod perpere iudicavit versatim melius discussion habeta emendare procuret.* I cannot regard the contents of this statement as so insignificant as Löning, II p. 269 f., who sees in it only the demand that the bishops should respond to unjust judges with ecclesiastical means of punishment. For the last sentence openly presumes that the judge is obliged, upon the bishop's intervention, to reinvestigate the case he has just completed from the beginning. This is certainly not one of the judicial duties of the bishop, but it is a disturbance to the legal system through the ecclesiastical function of the same. The bishop becomes the de facto overseer of the judge. An analogous clause was created at the second Synod of Tours, a. 567 c. 27.

[325] Cf. Löning, D. Kr. II, p. 535 f.

slaves;[326] the church censorship, that they enacted, had extensive consequences for the populace.[327]

The concessions toward the church thus approached the borderline where they had to deflect the impairment of the state. However, this borderline was not crossed; for the bishops never ventured out of the line of king's subjects.[328] As willingly as the princes [147] recognized their clerical power, they were far from considering this power equal to that of the king. They demanded an oath of fidelity[329] from the high as well as the lower clergy and committed the bishops to political service.[330] In all criminal cases, the clergy was subordinate to civic penal power;[331] the early beginning efforts of the synods to affiliate themselves with the customary courts had no success during the entire Sixth Century."[332,333,334]

---

[326] Cf. p. 143, note 6.

[327] Childeberti decretio § 2, M.G. Cap. Reg. Franc. p. 15: *Qui episcopo suo noluerit audire et excommunicates fuerit, perenni condemnation apud Deum sustineat et de palatio nostro sit omnino extraneus et omnes res suas parentibus legitimis amittat qui noluit sacerdotis sui medicamenta sustinere.*

[328] Ep. Leon. Sen. episc. ad Childeb. reg., M.G. Ep. III p. 437: He is surprised, *quod sine iussu glor. dom. principis nostri, filii vestri Theudoberthi regis, cuius somus regni ordenatione subiecti, iniugetis, ut ea quae anteacto tem-pore facta non sunt, nunc praesentia nostra aut consinsum debeant incoari.*

[329] Cf. Löning II p. 254 ff.; Weyl p. 34 f.

[330] Cf. Sickel, Gött. gel. Anz. 1890 p. 229.

[331] Sohm, Zeitschr. f. KR. IX p. 206 f. Löning, D. KR. II p. 510 f. Nißl p. 32 f., p. 104 ff.

[332] One sought to cut charges of clerics against clerics out of the secular courts (Conc. Elus. a. 551 c. 4, Matisc. I a. 583 c. 8, Autiss. a. 573—603 c. 35; on bishops' conflicts among one another Aurel. IV. a. 541 c. 12, Lugd. II a. 567–570 c.1), as well as to hinder the charges of clerics against laymen and laymen against clerics (Conc. Aurel. III a. 538 c. 35), or at least to make them more difficult (Aurel. IV a. 541 c. 20, Aurel. V a. 549 c. 17, Matisc. I a. 583 c. 7 and 9, matisc. a. 585 c. 10). The first Synod of Orléans (511) had handled the charges of laymen against clerics as permissible, cf. c. 6.

[333] Not until the edict of Chlothachar II v. 18 October 614 c. 4 (M.G. Cap. I p. 20) did it become the duty of the judge not to speak a verdict against a cleric per se, that is, without the participation of a bishop. Only when a lower clergyman was taken to task would such a verdict have been permissible. A particular clause referred to severe cases, in which the bishop should by all means be brought to the case. As unclear as this clause is, it seems to me that the exception was still out of the question that in such cases only the ecclesiastical censorship should take precedence: it can only be seen as leading toward civic punishment. Cf. on the interpretation of this clause Löning II p. 526 ff., Brunner II p. 316.

[334] Albert Hauck, *Kirchengeschichte Deutschlands*, [*Church History of Germany*] Bd. I 3rd and 4th edition, 1904, 1:137-147.

Appendix VII

Patrologia Latina

Volumen [Volume] 35, pgs. Col. 2417-2452

Sancti Aurelii

Augustini

[Saint Aurelius Augustine's]

-1841-

Expositio in Apocalypsim
B. Joannis

[Exposition of the
Apocalypse of Saint John]

[Saint Caesarius of Arles]

[This translated primary Latin document reveals what the Catholic's theological position was on the entire Apocalypse written by Saint Caesarius of Arles, 470/71, died at Arles, 27 August, 543. This is an extremely revealing document that was credited to St. Augustine but has been proven by G. Morin in the "Revue Benedictine, 45, 1933" and acknowledged and confirmed by Bertrand Fauvarque in: Rouche, Michel, ed. *Clovis, Histoire et Mémoire* (Actes du Colloque international d'historie de Reims), 2 vols. Paris: Univ. of Paris-Sorbonne Press, 1997, 2:280, by Bertrand Fauvarque, *Clovis' Baptism The beginning of the saint's millennium,* Paris: Univ. of Paris-Sorbonne Press, 1997, 2:280, that it was written by Saint Caesarius of Arles instead.]:

"Homily 1.

[Apocalypse chapter I.] In the reading of the revelation of the apostle blessed John, very dear brothers, we notice, and we will take care to explain according to the anagog with this bountiful the Lord bestowing this, that the revelation of Jesus Christ is announced to our ears, in order that the secret heavenly things are revealed to our hearts. "The apocalypse of Jesus Christ, which God has given to that one clearly to do for his own servants," that is to reveal. "Signifying the things which it is necessary to fulfill soon": this is showing. "To his servant John": John, is interpreted thanks to God. "Writing to the seven Churches, which are in Asia." Asia rising up is interpreted, through which human kind is represented. Those seven Churches and seven candelabra, this should be looked at carefully, because sevenfold is pleasing, which was given by God through our Lord Jesus Christ, for us for the human race, who believe: because he himself also promised to us to send the paraclete Spirit from the heavens, which he also sent to the Apostles, who were seen to be in Asia, this is in the elevated world, where he also granted the pleasing sevenfold to the seven Churches for us through his own servant John. "Thanks to you and may peace be multiplied by God the Father and by the Son of a human": that is, by Christ. Moreover whether the Son of a human, or seven candelabra, or seven stars, the Church is understood with Christ as its head. Moreover what he says, "Girded between the breasts with a golden sash": He who was girded, depicted Christ the Lord. The two breasts, understand as the two Testaments, which they receive from the heart of the Lord Savior as if from a perennial fountain, whence they nourish the Christian people for eternal life. Indeed the golden sash, is the chorus, or multitude of Saints. Indeed just as the chest is bound from a belt, thus the multitude of holy ones sticks to Christ, and it surrounds the two Testaments as if two breasts, in order that from themselves as if from holy udders they may be nourished. "His head," he says, "and hairs just as white wool and snow": he says the white hairs are the multitude of ones dressed in white, that is converts proceeding from Baptism. He said wool, because sheep are of Christ. He said snow, because just as snow falls from the sky beyond, thus also the grace of Baptism comes to no preceding ones who have merited. Indeed those themselves who are baptized, are Jerusalem, which daily descends in the likeness of snow from the heaven. Jerusalem, that is the Church therefore is said to descend from the sky, because from the sky is the supernatural gift, through which one is freed from sins, and is joined to Christ, that is an eternal head as a celestial spouse. Just as it is said on the contrary that the beast ascends from the abyss, that is, an evil people who are born from an evil people. For just Jerusalem is extolled up by descending humbly, thus the beast, that is the haughty people by ascending arrogantly are cast down headlong. "His eyes just as the flame of fire": he says the precepts of God in the eyes; just as it was written, "Lord, your word is a lamp for my feet"; and, "Your burned word" Psalms 118: [119]:105, 140. "And his feet are similar to the brass of Libanus, burned just as a fire in a furnace": in the burned feet is understood the Church; which on the imminent Day of Judgment, must be tested by the excess of oppressions, and examined by fire. And because the foot is the most recent part of the body and he said the feet were burned, therefore in the feet the Church of the most recent time it is understood must be tested with many tribulations just as gold in the furnace. The one who considers this matter well, now sees that it happens now from the multitude of iniquities. Therefore he expressed by bronze, [2418] what is led from the air and much fire and medicine to the color of gold: just as the church is rendered purer through tribulations and sufferings. In the golden zone girded on the chest, the spiritual knowledge and pure feeling given to the Church is possible also to be understood. "The double edged sword in truth proceeding from the mouth of himself," signifies that he himself is Christ, the one who also has now brought forth the good things of the Gospel, and earlier through the Law of Moses knowledge to the whole world: and similarly concerning this David says, "The first time God spoke, I heard these two things" Psalms 61:12. Therefore these are the two Testaments, which in order to capture either the new things of the time, or the old, are said to be a double-edged sword. "His voice as if the voice of many waters": many waters, are understood to be peoples; in the voice, the prediction of the Apostles. What moreover he said above, "His feet are similar to bronze, as if they have been ignited down in a furnace": they are also able to understood as the Apostles, who prophesied his word after the suffering. Indeed the prophecy walks through the agency of what are rightly named feet; just as also the prophet said, "How beautiful the feet of those evangelizing the peace, of those evangelizing the good things" Isaiah 52:7 and that thing, "We will worship in the place where his feet have stood" Psalms 131:7. That moreover he said, "He was holding in his right hand seven stars"; he wanted the Church to be understood. Indeed in the right hand of Christ is the spiritual Church to which when placed at the right hand he says: "Come, blessed ones of my Father" Matthew 25:34. Therefore the seven stars are the Church. Indeed we have said that the sevenfold Spirit of strength was given to him from the Father, just as Peter says to the Jews concerning Christ, "Therefore he who has glorified the right hands of God, has spread the Spirit received by the Father" Acts 2:33. Moreover the seven Churches, which he calls with his own words, he does not therefore speak of, because they alone would be the Churches; but what he says for the one, this he says for all. Finally whether in Asia, or in the whole world, the seven Churches are all, and one is Catholic; just as he says to Timothy, "How it is necessary that you are converted in the home of God, which is the Church of the living God I Timothy 3:15; and in Isaiah, the seven women which apprehended one man Isaiah 4:1, he understands that the seven Churches are represented, which is also one: the man, we understand to be Christ; the bread of the women, the Holy Spirit, which nourishes into eternal life. And in order that things which were spoken are inculcated are impressed upon you more firmly, I wish there to be a short recapitulation from them. Therefore the seven Churches, to which the holy John writes, are understood as one Catholic Church, on account of the sevenfold grace. What moreover he says, "Faithful witness," is Christ. The seven candelabra, are the Catholic Church. In the middle of the candelabra similar to the Son of a human, is Christ in the middle of the Church. That moreover he says it was girded above the breasts: the breasts are understood as the two Testaments, which receive spiritual milk from the chest of Christ, in order to nourish the Christian people into eternal life. In truth the golden sash, is the chorus or multitude of saints, who continue on continuously yet with the reading and oration. They are proven to stick to Christ. Those things now are sufficient for your dearness. What you have heard, remember with sacred conversation among you, until what is left, you are able to hear with the Lord granting. What he himself deems worthy to bestow, etc.

Homily II.

[Apocalypse 2 and 4.] Dearest brothers, in the candelabrum, about which you read when the Apocalypse was read, is understood the people. That moreover he says, "I will move your candelabrum"; this is, I will disperse the people in place of their sins. "And I will fight [2419] with them in the sword of my mouth": that is, I will bring my precepts, through which one's own sins or crimes are exposed. That in truth he said, "His face just as the sun shines in its strength" Apocalypse 1:16: and from the arrival or presence of Christ, because through the face each one is revealed and is known; and from the Church this is able to be received, for which Christ promised that clarity, about which he says, "Then the just will flash just as the sun in the kingdom of their father" Matthew 13:43. "The morning star"; he says is the first resurrection, which happens through the grace of Baptism. The morning star flees the night, and announces the light, that is it takes sin and has granted grace: if however grace has been received good works follow. Indeed just as it is not at all useful that a great tree blooms and does not bear fruit; thus it profits nothing to be called a Christian, and not to have Christian works. And therefore he says, "I advise to you to buy from me gold which has been refined" Apocalypse 3:18: that is, try to endure something for the name of Christ. "And anoint your eyes with salve": so that what you learn willingly through the Scriptures, you may fulfill with work. "That a gate has been opened in the sky," John the preacher of the New Testament saw. [By which eyes did he see? So far as concerns the represented evidence, not of flesh, but of the mind. So far as concerns in truth the correctness of the matter itself which had already been revealed in the Lord appearing as flesh, not only did he see with the eyes of flesh, but also he handled with his hands. In truth what is designated through the gate in this place, unless the mediator of God and of men Christ Jesus, with the Lord himself saying, "I am the gate" John 10:9, and the remaining things. Therefore it is considered justly not closed, but opened, because our mediator certainly made known the same thing by being born, by dying for all the faithful, because he himself was the redeemer of the world. What is designated through the heaven, if not the Church? Just as he himself says, "The heaven is a throne for me" Isaiah 66:1; or, "The soul of the just," just as Salomon bears witness, "is the seat of wisdom." Paul also answers calling Christ the Strength of God, and the Wisdom of God I Corinthians 1:24. It remains far from doubt that the heaven is the Church of selected ones, in which the gate is seen as opened; because in it our Redeemer, having been born and having suffered, is preached and believed to have ascended to the heavens. Moreover what John heard when placed in this vision, he makes clear when he says, "And the first voice which I heard, as if of a trumpet speaking with me, saying,] "Rise up to here": When it is shown open, it is clear that it was closed before to humans. "The throne which was placed," is the seat of the one judging, above whom he saw the likeness of the jasper and of carnelian. Jasper has the color of water, and carnelian, of fire: in these two stones two judgments are understood; one which has been done already through water in the flood, the other which will be through fire in the consummation of the age. It is possible in this place also that the life of the servants of God is understood; because with respect to the likeness of water and of fire sometimes in this life all the holy ones have successful things, sometimes they suffer adverse things. ["And there was a rainbow in the circuit of the seat similar to the appearance of an emerald." The rainbow is therefore called in the Greek and Latin tongue a bow, which is seen   to appear on the day of rain. And what is designated through this unless the reconciliation of the world, which is recognized as made through the dispensation of the Word incarnate? If this is looked at carefully, the effect of the rainbow itself is seen certainly to indicate this. The bow therefore appears at that time, when the rainbearing cloud was illuminated by the rays of the sun. Therefore when the sun illuminates the cloud, the rainbow, that is the bow appeared: because of course it has illuminated the Word of the Father, which is the radiance of eternal light and the sun of justice, has illuminated by supporting human nature, as the very protection of its humanity, which in fact is called a cloud by the prophet Isaiah 19:1, became the reconciliation of the world. Moreover well is it called rainbearing, because it is certainly full of the eloquences of preachings. If indeed fittingly to the reconciliation of the human race in the new Testament the bow is described to have appeared figuratively: which in the Old also therefore is understood placed in the clouds by the Lord, [2420] in order that through it peace is recognized as returned to the lands after the inundation of the flood; in order that namely by its appearance the omnipotent God mindful of his agreement, allowed the land to be destroyed by the immensity of waters in no way further. Of course if one letter is added on the end to this name and it is called irini, the interpretation seems to sound especially like this itself: for peace is named by the Greek word [eirene]. And indeed in the Old Testament the Lord says to Noah, "Behold, I will establish my agreement with you" Genesis 9:9. And it should be noted how apt the connection of shapes is. Because indeed the lightning, voices and thundering from the throne are said to proceed as if from a cloud in the following, conveniently here with the sun irradiating the likeness of the bow, the same throne is said to have returned: this bow of course, although it is of diverse color, and shines mostly with two, that is, of water and of fire, and is designated through the flood, and following through fire; this however is compared not without merit to the appearance of emerald, in order that through it, as we have said, divinity is shown when the world is repopulated. Indeed the stone emerald is of a very green color: and this color certainly, as I have already said in the preceding versicle, is not inconveniently fit to the nature of divinity.] "The glass sea," is the gift of Baptism: which therefore is said to be before the throne, because it is given before the arrival of the judgment. Which indeed after these things he says, "I have the keys of death and of the underworld"; this therefore he says, because he who believes and is baptized, is freed from death and from the underworld; and because the Church itself, just as it holds the key of life, thus also of the underworld: indeed it was said to the very one, "For the one for whom you have dismissed the sins, they are dismissed; and whose you have retained, they have been retained" John 20:23. Wherever he places the angel of the human in the Apocalypse, he is the human himself of the Churches. In the name of angels only did he want the Catholic Churches to be understood, in order to order the angels to pay penitence. Indeed the Angels, who are in the heaven, are not needful of pentitence; but the humans who are not able to be without sin. For because also the Messenger Angel is interpreted, whoever either bishop or presbyter or even a layperson frequently speaks about God, and he announces how he arrives at eternal life, is rightly called an angel of God. And nevertheless because no one is able to be without sin, it is said to him, that is to a human, that he should do penitence: because he who considers revered things well, knows that not only lay, but also priests ought not to be for one day without penitence. Because in the way in which there is no day in which a human is able to be without sin, thus no day ought to be without remedy of satisfaction. Moreover the seven candelabra, and the one candelabrum, we are able to understand to be the sevenfold Church: and therefore the ones he seems to say are for the seven Churches, he says are for one Church scattered in the whole world; because in the number of seven all plenitude consists. Therefore he says the angels are the Church: in whom he shows there are two parts, which is of good and of evil. And especially he not only praises, but also rebukes, in order that praise is directed to the good, rebuke to the evil: just as the Lord in the Gospel, said that every body of the priors was one servant blessed and worthless, which the Lord when he comes himself will divide. How is it able to happen that one servant is divided, when it is not possible to live while divided? But he says one servant is the whole Christian people: which people if all are good, would not be divided. But because not only does it have good, but it also has bad, it must be divided: and the good will hear, "Come, blessed of my Father, take the kingdom"; in truth the plunderers and adulterers, who have not made compassion, will hear, "Depart from me, ones spoken ill of, into the eternal fire." What moreover is said in the Apocalypse individual Churches, dearest brothers, applies to individual humans organized in the one Church. "The one who holds seven stars in his hand says these things": this is the one who holds you in his hand, which is in power, and governs. "The one who walks in the middle of the golden candelabra": that is, [2421] in the middle of you; because those candelabra signify the Christian people. That moreover he says, "I will move your candelabrum from its place, if you have not done penitence": see that he did not say, he removes, but he moves; because the candelabrum signifies the one Christian people. And he says that the candelabrum itself is moved, not removed: and through this it is understood that in the one and same Church the evil are moved, the good are confirmed; and that by a secret, but nevertheless just judgment of God, that which is removed for the evil, is increased for the good; as that which was written is fulfilled, "To the one who has, will it be given; moreover to him who does not have, even what he seems seen to have, will be removed from him" Matthew 25:14-41. That moreover he says, I will give to the one conquering to eat from the tree of life"; that is, from the fruit of the cross. "And this is," he says, "in the paradise of my God": he says paradise is the Church; for all things have been made in its form. For what he says, "I know your works, and tribulation, and poverty; but you are rich"; he says to all the Church, which is poor in spirit, and possesses all things. What moreover he says, "You will have ten days of oppressions"; ten days, the whole time he placed, because the number of ten is perfect: in which the Christian people, just as the Apostle says, through many tribulations enter into the kingdom of heavens Acts 14:21. For he says that to the angel of the Church of Pergamum, "I know where you live, where the entrance of Satan is" Apocalypse 2:13: he speaks to all the Church in the word of one, because Satan lives everywhere through his own body. The body moreover of Satan is humans who are haughty and evil; just as also the body of Christ is the humble and good people. "I will give to the conquering to eat from the hidden manna": that is, from the bread which descends from the heaven. The figure of this was manna in the wilderness because, just as the Lord himself said, the many who ate it died John 6:41. But also now whoever eats it unworthily eats judgment for himself I Corinthians 11:29. The same bread is also the tree of life. We are also able to receive immortality through manna. "And I will give to him an honest calculation": that is, a body sparkling by Baptism. "And over the calculation a new name was written": that is, knowledge of the Son of human. "And no one knows this, unless he receives it": namely through revelation; and therefore it is said concerning the Jews, "If indeed they had known, they would never have crucified the Lord of glory" I Corinthians 2:8. That moreover he says to the angel of the Church of Thyatira, "I have against you, that you have conceded to the woman Jezebel"; he speaks to the priors of the Churches, who are extravagant and fornicating, and doing any other kind of evil, do not impose the strictness of the teaching of the Church. This is possible to be understood also concerning the heretics, "She says that she is a prophet": that is, a Christian. Indeed now many heresies delude themselves by this name. "Nor have you learned the depth of Satan": that is, you have not cast out his teaching, as if heresies. "I do not send the other weight above you": that is, above that which you are able to sustain. "Hold onto the true thing which you have until I shall come. He who conquers, and he who preserves my works up until the end, I will give to him the nations; and he will feed them in the firm rod, and crush them just like a potter's vase, just as I also have received from my Father." In Christ the Church has this power; just as the Apostle says, "With that one he has given all things to us" Romans 8:32. He says firm rod on account of the rigor of justice: and from the rod itself the good are corrected, the evil are broken.

Homily III.

[Apocalypse 3 and 4.] Now, dearest brothers, I have heard the blessed John, rebuking a sinner human terribly: and therefore I trusted with great fear, and I am fearful with a tremor what was said, "I recognized your works, because you have a name which you live, and you have died." He does not die, unless he has committed a moral crime, according to that which was said, "The soul which has sinned, itself will die" Ezekiel 18:20. What is worse, many are known to carry dead souls in live bodies. "Be vigilant, and strengthen the rest of the things which were going to die. The one who says these things is a holy and true one who has the keys of David": that is, kingly power. "And he opens, and no one shuts"; he shuts, and no one opens": it is clear that Christ would open to those knocking, and to hypocrites, that is the pretend he would shut the door of life. "Behold I have given a gate opened before you": this [2422] therefore was said, so that no one would say, because the gate which God opens for the Church in the whole world, someone would be able perhaps to shut it partly. "Because you have a little virtue": this is praise of God because the gate of the Church would open for a little faith. "And I will write the name of my God above that": we are signified as Christians everywhere. "And the name of the new citystate of my God is Jerusalem, which descends from the heaven": the new celestial Jerusalem, he says is the church, which is born from the Lord. Moreover he said new, on account of the newness of the Christian name, and because they are made new from old ones. "You are neither cold nor boiling hot": that is, you are unuseful. Indeed a persona of unfruitful rich people is able to be received even beyond those who have resources, and they do not thence make compassions. They are not poor, who have resources: they are not rich, who do not work hard from riches. "I am giving to you a plan, in order that you may buy gold for yourself": that is, so that by making charity donations, and by persisting in good acts, you yourself may become gold; that is, you may receive understanding from God, and through good familiarity you may be worthy of suffering martyrdom. "And behold," he says, "the gate is open in the sky." The open gate he says is Christ, because it is a door. He says the heaven is the Church where heavenly things are carried out; just as the Apostle says, "To renew all things which are in the heavens and which are on the earth" Ephesians 1:10: the sky is understood as the first Church from the Jews, the land in truth from the Gentiles. "Ascend to this place, and I will show to you": this is not fitting only for John, but for the Church or all who believe. Indeed the one who has seen the gate open in the sky, has believed that is that Christ has been born, and suffered, and has risen again; he ascends into the height, and he sees future things. [By what steps unless of faith and belief? And if openly it was said to anyone of the chosen, In order to know the sacraments of Christ and of the Church climb with faith, reach with belief. Indeed rightly is John invited by the first voice, to climb to the gate of heaven and to heaven: because of course every one of the chosen, in order to reach with the unhurt foot of faith through the Gospel to the sacraments of true faith, the teachings of the old document, which precedes the new, is strengthened.] "And behold the throne has been placed in the sky": that is, in the Church. "And the one, who was sitting, was similar to the appearance of the stone jasper or carnelian": those comparisons are fitting for the Church. Jasper has the color of water, and carnelian that of fire: through these, just as it has already been said, he wants the two judgments to be understood; one through water, which has already been made through the flood; the other which will be through fire. [Why through jasper unless the divinity of our Mediator is represented?] "In the circuit of the throne I have seen twenty-four seats, and above the seats twenty-four elders sitting." He says the elders are the whole Church, just as Isaiah says, "Since he was glorified in the middle of his own elders" Isaiah 24:23. The twenty-four elders moreover, are the priors and the peoples. In the twelve, understand the Apostles and priors; and in the other twelve, understand the rest of the Church. "And lightning and voices proceeded from the seat:" indeed heretics proceed from the Church, because they have exited from us. There is also another meaning, that the lightning and voices are understood as the preaching of the Church. In the voices the words are understood, in the lightning the miracles. "In the sight of the throne a glass sea": the glass sea, the font of Baptism; he said before the throne, that is before the judgment. But also understand sometimes the holy soul as the throne: just as it was written, "The soul of the just is the seat of wisdom (Sap. 7); sometimes the Church in which God holds the seat. "And in the middle of the throne are four animals": that is, in the middle of the Church as Evangelist. Full of eyes in front and back": that is, inside and outside. The eyes are the precepts of God. "In front and back": that is, things looking in the past and future. In the first animal similar to a lion, the strength of the Church is revealed. In the calf, the passion of Christ. In the third animal, which is just as a human, the humility of the Church is signified: because nothing is coaxed by itself to understand the haughty, no matter how it holds the adoption of sons. [2423] The fourth animal, he said was the Church. "Similar to an eagle": that is, flying and free, and raised from the earth by two wings, as if elevated by the rudders of the two Testaments, or of the two precepts. For also John the evangelist when he had looked carefully concerning those animals saw that a fourfold mystery was fulfilled in Christ, and when he had seen a human being born, a calf suffering, a lion ruling, then he also saw an eagle returning to the heavenly things. "And they were holding each one of them their individual wings six each through the circuit." In the animals are shown twenty-four elders: for the six each wings in the four animals, are twenty-four wings. For indeed he saw the animals through the circuit of the throne, where he had said that he had seen the elders. For how is an animal with six wings able to be like an eagle, which has two wings, if not because they are four animals as one, which have twenty-four wings, in which we understand twenty-four elders, who are in the Church which resembled the eagle? And otherwise the six each wings are testimonies of the Old Testament. Indeed just as an animal is not able to fly, unless it has feathers; thus neither does the preaching of the New Testament have faith, unless it has the previously announced testimonies of the Old Testament, through which it is raised from the earth, and flies. Indeed always what was said before is the future, and after the deed is discovered, it makes faith undoubtable. Indeed unless what the prophets had preached, had been accomplished in Christ, the preaching of those would be futile. The Catholic Church holds this, both the earlier preachings, and the later things that were fulfilled. It flies deservedly, and is brought from the earth as one animal into the sky. "And those animals did not have rest": It is the church, which does not have rest, but always praises God. We are also able to understand that the twenty-four seniors are the books of the Old Testament, both the Patriarchs and Apostles: the lightning and thundering, which are said to go out of the throne, the preachings and promises of the New Testament. "Sending his own crowns before the throne": this therefore, because whatever dignity the holy have, they attribute the whole to God; just as also those in the Gospel were spreading palms and flowers under his feet Matthew 21:8, that is, they attributing everything which they had conquered to the very one. "Because you have created everything, and it was from your will, and was created"; was according to God, by whom everything was possessed because it came about; it was created moreover, in order to be seen also by us, just as Moses says to the Church, "Isn't this one himself your Father, who made you, and possessed you, and created you Deuteronomy 32:6? He possessed in foreknowledge, he made in Adam, he created from Adam.

Homily IV.

[Apocalypse 5.] "And I saw above the right hand of the one sitting on the throne a book written inside and outside": understand each Testament, the Old from outside, the New from within which it was hidden within the Old. "Marked," he says, "with seven seals": that is, obscured with the fullness of all mysteries, that which up until the suffering and resurrection of Christ remained sealed. For in the way a will is not pronounced, unless what those who will die do, and is sealed up until the death of the testator, and after the death of himself is opened: thus also after the death of Christ all mysteries are revealed. "And I saw the brave angel shouting with a great voice: Who is worthy to open the book, and to release its signs?" Why the signs are released first, and then the book is opened, is a certain reason, because Christ opened the book at the time, when having approached the work of his father's will, he was conceived and born; then he released his father's signs, when he was killed for the sake of the human race. "And no one was able neither in the sky, nor on earth, nor under the earth": that is, neither an angel, nor one living on the lands, nor a dead one. "To open the book, nor to see that one": that is, to contemplate the splendor of the grace of the New Testament. "And I wept much, because no one was found worthy to open the book and to see it": The church wept, whose shape John had, burdened and weighed down by sins, imploring the redemption of its own. "And behold one of the elders": one of the elders understand to be the entire body of the Prophets. The prophets [2424] indeed consoled the Church, announcing Christ from the tribe of Judaea as the root of David. Because he himself in us conquers every sin in us, and if anyone has anything good, he has it from that very one. "And I saw, and behold in the middle of the throne both four animals, and in middle of the elders a lamb standing as if killed": the thrones, animals, elders, and lamb as if killed. The church is with its own head, which dies for Christ, in order to live with Christ. The martyrs also are able to be received in the Church to be received as if a killed lamb. "Having," he says, "seven horns and seven eyes, which are the spirit of God, who was sent into all the earth": that no one is able to have the Spirit of God except the Church, is known clearly from this. "And he came, and he received from the right hand of the one sitting on the throne a book": we received the one sitting on the throne, both the Father and Son and Holy Spirit. Therefore the Lamb has received from the right hand of God. That is he has received from the Son the work of the book which is about to be finished, with that one himself saying, "Just as the Father sent me, I also send you" John 20:21: because he himself finishes in those what he gives. "Having individual lyres": that is, strings of praises. "And golden saucers": these are the vases in the home of the Lord, in which because it was customary that incenses be offered, therefore we understand the orations of the saints well in them. "And they were singing a new song": that is the New Testament; singing a new song, that is professing their own declaration publicly. And truly it is new, that the Son of God becomes human, and dies, and rises again, and ascends into heaven, to give remission of sins to humans. Indeed the lyre, that is, the string extended in the wood, signifies the flesh of Christ joined to the suffering: the saucers moreover the confession, and the progeny of the new priesthood. The resignation of the seals is the disclosing of the Old Testament. "I both saw and heard the voice of many angels": he says the angels are humans, who are also said to be sons of God. "The Lamb who was killed is worthy, to receive the power and riches and wisdom," etc. He does not speak concerning God, in whom there are all the treasuries of wisdom Colossians 2:3, in order that he himself may receive: but concerning the human who was received, and his body, which is the Church, or concerning his martyrs, who were killed on behalf of his name; because on his own head the Church receives the whole, just as it was written, "He gave everything to us with that one" Romans 8:32. Indeed the Lamb himself receives, who says in the Gospel, "There was given to me all the power in heaven and on earth" Matthew 28:18. To the advantage of humanity moreover, not to the advantage of divinity he received. "All," he says, "I heard speaking to the one sitting on the throne," that is, to the Father and the Son: "and to the Lamb," that is, the Church with its own head. "Benediction and honor and clarity forever": for whom there is honor and glory and rule forever. Amen.

Homily V.

[Apocalypse 6] Just as just now, while the divine reading was being read, you have heard, thus saint John says, "And behold there is a white horse, and the one sitting on him, was holding a bow; and there was given to him a crown, and he went out conquering": the white horse is the Church, the rider is Christ. That horse of the Lord with the warlike bow was promised before through Zechariah in this way, "The Lord God will visit his flock, the home of Israel, and he will arrange them just as if a splendid horse in war: and from him he will inspect, and from him he will arrange, and from him a bow in anger, and from him every one will go following" Zechariah 10:3-4. We understand the white horse therefore as the Prophets and Apostles. The crowned horseman holding a bow, we recognize not only as Christ, but also as the Holy Spirit. Afterwards indeed the Lord ascended into heaven, and he revealed the universal mysteries; he sent the Holy Spirit: whose words through eulogists as if arrows would reach to the heart of humans, and they would conquer incredulity. Moreover the crown above the head must be understood as predictions through the Holy Spirit. "And when he had opened the second seal, I heard the second animal, saying": "Come and see. And there went out a red horse": and it was given to the one sitting on him to carry peace from the land, and in order that they kill in turn, there was also given to him a great sword." Against the victorious and conquering Church there went out the red horse, that is the sinister and evil people, blood-stained from its rider the devil: although we read according to Zechariah the red horse of the Lord: but that one was stained by his own blood, the latter by another's. "There was given to him [2425] a great sword, to carry peace from the earth"; namely his own peace, this is of the world: for the Church has eternal peace, which Christ left for it. Therefore just as it was said above, he calls the white horse the Church; its rider, Christ or the Holy Spirit. The bow which he had in his hand, are his precepts: which through the whole world just as sharp arrows were directed to kill sins of a powerful one, and to stir up the hearts of the faithful. The crown on his head is the promise of eternal life. The red horse, the evil people; its rider, the devil: which he therefore said was red, because it was reddish by the blood of many. That moreover there was given to him a sharp sword, and to bring peace form the land, this is, that with the devil persuading, evil men do not cease to stir up when among themselves perpetually contests and discords up until death. And on a black horse, there is understood a sinister people, agreeing with the devil. That moreover, "he was holding

a scales in his hand," this therefore, because the evil depict themselves to hold the scales of justice, thus they deceive very many.
That he said, "Do not harm the wine and the oil"; in the wine there
is understood the blood of Christ, in the oil the ointment of anointing. In wheat or barley, the whole Church whether in great ones
or in very small ones, or certainly in priors and in the peoples: and
on a pale horse, are understood evil humans, who do not stop stirring up persecutions. Those three horses are together, those who
went out after the white one and against the white one: and they
have the devil as a rider, who is death. Therefore the three horses
are understood as hunger and wars and pestilence: that also the
Lord predicted in his Gospel, the things which both happen now,
and will happen further on the imminent Day of Judgment. That
he said moreover that he had seen under the altar of God the souls
of the killed, they are understood as martyrs. That moreover he
says, "A great earthquake," is the very recent persecution. That he
says the ground was made black, and the moon bloody, and that
stars had fallen from the sky; the sun and moon and stars, are the
Church diffused in the whole world. That moreover he says that
they had fallen; not all fell, but it is understood all from a part.
Indeed in every persecution the good persevere, and the evil as
if from the heaven, that is from the Church fall. Finally it follows,
"Just as a fig tree loses its young fruit when it is shaken by the
wind": thus the evil fall from the Church, when they have been
shaken up through some tribulation. Moreover that the heaven
withdrew as a book; the Church is what is separated by the evil
and just as an unrolled book, it contains in itself divine mysteries
known to itself. That moreover he says, "The kings of the earth
fled, and they hid themselves in the caves of the earth"; this signifies that the whole world will have refuge in the good and holy
ones towards the Church, so that one who has been established
under its protection, is able to arrive at eternal life, with our Lord
Jesus Christ helping, who lives and rules forever. Amen.

Homily VI.

[Apocalypse 6-8] "And I saw another angel ascending from the
rise of the sun. Another angel" he understands to be the Catholic
Church: "from the rise of the sun," from the suffering and resurrection of the Lord one shouting to four angels of the earth. "And
he shouted with a great voice saying to the four angels, to whom

there was given the power to harm the earth and sea: Do not harm the earth, nor the sea." Moreover he receives the sword generally, whether against those whom he kills in life, or those whom he persuades to struggle among themselves for temporal things up until death. Concerning the third seal he says that a black horse had gone out, and the one who was sitting on it had in his hand a scales: "A scales," he says, he had in his hand," that is, a proof of equality; because while he depicts that he holds justice, he harms through the simulation. Moreover while in the middle of the animals, that is in the middle of the Church it is said, "Do not harm"; it is shown that the spiritual evils do not have power against the servants of God, unless they have received from God. "Do not harm the wine and oil": in the wine and oil, unction of anointing and the blood of the Lord; in the wheat moreover and barley he spoke of the Church, whether among great or among few Christians, or among priors and peoples. Concerning the fourth seal, "A pale horse. And the name of the one who [2426] was sitting on it was the Death, and the underworld was following him: and there was given to him the power over the fourth part of the land, to kill with a sword, hunger, and death, and beasts of the land." Those three horses are together, the ones who went out after the white one and against the white one: and they have one rider the devil, who is death. For it is clear in the sixth seal, that the horseman is the devil and his comrades; he says that the horses fight against the final battle. Therefore the three horses are understood as hunger and wars and destructions, just as they are preached by the Lord in the Gospel. The white horse is the word of prophecy in the world. In the red horse and his rider were signified the wars which will be, by no means become, when now nation rises against nation. Through the pale horse and his rider, a great pestilence and mortality is expressed. "And the underworld follows that one": that is, he waits for the devouring of many. "And when the fifth seal had opened, I saw under the altar of God the souls of the ones killed." He says the altar of God is the Church, under whose eyes martyrs have resulted. And although the souls of the holy are in paradise, nevertheless because the blood of the holy ones is poured over the earth, they are said to shout under the altar: just as that thing is, "The blood of your brother shouts to me from the earth" Genesis 4:10. "And when the sixth seal had opened, a great earthquake happened": that is, a very recent persecution. "And the sun was made black just like a haircloth sack, and the moon became total just as blood, and the stars fell into the earth." Which is the sun and moon, and the stars, that is the Church: but a part is understood from the whole. Indeed not the whole Church, but the ones who are evil in the Church, they themselves fall from heaven. Moreover he said the whole, because in the whole world there will be a very recent persecution. And at that time those who were just, will remain in the Church as if in the sky: in truth the desirous, unjust and adulterous consider to agree to sacrifice to the devil. And at that time those who were saying that they were Christians only with words, as if stars will fall from the sky, which is the Church. "Even as a fig tree when shaken by a great wind loses its young fruit." He compared a shaken tree, to the Church; a great wind, to persecution; young figs, to evil men, who must be shaken off and withdrawn from the Church. "And the heaven withdrew as an unrolled book." And in this place he says the heaven is the Church, which withdrew from the evil, and within itself contains the mysteries known to only itself, just like an unrolled book, which the wicked neither wish to understand entirely, nor are they able. "And every mountain and islands were moved from their places." What is the heaven, this the mountains, this the islands signify; that is the Church when the very recent persecution was made had all withdrawn from its place, whether among the good by fleeing persecution, or among the evil by yielding to faith. But it is able to be appropriate for each part; because even the good part is moved from its own place, fleeing, that is, losing that which it has: just as that statement, "I will move your candelabrum from its own place" Apocalypse 2:5. "And the kings of the earth and the magistrates: the kings, powerful men we understand. Indeed from every rank and condition they are converted to Christ. For the rest those who at that time will be kings, besides the one persecutor, "hid themselves in the caves and rocks of the mountains." They all flee in the present age to the faith of the Church, and in the hidden mystery of the Scriptures are protected. "And they say, Fall: that is, cover us. "And hide us": that is, in order that an old man may be hidden from the eyes of God. And otherwise: He who considers the future judgment, turns to the mountains, that is to the Church, so that his sins may be hidden through penitence in the present time, so that they are not punished in the future. "Until we mark servants of our God on their foreheads": he warns the Church; and he says to evil men, that are to the sinister part that harms, "Do not harm." This is the voice, which in the middle of four animals says to the one harming. "Do not harm the wine and oil": in the wine and oil, all who are just are understood, whom neither the devil nor evil humans will be able to harm, unless whenever God has permitted for their proof. "Do not harm the wine," he says, "and oil": the Lord commands all his spiritual land not to be harmed, until they all are indicated. "And I heard the number of witnesses, one hundred forty-four thousand witnesses from every tribe of the sons of Israel." One hundred forty-four thousand, is entirely all the Church. "Afterwards I saw, and behold there was a bountiful people, whom no one was able to number, from all [2427] the nations and peoples and tongues": he did not say, After these things I saw another people; but, I saw the people, that is the same one hundred forty-four thousand which he had seen in the mystery, this he sees innumerable from every tribe and tongue and nation, because all the nations were introduced to the base by believing. The Lord in the Gospel shows the Church both from Jews and from the Gentiles, in twelve tribes of Israel, saying: "You will sit over twelve thrones, judging twelve tribes of Israel Matthew 19:28. "Wrapped in white stoles": white stoles, he understand as a gift of the Holy Spirit. "And all the angels were standing away from the circuit of the throne": the angels, he says are the Church; because he was describing nothing else except itself. "And one of the elders responds to me saying: Those who are wrapped in white stoles, who are they?" One of the elders who responds, reveals the office of the priesthood; because they teach the Church, that is the people in the Church, what is the reward of the labor of the holy: saying, "These are the ones who came from great tribulation and washed their stoles in the blood of the lamb." Indeed they are not, as some think, martyrs only, but all the population in the Church: because he said that they washed their own stoles not in their own blood, but in the blood of the lamb, that is in grace of God through Jesus Christ our Lord, just as it was written, "And the blood of his Son cleansed us" I John 1:7. "And the one who sits on the throne, dwells over them: for they themselves are the throne, over whom God dwells forever, that is in the Church. "Neither will the sun fall over them, nor the heat": just as Isaiah says about the Church, "It will be in the shade away from the heat" Isaiah 25:4. "And he will lead to the fountains of waters of life": all these things also come about in the present life of the Church spiritually; since we rise again when sins are dismissed, and when we have been despoiled of the sorrows of the prior life and of the old human, we are dressed in Baptism in Christ, and we are filled with the joy of the holy. "And when he had opened the seventh seal had opened, there was silence in the sky": that is, in the Church. "As if it were the middle hour": in the half hour, he shows the beginning of eternal quiet. "And I saw seven angles, who stand in the sight of God." Seven angels, he said are the Church. "The ones who have received seven trumpets," that is a completed prophecy: just as it was written. "Exalt, just as if a trumpet, your voice" Isaiah 58:1. "And another angel came, and stood before the altar": the other angel, whom he speaks of, does not come after those seven, because he himself is the Lord Jesus Christ. "Having a golden censer": This is the holy body. Indeed the Lord himself became the censer, from which God received the odor of sweetness; and he became favorable for the world, because he brought himself into the odor of sweetness Ephesians 5:2. "And the angel received the censer, and filled it from the fire of the altar": Jesus received the body, that is the Church, and in order to complete the will of the Father, filled it with the fire of the Holy Spirit. "And there were voices and thunderings and lightning and earthquake": all these things are spiritual prophecies and strengths of the Church. "And seven angels, who held seven trumpets, prepared themselves to sing with the trumpet": that is, the Church prepared itself to preach. "And the first angel sang with the trumpet, and there was made hail and fire mixed with blood": there developed the anger of God, which had in itself the death of many. "And it was sent into the land, and a third part of the land burned, and a third part of trees, and all the green grass burned": what is the land, and this the trees, and this grass, that is humans. Moreover the green grass, understand as bloody and extravagant flesh, according to that statement, "All flesh is grass" Isaiah 40:6. "And the second angel sang with the trumpet, and just like a great mountain burning with fire was sent into the sea, and a third part of the sea became blood": the burning mountain, is the devil. And what is the third part of the earth or of trees, this is the third part of the sea. And the humans having souls, he said were the wicked; in order to show in the flesh the living, but spiritually dead. "And they broke to pieces a third part of the ships": the heretics corrupted with their doctrine those who acquiesced to them. "And the third angel sang with the trumpet, and there fell from the sky a great burning star like a small torch": from the Church he says that haughty and wicked humans had fallen. In truth he said a great star; because the personas of older ones and of those holding power [2428] or riches. "And the name of this star is called absinth, and a third part of the waters was made into absinth"; a third part of humans was made similar to the star which fell over it. "And many of the humans died from the waters, since the waters became bitter." Humans died from the waters. This is clearly able to be understood, in these who are rebaptized. "And the fourth angel sang on the trumpet, and a third part of the sun was struck down, and a third part of the moon and third part of the stars": the sun, moon and stars, is the Church, of which the third part was struck down; in the third part, are understood all the evils. Moreover it was struck down, that is dragged by its evils and pleasures: in order to that it was made known in its own time, when the sins are overflowing and increasing. "And I saw and heard a voice of one eagle flying in the middle of the sky, and saying, Woe! woe! woe to those living on the earth!" He understands the eagle to be the Church flying in the middle of the sky that is running to and fro in the middle of his, and predicting the plagues of a very recent time with a great voice. Indeed when the priest announces the Day of Judgment, the eagle flies in the middle of the sky. Just as therefore it was said above, another angel whom he said had ascended from the rise of the sun is the Church, ascending from the rise of the sun that is from the suffering or resurrection of the Lord. Moreover what he says. "Do not harm the earth, nor the sea"; the Church shouts this everyday to evil men by preaching. That it says, "Do not harm the wine and oil"; in the wine and oil, all who are just people in the Church are understood; and no one will be able to harm them, unless God has allowed for the testing of them. That moreover he says, a hundred forty-four thousand had been signified: all the Church is understood. Whence also in those concerning which he spoke that he had seen many people whom no one was able to number, the same Church was indicated. That moreover he said that they were wrapped in white stoles; in the stoles the gift of the Holy Spirit is understood: the angels standing around the throne, he said were the Church, because besides that nothing else was he describing. The elder who is responding and said, "Who are those, and whence have they come," indicates the office of priests, who teach the people in the Church. What he said moreover, "They washed their stoles," he said concerning the whole Church, not concerning martyrs only. Finally he does not say in his own blood, but "in the blood of the lamb," because it is fulfilled through the sacrament of Baptism in particular. "And the one, who sits over the throne, dwells over those": indeed they themselves are the throne, over whom God dwells. "Neither does the sun fall over them, nor any heat: and he will lead them to the fountains of the waters of life": all these things also in the present age, and in these days come spiritually to the Church; while thus through the grace of God it is defended, in order that it is exercised by the persecutions of this world more than it is conquered. That he says in the half hour silence was made in the sky; he says in the Church, and signifies the beginning of eternal quiet. And with the seven angels singing with trumpets: in the angels the Church, in the trumpets the preaching of the Church is understood. The other angel, whom he said had stood before the altar, is Christ the Lord. "Holding the golden censer": namely the holy body, through which God the Father has received the incense of suffering, the odor of sweetness. Moreover he says that, "There were voices, lightning and thundering"; they are spiritual predictions of the Church. The seven angels, who prepared themselves to sing, are the Church: in which through the whole world against all sins or crimes there develops spiritual preaching. Moreover that a third part of the land burned when the first angel was singing, signifies humans haughty and devoted to pleasures, whom God allows with a just judgment to be burned by the fire of luxury and desire. Moreover that, when the second angel sings, a burning mountain fell into the sea; that mountain is understood to be the devil, the sea as that world. A third part of the sea, just as it was already said above, is the wicked and impious humans. Moreover that, when the third angel was singing, a great star fell from the sky, is understood as great men, who fall from the church as though from the sky by evil habits and wicked acts. That he says, "Many men have died from the waters, since the waters have become bitter"; this is able to be understood among those who are rebaptized. That moreover, when the fourth angel sings, a third part of the sun, and moon and stars was struck down; in these the Church is understood, in which everyday those who are evil or pretend, are struck down in the soul when the devil persuades by the wounds of sins [2429]. That moreover he speaks of the Eagle flying in the middle of the Sky, and shouting Woe! woe! woe! He wanted to be understood as the Church flying in the middle of the sky, that is, in his midst, and announcing through the constancy of preaching the plagues of the very recent time. Indeed when the priest in the Church of God announces the Day of Judgment, an eagle flies in the middle of the sky. Let divine piety grant, that while both the priests are eager to predict perpetually, and the people to fulfill faithfully those things which are predicted, at the same time they deserve to arrive at eternal things, with the Lord Jesus Christ being present, who lives, etc.

Homily VII.

[Apocalypse 9 and 10] Now, very dear brothers, when the Apocalypse was read, I heard that when the fifth angel was singing with a trumpet, a star fell from the sky above the earth. One star is the body of many falling through sins. "And there was given to him the key of the pit of the depths": the star, the abyss, the pit are the humans. Therefore a star fell from the sky: that is, the sinner is the people from the Church. "And he received the key of the pit of the depths": that is, the power of his own heart, in order to open his heart, in which the devil who was tied up should not be restrained to make his wish. "And he opened the pit of the abyss": that is, he revealed his own heart without any fear or shame of sinning. "And smoke ascended from the pit": that is it ascended from the people because it covers and obscures the Church, in such a way as it would be said. "And there was obscured the sun and the air from the smoke of the pit." He said the sun was obscured, not that it had fallen. Indeed the sins of evil and haughty humans, which are committed indiscriminately throughout the world, obscure the sun, that is the Church, and make obscurity meanwhile for the holy and just people: because such is the number of evil ones, that several times the good scarcely appear among them. "Just like," he says," the smoke of a great furnace. And from the smoke of the pit there went out locusts into the earth, and power was given to them, just as the scorpions of the earth have power": that is, to harm with poison. "And it was commanded to them, not to harm the grass of the earth nor every tree, if not humans. And it was given to them not to kill them." And that there are two parts in the church, namely of good and of bad; one part thus is struck down in order to be corrected; the other is left to its own pleasures. The part of the good is dragged to humiliation for the awareness of the justice of God, and the memory of penitence, just as it was written, "It was good for me that you humiliated me, so that I would learn your justifications Psalms 18:17 "It was given to them not to kill, but to torment: and the torment of them was the torment of a scorpion, when it strikes a human": this then would happen, when the devil passes poisons through vices or sins. "And humans will seek death": in truth he called death a relief. Therefore they will seek death, but for the evil things, that is tribulations, in order that they themselves rest, while the evils die. "Over the heads of these," he says, "as if they are crowns similar to gold." The church was represented earlier in twenty-four elders, who have golden crowns; moreover those similar to gold, are the heresies, which imitate the Church. "And they had hairs, as if the hairs of women": in the hairs of women not only the effeminate gender, but also each gender he wanted to show. "And they had tails similar to scorpions, and stings in their tails": he says the tails of the heretics were the ecclesiastic superiors, just as it was written. "The prophet teaching the lie, this is the tail" Isaiah 9:15; and those who are pseudoprophets, these fulfill the cruel orders of kings. "Having over themselves a king as an angel of the abyss": that is, the devil or king of the age. The abyss is the people. "For whom the hebrew name is Abaddon, in Greek or Latin Perdens (Destroying One). Woe the one went away, and behold two alas come, after these things." And the sixth angel sang with a trumpet": from here there begins a very new prediction. "And I heard one angel of the four horns of the golden altar, which is in the sight of God, saying to the sixth angel, who was holding a trumpet: Release the four angels, who were bound up in the great river Euphrates" The altar which [2430] is in the sight of God, he wants to be understood as the Church, which in the time of very recent persecution would dare to condemn the words or orders of the very cruel king, and to depart from those who were obeying. "Release the four angels in the river Euphrates." The Euphrates River he said was the sinner people, in which Satan and his own wish was bound. The Euphrates moreover is the river of Babylon, just as Jeremias in the middle of Babylon drops a book into the Euphrates, Jeremiah 51:63. "And the four angels were released," that is the persecution was begun. "Prepared for the hour and day and month and year, to kill the third part of humans": these are the four times of the space of three years, and a part of time. "And the number," he says, "of the armies twice myriads of myriads, I heard their number": but he did not say, how many myriads. "In order to kill a third part of humans": this is the third part of the haughty, from which the Church descended. "And I saw horses in the vision, and those who were sitting over them, were holding fiery reins, both the color of hyachinth and sulfurous." He says the horses are humans, the riders in truth worthless spirits, armed with fire, smoke and sulfur. "And the heads of horses were as if of lions": for savaging in persecution. "From their mouth there went out smoke, fire and sulfur": that is, blasphemies egress from their mouth against God. "Their tails are like serpents." We called their tails priors, their heads the leaders of the world. And in these the devil is harmful, and without these he is not able to harm: indeed either the sacrilegious kings by ordering badly, or the sacrilegious priests harm by teaching badly do harm. "And I saw," he says, "another brave angel descending from the sky, wrapped in a cloud, and a rainbow," that is a bow, "on its head, and his appearance was as the sun": wrapped in a cloud, is understood as the Lord wrapped in the Church. We read indeed the holy, the clouds; just as Isaiah says, "Who are these, who fly as clouds" Isaiah 60:8? Therefore dressed by a spiritual cloud, that is, understand Christ with a holy body. "And the rainbow over his head": that is, either a judgment which becomes and which will be, or a promise thoroughly protecting. Indeed he describes the church in the Lord, saying, "And his appearance just as the sun"; that is, concerning the resurrection. Just as the sun indeed appeared when he rose again from the dead. "And his feet as if columns of fire." He says the feet are apostles, through whom his teaching disperses in the universal world: or certainly, because the foot is the most recent part of the body, he says the Church after the fire of the most recent persecution is the future clarity of saints. "And he placed his own right foot over the sea, but the left over the earth": that is, to announce across the sea, and in the universal world. "And he shouted with a great voice, in the way a lion roars": that is, he announced strongly. "And when he had shouted, seven thunders spoke as his own voices," which are also seven trumpets. "And I heard a voice saying from the sky," the signs which the seven thunders have spoken, do not record them": on account of those to be made weary, in order that the words of God are not visible everywhere to all the impious. Finally in another place on account of his servants: "You should not have indicated," he says, "the words of this prophecy." And he shows by whom he had ordered to be indicated, and to which not: "He who has persisted," he says, "to harm, should not harm; and he who is among defilements, let him become dirty still" Apocalypse 22:10-11. This is, On that account I speak in those parables, in order that he who is just, may do more just things, and similarly a holy one more holy things: this is, Your happy eyes, since they see, and ears, since they hear: indeed to those the words of the book have not been indicated, yet to the evil they have been indicated. "And that angel swore, since the time will be no longer: but in the days of the seventh angel, when he began to sing with a trumpet": the seventh trumpet is the end of persecution and the arrival of the Lord. On that account the Apostle said there would resurrection in the most recent trumpet I Corinthians 15:52. Which moreover just as it was said above, when the fifth angel was singing with a trumpet he said a star again had fallen from the sky; and also this star is the body of many stars from the sky, that is falling from the Church and it indicates the haughty and impious people. Moreover that "there was given to him a key of the abyss"; he was allowed in the power of his own heart, to open his own heart to the devil, and apart from any reverence to practice every evil. Moreover that the smoke ascends from the pit: that is, from the evil people: and [2431] it obscured the sun and moon; he said the sun was obscured, not that it had fallen. This therefore, because the sins of bad and haughty humans seem to obscure the sun, while they make obscurity for the holy and just ones meanwhile through many tribulations. But they do not agree with those to consent to evil. That moreover he says, "That from the smoke of the pit locusts had gone out, and had received the power of harming: and it was given to them not to kill them"; this therefore, because two parts are in the Church, namely of good and of evil ones. One part thus is struck down in order to be corrected; another is left to their own pleasures. Moreover what he said, "The torture of the women as if the torture of a scorpion, when he strikes down a human": this then would happen, when the devil offers poisons to extravagant humans through vices and sins, in the mode of a scorpion. "And above the heads of the women as if crowns similar to gold." Twenty-four elders, in whom the Church was represented, had golden crowns: those moreover similar to gold, heresies namely which imitate the Church. Moreover that they had the hairs of women; in the hairs not only the effeminate gender, but also either gender he wanted to show. In the tails of those, which were as if scorpions, generals or leaders of heretics are understood: just as it was written, "The prophet teaching a lie this is a tail. They had above themselves a king of the abyss": that is, the devil. In the abyss the evil people are understood, whom the devil dominates. The altar which he said was in the sight of God, he wants to be understood as the Church, which just like cleansed gold, in the time of the most recent persecution would dare to despise the orders of a very cruel king, and to depart from those submitting. Moreover that he says that four angels were bound in the Euphrates River; the Euphrates River signifies the sinner people, in whom Satan and his own wish were bound. Moreover the Euphrates is a stream of Babylon, which is interpreted as the Confusion. Whence they pertain to the river itself, whosoever practices things worthy of confusion. Moreover that he says that he had seen the horses, and those who were riding on them, had fiery reigns both of hyacinth-color and sulfurous; the horses he says are the haughty humans, and the rider of them is the devil and his angels. Moreover that he says the heads of horses as of lions was said on account of the violent persecution of evil humans. "And from their mouth there went out fire, smoke and sulfur": that is, blasphemies go forth from their mouth against God. In the tails, which were similar to serpents, just as it was already said above, are princes and the priors of heretics, through whom the devil was accustomed to harm. Indeed either sacrilegious kings by ordering poorly or sacrilegious priests by teaching poorly do harm. The angel, whom he said was wrapped in a cloud, is out Lord and Savior, wrapped in a cloud, which is the Church: because it was written concerning the holy, "Who are those, who fly as clouds?" Moreover that he said, "His appearance as the sun," he said on account of the resurrection of the Lord; just as the sun indeed appeared, when it resurrected from the dead. In his feet, which were just as the columns of fire, the Apostles were depicted, through whom his teaching dispersed in the universal world. Moreover that, "he placed his own right foot over the sea," this signified, that his announcement would go all the way to across the sea, and into the universal world. Moreover that, "just like a lion roaring he shouted," this therefore because he announced strongly from the power. That moreover he said, "The signs which were spoken seven thunderings," was said on account of the ones who would be wearied, concerning whom in the Gospel, "Do not give the holy thing to the dogs" Matthew 7:6: that is, that not for all the wicked everywhere should the word of God be open. Finally in another place on account of his servants he said: "You should not have expressed," he says, "the words of this prophet." And he shows to whom he ordered to be expressed, and to whom not: "He who has persisted," he says, "to harm, should not harm: and he who is in defilements, should still become dirty." Behold for whom the word of God was signified. On account of this I speak in parables to those, so that he who is just, may do more just things, and similarly the holy more holy things. Behold for whom it was not signified. Let me beseech this matter so that the Lord grants also to fulfill among us [2432] on behalf of his piety, who lives with the Father and the holy Spirit and rules. Amen.

Homily VIII.

[Apocalypse 10 and 11] The voice "from the sky," is the empire of God, who touches the heart of the Church, and orders to receive it, because the Church predicted future peace with an open book. "And I went away to the angel, so that he might give the book to me": the Church says this from the persona of John, desiring to be taught thoroughly. "And then he said to me, Receive and consume that one": that is, make known your innermost parts, and describe in the extent of the heart. "And he will make your stomach grow bitter, but in your mouth it will be sweet as honey": that is when you have understood, you will be delighted with the sweetness of divine eloquence, but you will feel bitterness when you have begun to preach and work because you will have understood; just as it was written, "On account of the words of your lips I guarded the harsh paths" Psalms 16:4. And otherwise, "It will be," he says, "sweet as honey in your mouth, and bitterness in your stomach." In the mouth are understood the good and spiritual Christians, in the stomach the carnal and extravagant ones. Thence it is that when the word of God is preached, is sweet to the spiritual ones: to the carnal in truth, whose stomach is God according to the Apostle Philippians 3:19, it seems bitter and harsh. "And there was given to me a staff similar to a rod, saying: Rise and measure the temple of God and the altar, even as you are worshiping in it. Rise," is the appeal of the Church. Indeed this John who was sitting was not hearing. "Measure the temple, and the altar, even as you are worship in it": He orders the church to be counted, and to be prepared for the end, even as they are worshiping in it. But because not all who are seen worship, therefore he said, "The hall which is outside the temple, throw outdoors, and do not measure that." The hall is those very ones who seem to be in the Church, and are outdoors, whether the heretics, or Catholics living badly. "Since it was given to the nations, they also will trample the holy city-state in forty-two months." Those who will be excluded, and to whom it will be given, both will trample it. "And I will give to my two witnesses": that is, to the two Testaments. "And they will prophesy for one thousand two hundred sixty days": he said the number of the most recent persecution, and of the future peace, and of the whole time from the suffering of the Lord; since each time holds the same number of days, which will be said in its own place. "With sackcloths," that is by hair shirts, "clothed." Which in "Greek", that is, they should have been appointed in confession; because he said from the sense of humility they were clothed in sackcloths. Next he shows who are these two witnesses, saying,

"These are two olive trees and two candelabra, standing in the sight of the land of the Lord": these are the ones who stand, and not the ones who will stand. The two candelabra are the Church, but for the number of the Testaments he said two. Just as he said four angels were the Church, although there are seven lands for the number of angels: thus from the seven candelabra, if he names one or more for the places, the whole is the Church. For Zecharias saw one sevenfold candelabrum, and these two olive trees Zechariah 4:2-3, that is, the Testaments poured oil on the candelabrum, that is the Church. Just as there are in the same place seven eyes, thanks to the sevenfold Holy Spirit, which are in the Church, looking closely at the whole earth. "And if any wishes to harm them or kill them, fire will go out from their mouth, and it will devour their enemies": that is, if any either harms or has wished to kill the Church, he will be consumed by the prayers of its mouth with divine fire either for correction in the present, or for damnation in the future century. "These have the power to shut up the heaven with clouds, so that it may not rain in the days of the prophecy of the very ones. They have," he says; not, they will have; he says this therefore, because he indicated the time which is being done now. But also the heaven is shut up spiritually, so that it doesn't rain, that is so that he descends not with a hidden, but nevertheless with a just judgment of God as a benediction from the Church over the sterile earth. "And when they have ended their testimony, the beast which ascends from the abyss, will make battle with them." He shows all these things openly happened before the very recent persecution, when he says, "When they finished their own testimony": at least that which they offer up until the revelation of Christ. "And he will conquer those, and he will kill them: he will conquer," [2433] in relation to those who have succumbed; "he will kill," in relation to those who have acknowledged God. "And their body will be hurled forth in the streets of the great city-state": he says one body of two, sometimes bodies, in order both to preserve the number of Testaments, and to show the one body of the Church. "In the streets of the great city-state": that is, in the middle of the Church. "And they see because of the peoples and the tribes and the tongues the body of them, through three and a half days": that is, three years and six months. Indeed he mixes up the time, now present, now future: just as also God says, "The hour will come, in which all who have killed you, will be judged to offer themselves as compliance to God John 16:2. And he is now, and he will come. "And they do not allow their bodies to be placed in a grave." He said their wish for attack: not why they would prevail to act so that the Church is not in memory, just as also that, "You neither enter, nor allow others to enter Matthew 23:13: since many entered even while those were attacking. Thus therefore they do not allow to be placed in a grave. "And inhabiting the earth they rejoice over those, and feast, and send gifts in turn." This was always done, and they now send in turn, and they will rejoice very recently and will feast; for as often as the just are afflicted, the unjust exult, and feast. "Since these two Prophets have tortured them": through the plagues, which afflict the human race for the contempt of the Testaments of God. Finally even the sight itself of the just burdens the unjust, just as they themselves say, "It is oppressive for us even to live" (Sap. II, 15). Moreover they will rejoice everywhere, just as they have had nothing already which they bear impatiently, when the just are disturbed and killed, and when their heredity is taken hold of. "And after three and a half days the spirit of life entered from God into them." It was already said about the days. From here the angel narrated up to the future, and brings in a deed which he hears will happen. "And they stood above their feet, and great fear fell over them when they saw. And I heard a great voice speaking from the sky, Ascend to here: and they ascended into the sky in a cloud." This is what the Apostle said, "Let us seize in the clouds a meeting with Christ I Thessalonians 4:16. Before the arrival however of the Lord it was written that it was possible for no one to reach to this: "Christ is the beginning, and then these are the ones who are of Christ in his arrival" I Corinthians 15:23. Whence there is excluded every suspicion of certain ones, who think that these two witnesses are two men, and before the arrival of Christ the heaven had ascended in clouds. Moreover, how were the ones inhabiting the land able to rejoice from the death of the two, when they died in one city-state, and to send gifts in turn, if there are three days, who before they rejoice about the death, will be made sad about the resurrection? Or what kind of banquets or pleasure is there able to be in the streets of the banqueting, when human cadavers return disease to the feasts with a three-day stench? Whence the Lord grants to free us. Amen.

Homily IX.

[Apocalypse XI and XII.] What we have heard, brothers, in the reading which has been recited, "That a great motion of the earth happened in that hour"; in that earthquake a persecution is understood, which the devil was accustomed to exercise through evil humans. "And a tenth," he said, "part of the city-state fell, and there were killed seven thousand names of men in the earthquake." The number both of ten and of seven is perfect: because if it weren't, the whole would have had to have been understood in part. There are indeed two buildings in the Church; one over the rock, the other over the sand; the one which is above the sand is said to have fallen down. "And the rest were afraid and gave renown to God." Those people who were built over the rock gave renown, and they were not able to fall, with those who were over the sand. Therefore moreover he said, "They were afraid," because the just one when he sees the destruction of the sinner is motivated more in his observation of the precepts, just as it is said. "And he will wash hands in the blood of the sinner" Psalms 57:11. "And there was revealed," he said, "the temple of God in heaven"; that is, the mysteries of the incarnation of Christ in the Church have become clear: whence the Church is shown to be the heavens. "And there was seen the box of his testament in his temple"; that is, it was understood that the Church was the box of the testament. "And there were brought about lightning [2434] and thundering and earthquake": these all are powers of foretelling and of lightning and of the wars of the Church. "And a great sign was seen in the sky, a woman clothed by the sun, and the moon under her feet": It says that the church has, its part, that is, has deceitful men and evil Christians under its feet. "And on her head a crown of twelve stars." Those twelve stars can be understood as the twelve Apostles. Clothed by the sun, moreover, signifies the hope of resurrection, on account of that which was written, "Then the just will shine just as the sun in the kingdom of their Father" Matthew 13:43. "A great red dragon": is the devil seeking to devour the son of the Church. "Having," it says, "ten horns and seven heads": the heads are kings, the horns indeed are kingdoms. For all kings in seven heads, all kingdoms of the world in ten horns it says. "And its tail was dragging a third part of the stars of the sky, and it sent them [the stars] into the earth": the tail is the wicked prophets, that is the heretics, who since they cling to themselves through repeated baptism throw the stars of heaven into the earth; they themselves are under the feet of the woman. Many believe that those humans are the ones, whom the devil made comrades since they agreed with him: many believe that, the angels are those who were cast headlong with that one when he fell. "Ready, being in labor she is in torment in order that she may give birth": through the whole time daily the Church gives birth in prosperity and in adversity. "And the dragon stood before the woman who was going to give birth, in order to devour her son when he had been born": for the Church is always giving birth in torments, to Christ through limbs, and always the dragon seeks to devour the one being born. "And the woman begot a male child": that is, Christ. Then his body, that is the Church, always creates the limbs of Christ. However he said a male, a victor against the devil. "And the woman fled into the wilderness": we receive that world as a not unfitting wilderness, where up until the end Christ governs the Church and nourishes it, in which the world the Church itself tramples the haughty and impious men as if scorpions and vipers, and every power of Satan through the help of Christ, and it breaks them to pieces. "And there was a war in the heavens": that is, in the Church. "Michael and his Angels were fighting with the dragon": understand Michael, to be Christ; and his Angels, holy humans. "And the dragon fought and his angels": that is, the devil and humans who were following his wish. For let it be absent that we believe the devil with his angels dared to fight in the heavens, he who did not dare on earth to attack one Job, unless he asked from the Lord to harm. "And they were not strong enough, nor was their place found any longer in the heavens": that is, among holy humans, who since they believe, do not receive the devil once he has been expelled and his followers any longer; just as Zecharias said, so that the idols that have once been banished do not receive a place any longer. "And there was expelled the great dragon, an ancient serpent which is said to be the devil and Satan, and his angels with him": the devil and all the dirty spirits were expelled with their leader from the hearts of the holy into the earth, that is, into humans who understand earthly things, and determine their total hope on the earth. "And I heard a great voice speaking from the sky, Now there has been come about safety and strength and the kingdom of our God": that is, of the Church. He shows in what sky those things happen. For in the presence of God indeed there was always both strength and the kingdom and the power of his Son: but in the Church he said that the safety of Christ was made through victory, and concerning those who see this safety the Lord said, "Many just people and Prophets have desired to see what you see Matthew 13:17; they said, Now the safety of our Lord was made. Since the accuser of our brothers was excluded," etc. If however, as certain ones think, the voice of Angels is in the upper sky, and not of the holy in the Church, they would not say, "the accuser of our brothers," but, our accuser; nor, "he accuses," but, he was accusing. Because if the Angels have named the just ones placed on earth our brothers, there was not joy that the devil was sent into the earth, whom the holy ones could prove more troublesome when he was placed with themselves on the lands, than if, as it is said, he were still in the sky. Thus indeed they speak evil of the earth when they say, "Woe to you, earth and sea!" that is, you who are not said to be the sky, were still in the sky. "Because the devil, having great anger, knowing that he has a short time, descended to you. He descended," it says, to protect the allegory. All of the rest are in the sky that is in the Church, [2435] which is said to be the sky rightly: whence having been thrown down by the holy ones the devil descended into his own people, who are the earth for the earthly love. Moreover he said that he was thrown down from the sky not thus, as for the fact that the heaven would now become among men who have been made, but because they are, not because they become. Indeed the holy are not able to become the sky, unless when the devil has been excluded. Therefore not with the first name, but with the second did he name them the sky, among whom the place of the devil has not been found beyond. From this danger the Lord sees fit to free us under his own protection, who lives, etc.

Homily X.

[Apocalypse XII and XIII.] Now, most dear brothers, we have heard that when the dragon had seen that he was excluded from the sacred into the earth that is from the heaven into sinners he chased after the woman who produced the male. For by the extent the devil is thrown out of the holy, so much more does he chase after them. "And there were given to the woman," that is to the Church, "two wings of a great eagle, in order to fly into her deserted place, where she is nourished through the season and times and half of time by the shape of the serpent": the time, is also understood both as a year and a hundred years. The two great wings are the two Testaments of the Church which she received, when she evaded the serpent into the wilderness. "Into its own place" he said, that is, in this world, where serpents and scorpions live: because it was said to that one, just as the Lord says, "Behold I send you just as sheep in the middle of wolves" Matthew 10:16; and Ezekiel says, "Son of human, you live among scorpions" Ezekiel

2:6. "And the serpent sent out of its mouth after the woman water like a river": that is, violence of persecutors. "And the earth helped the woman, and opened its mouth, and absorbed the river which the dragon sent from its mouth." He says the holy earth, which are the holy people. As often as indeed the persecutions of the Church are inflicted on the Church, by prayers of the holy earth, that is by the orations of all the holy ones they are either removed, or moderated. For also our Lord Jesus Christ who interrupts on behalf of us, and also removes these persecutions, sits with the earth itself from the right hands of virtue. Moreover otherwise, that the woman has flown into the wilderness he understands to be the Catholic Church itself, in which in a very recent time under Elias the Synagogue is going to be believed in. The two wings of the great eagle, he wants to be understood as two prophets, namely Elias, and the one who is going to come with him. The water which has been sent out from the mouth of the dragon signifies the army of ones pursuing her: the water which was absorbed, the revenge made concerning the persecutors. "And the dragon was angered against the woman, and went away to make war with the rest descended from his offspring": that is, when he had seen that he was not able to continue the persecutions, which he was in the habit of sending through the Pagans, because they were removed by the mouth of the holy earth, that is by holy orations, he brought about the heresies. "And he stood over the sand of the sea": that is, over the multitude of heretics. "And I saw the beast ascending from the sea": that is, from the evil people. He said "ascending," this is being born. Just as a flower ascends into a good portion from the root Jesse. He says the beast ascending from the sea, is the wicked, who are the body of the devil. "And the beast which I saw, was similar to a leopard, and its feet just as a bear's, and its mouth just as the mouth of a lion": he resembled a leopard on account of the variety of nations, a bear on account of the malice and madness, a lion on account of the strength of body and the haughtiness of the tongue. And because in the times of the Antichrist the kingdom of that one will be commingled with a variety of nations and peoples, the feet just as if of a bear, are its leaders; its mouth, his command. "And the dragon gave to him its strength": just as we see now that the heretics are powerful in this age, who have the strength of the devil. Just as once the Pagans, thus now those destroy the Church. "And I saw one of its heads as almost beaten into death; and the affliction of its death was cured": what it says almost killed, are the heretics, who pretend that they praise Christ: and as long as they do not thus believe as the Catholic faith holds, they blaspheme; when they preach him and beat him that he has arisen again: because also Satan himself transfigures himself into an angel of light II Corinthians 11:14. And otherwise: the heresies are beaten through the Catholics, are crushed with the testimonies of the Scriptures, but those nevertheless as if renewed by the affliction of Satan complete the works of Satan, and do not cease to blaspheme, and [2436] to attract those whom they can to their dogma. "And all the earth wondered at and followed the beast, and they worshiped the dragon which gave power to the beast": the heretics have power without condition, but especially the Arians. "And they worshiped the beast, saying, who is like the beast? or who will be able to fight with it?" Therefore because the heretics delude themselves with this, that no one believes more than those, and that no one conquers the nation of those, which bases its reputation on the name of the beast: to which it was given by the devil himself, and was permitted by God, to speak great things and blasphemies; just as the Apostle says: "It is necessary that there are heresies, so that those who have been proven, may be manifest in you" I Corinthians 11:19. "And there was given to him the power to make forty-two months": the time of the very recent persecution we understand in those forty-two months. "And then he opened his mouth into blasphemy against God": here it is clear that those who have withdrawn from the Catholic Church are signified; when those who before secretly within the church seemed as if to hold the correct faith, produce blasphemy in persecution against God with an open mouth. "And into his tabernacle and towards those who live in the heaven": that is, toward the holy who are contained within the Church, which has been called the heaven, because they themselves are also the tabernacle of God. "And it was permitted to him to make war with the holy ones and to conquer them": we understand that it is a part from the whole, which is able to be conquered; for not good Christians, but those who are evil are conquered. "And there was given to him the power over every tribe and tongue, and all living on earth will worship it": he said all, but the ones living on earth, not in the heaven. "The name of them was not written in the book of life of the Lamb": he spoke concerning the devil or his people, his name was not written in the book of life. "From the origin of the signified world": because in the presence of God the Church was preordained before and was signified. Because he himself to stand over, etc.

Homily XI.

[Apocalypse 13 and 14.] In the reading which was just now recited, very dear friends, we have heard saint John saying, "And I have seen the other beast ascending from the land": which is the sea, this the land. "And it had two horns similar to a Lamb's": that is, two Testaments in the likeness of a Lamb, which is the Church. "And it spoke like a dragon": this is that one which presents the lamb under the Christian name, in order to pour out the poisons of the dragon in secret; this is the heretical Church. Indeed it would not imitate the lamb's likeness, if it spoke openly: now it feigns Christianity, by which it deceives the incautious more securely. Therefore the Lord says, "Beware of pseudoprophets," etc. Matthew 7:15. "And he makes the earth and those who are in it to worship the earlier/preferable beast, whose affliction of his death has been healed: and he will make great signs, so that he may make fire descend from the sky into the earth": and because the sky is the Church, what is the fire descending fro the sky, except for heresies falling from the Church? Just as it was written, "They departed from us, but they were not from us" I John 2:19. Indeed the fire descends from the sky when the heretics who withdraw from the Church like fire, persecute the Church itself. Therefore the beast with its two horns, acts so that the people worship the likeness of the beast, which is the invention of the devil. "In order that he give to them a mark upon their right hand or upon their forehead": for he disputes the mystery of the crime. Indeed the holy who are in the Church, receive Christ in the hand and in the front; the hypocrites however receive the beast under the name of Christ. "If any have not worshiped the beast, nor his image, nor have received an inscription on the forehead, or on their hand, let them be killed": he does not shrink away from the faith, in order that the beast itself is understood as the wicked city-state, that is the congregation or the conspiracy of all the wicked or haughty, which is said to be Babylonia, and should interpreted as the Confusion; and whoever wanted to exercise things worthy of confusion relate to this very one. He himself is the people of the unfaithful, contrary to the faithful people and the city-state of God. His image in truth is a simulation, namely among those humans, who just as if they profess the catholic faith, also live unfaithfully; indeed they depict themselves to be what they are not, and are called not true in image, but false in the image of the Christian: concerning them [2437] the Apostle says, "Having indeed the appearance of piety, but denying its strength" II Timothy 3:5; a not small portion of them is contained in the catholic Church. The just however do not worship the beast, that is, they do not agree, they are not placed under: nor do they receive the inscription, namely the mark of the crime, on their front on account of their profession, on the hand on account of their action. Thus therefore let them act, "So that no one is be able to be bought, unless he has the name or mark of the beast, or the number of his name. This is wisdom. He who has understanding, let him compute the number of the beast: indeed the number is of a human": that is, of Christ the son of a human, whose name the beast has made among heretics for himself. Let us therefore make the number which he said, in order to find the name and mark when the number has been received. "His number," he says, "is six hundred sixteen." Let us make this according to the Greeks especially because he writes to Asia, "And I," he says, am alpha and omega." Six hundred and sixteen in Greek letters thus would be 'chist.' And these marks when understood are the number: moreover when reduced into a monogram, they also make the mark, and the number, and the name. This sign of Christ is understood, and the likeness of itself is shown, which likeness the Church honors in the truth. The adversity of the heretics makes itself similar to it, when those who persecute Christ spiritually, nevertheless seem to take pride in the sign of the cross of Christ. This therefore, because it was said, "The number of the beast is the number of the human. And I have seen, and behold the Lamb standing on the mountain Sion, and with it one hundred forty-four thousand, having its name and the name of its Father written on their foreheads." He revealed what is the imitation of the mark on the fronts, while he says both God and Christ have been written on the fronts of the Church. "And I have heard a voice from the sky as if of many waters": that is, one hundred forty-four thousand. "And as great thunderings: and the voice which I heard as if of harpists playing on their lyres." What moreover he said, "These are those who have not defiled themselves with women," etc., we should understand as virgins in this place chaste in body not only, but especially all the Church, which holds the pure faith, just as the Apostle says, "I indeed have pledged you to one husband, to present to Christ a chaste virgin" II Corinthians 11:2: polluted with no adulterous intermingling of heretics, nor contracted in evil with soothing and fatal pleasures of this world up to the end of their life apart from the remedy of penitence by unhappy perseverance. He adds after this, saying: "And in the mouth of themselves there was not found a lie." He did not say, there was not; but, "there was not found." Indeed such kind as the Lord finds when he calls forth from here, such he also judges: for either through Baptism, or through penitence we are able to be made virgins in the inner human and without a lie. Now again a recapitulation. "And I saw," he says, "another angel flying in the middle of the sky": that is, the foretelling running to and fro in the middle of the Church. "Having an eternal Gospel; in order that he may evangelize to those living on the earth, saying" Fear the Lord," etc. Some wish the angel flying in the middle of the sky to be understood as Elias; and the other angel who follows him, the comrade of Elias, who will preach in this time. "And another angel followed": that is, the prediction of future peace. "Saying, It fell, that great Babylon fell": He says that Babylon the wicked citystate, just as it was said above already, is the company of the devil, that is, the people agreeing with himself: and all the concupiscence and corruption, which he seeks after for the destruction of his own and the human race. For just as the Church is the citystate of God and all the heavenly conduct: thus to the contrary the citystate of the devil is Babylon in all the world, just as the Lord says, "Behold I will place Jerusalem as a stone able to be trampled in all the races" Zechariah 12:3. Therefore the church says, "It fell, that great Babylon fell." As if already completed he says, what was still the future: just as that, "They divided my clothes for themselves" Psalms 21:19. "What he drank from the wine of his anger of fornication is all the races": all the races, are the city-state of the world, that is all the haughty and impious ones, whether outside the Church, or constituted into the Church. "And I saw, and behold a white cloud, and above the cloud sitting the Son of a human," that is, Christ. Indeed he describes in his clarity [2438] the Church extraordinarily turning white after the flames of the persecutions. "Having on his head a golden crown": they themselves are the seniors with golden crowns. "And in his hand a sharp sickle": that sickle separates Catholics from the heretics, the holy from the sinners, just as the Lord says about harvesters. If moreover it should be thought that Christ himself especially was seen in the white cloud ass a harvester; who is the grape picker, if not the same, but in his body which is the Church? By chance it is not understood badly, if those three angels who went out, we understand as the triform meaning of the Scriptures, alike historial, moral, and spiritual: for the sickle is the disagreement. "And he sent into the great winepress of the anger of God": not into the great winepress; but he sent the one himself into the winepress, which is each haughty one. "And the winepress was trampled outside the citystate": that is, outside the Church. Indeed when the dissension was made, every human of sin went out to the outdoors. Moreover the trampling of the winepress is the retribution of sinners. "And the blood went out from the winepress up to the reigns of the horses": the revenge will go up to the rulers of the peoples. Indeed up to the devil and his angels revenge of the poured out blood will go in the most recent struggle. "Through six hundred thousand stades": that is, through all four parts of the world. Indeed the fourness has been made four, just as there is in the four fourfold and entire faces. Indeed the forty-four are the six hundred thousand.

Homily XII.

[Apocalypse 15 and 16.] In the reading which was recited, dearest brothers, saint John said that he had seen "another great and wonderful sign in the sky: seven angels": that is, the Church. "Having seven very recent afflictions, since in these the anger of God was ended": he said very recent, because the anger of God always strikes down the obstinate people with seven afflictions, that is, completely; just as God himself repeats frequently in Leviticus, "And I will strike you down seven times, on account of your sins" Leviticus 26:24. "And I saw even as a glass sea": that is, a very clear font of Baptism. "Mixed, with fire": that is, with spirit or trial. "And the victors of the beast over the glass sea": that is, in Baptism. "Holding the cithers of God": that is, hearts of ones praising which were dedicated to God. "And singing the canticle of Moses the servant of God, and the canticle of the Lamb": that is, each Testament. "Great and wonderful are your works": indeed these are in each Testament, which the ones mentioned above sing. He repeats what he had proposed, saying: "After these things I saw, and behold there was revealed the temple of the tabernacle of the testimony in the sky." We have already said that the temple should be perceived as the Church; the angel who went out from the temple and ordered to the one sitting above a cloud, was said to be, the rule of the Lord. Indeed he is the outcome of the order, just as the evangelist says, "There went out an edict from Caesar Augustus" (Luc. 2. 1). "Dressed in clean and shining linen and having bound over their chests golden sashes": he clearly shows the Church in the seven angels. Thus indeed he described the beginning from Christ: "Having," he says, a golden sash above their breasts. And one of the four animals gave to the seven angels golden saucers, full of the wrath of God" Apocalypse 1:13: those are saucers which the seniors and animals carry with odor, which are the Church; and they are also the seven angels. And that which are odors, this is the anger of God; this is also the word of God. But also these all give life to the good, to the evil brings death: just as is that [statement], "For some the odor of life into life, for the others the odor of death into death II Corinthians 2:16. Indeed the prayers of the holy, who are the fire going out from the mouth of witnesses, are the anger for the world and the wicked. Therefore, because this is not enough for the haughty and wicked, that those who are holy, they do not esteem, nor imitate, but also wherever they could. All those plagues are spiritual, and happen in the mind. For in that very time every wicked populace will be harmed by every affliction of the body; because it will not be worthy to be whipped in the present age, as one who received the entire power of being cruel; but spiritually, that is, voluntary and mortal sins, which are ulcers in their souls, all the wicked and haughty suffer. "The second one poured his saucer into the sea," and the remaining things. The sea, rivers, fountains of waters, sun, throne of the beast, Euphrates river, [2439] air, over which the angels poured the saucers, are the earth and humans: because to all the angels it was commanded to pour onto the earth. However all those afflictions must be understood to the contrary: indeed the affliction is incurable, and the anger great, to receive the power of sinning, especially among the holy, and not to be corrupted; still greater is the anger of God, and the poultices of errors to be supplied to injustice. This affliction of the anger of God, these wounds, that each is stabbed through and rejoices and is pleasing to himself in sins. Thus the prosperity of the evil, are the ulcers of the souls: and the adversity of the just, are the rewards of eternal joys. In the third true angel and conversion of waters into blood, understand all the angels of the peoples, that is, weaker humans bloody in mind. "The fourth angel poured out his saucer over the sun, and humans were burned with a great burning": this is the future still in the fire of hell. For the devil in the present when in the soul he kills his lovers in the soul, not only does not burn in body, but praises as much as he is permitted: this glory and happiness the Holy Spirit has defined as afflictions and griefs. "And they blasphemed the name of God who has the power in these afflictions, nor did they give penitence."

Because not in the body, but in the mind they are struck down with those afflictions by God: therefore neither are they mindful of the Lord, but they advance into worse; and on that account they blaspheme, persecuting his saints. "The fifth poured his saucer out over the seat of the beast, and his kingdom was made cloudy": the throne of the beast is of the Church itself, which is the congregation of the haughty, which is blinded with afflictions of every kind. "They were devouring their own tongues from their own griefs": that is, the blaspheming ones were harming themselves out of the anger of God, because they were thinking of joys after having been transfixed. "And they did not pay penitence": certainly they were stubborn with happiness. "And the sixth angel poured his saucer over that great river Euphrates": that is over the populace. "And his water was dried": just as he said above, the harvest of the land dried up, that is, it was prepared to be put on fire. "In order that there is prepared the way of those who are from the rise of the sun": that is, for Christ: indeed when these are completed the just, set out to meet Christ.

Homily XIII.

[Apocalypse 16 and 17.] Saint John, very dear brothers, while he was speaking about the saucers or afflictions of the seven angels, recapitulates in the accustomed manner since the seventh angel was omitted speaking briefly from the beginning: "And I saw from the mouth of the dragon, and from the mouth of the beast, and from the mouth of the pseudoprophet the three spirits unclean in the manner of frogs." He saw one spirit, but in place of the number and portion of one body. The dragon, that is the devil: for both the beast, that is the body of the devil, and the pseudoprophet, that is of the body of the devil put in charge, is one spirit, as if of a frog. "Indeed there spirits of demons making signs." For in fact frogs besides their own horror also are in an unclean place. And since they seem inhabitants and native of waters, not only are they fugitives of waters and unable to take dryness, but also in the waters themselves, are involved in the defilements and slime of water. Thus they do not live as hypocrites in water, as they are thought; but in defilements, which they put aside when they trust the water. Also similar to frogs are humans, who in crimes or offenses, which others through penitence or Baptism put aside, are not ashamed to be involved in. Indeed when someone converts himself to God, and is sorry that he was haughty, adulterous, drunken or greedy, the one who imitates those sins which another left behind by confessing, thinking with himself and saying, "I do what I want, and later just as that one does penitence, I myself do also: and suddenly while the final day has come upon him, confession perishes, and damnation remains: that one who is such a kind, while he wishes to imitate others not for the good, but for the bad, in the mud, whence the other was liberated, just as a frog is involved, he also wallows. Therefore the frogs signify the spirits of demons making signs. "And they go out to kings of the entire world to gather them for the war [2440] of the great day of the Lord." The great day he speaks of is the entire time from the suffering of the Lord.

But a day must be taken in the places: now and then he says the Day of Judgment, sometimes the most recent persecution, which is going to be under Antichrist, sometimes the entire time, just as through Amos the prophet: "Woe," he says, "to those who long for the day of the Lord! And just as the day of the Lord" Amos 5:18 and the remaining things which follow there. All these things are in this life for these days in which are the shadows of the Lord: those who long for the day of the Lord, that is those who delight in this age, for whom it is sweet, who in that when they serve pleasure and luxury take wealth, who think it must be demanded of religion, to whom it is said. "Woe to you who have been satisfied" Luke 6:25 not those to whom it is said, "Blessed are those who grieve" Matthew 5:5. He recapitulates again from the same persecution saying: "And there was lightning and thundering, and a great earthquake, such as was not made from when humans were made, and that great city-state was made into three parts." This great city-state is understood as entirely all the populace which is under the sky, which would become into three parts when the Church was divided, in order that there be Gentiles as one part, heretics and pretended Catholics in another, the Catholic Church in the third. Indeed he continues, and shows what the three parts are, saying: "The city-states of the nations have fallen, and that great Babylon has come into mind for God to give to it a drink of the wine of his wrath, and every island flees, and the mountains have not been found." The city-states are the nations of nations, Babylon the abomination of devastation, the mountains and the islands are the Church; in the city-states every defense of the nations and hope of the nations he says has fallen. Indeed they do not hold different from Christians, but good and bad city-states among humans are described. Therefore at that time Babylon fell or drank the wrath of God, when it received the power against Jerusalem, which is the Church. "The islands were not found": that is, they did not survive. "And a great hail as large as a silver dollar coin descended from the sky over humans": he says that the hail is the wrath of God. He says that all the afflictions are those forms of spiritual afflictions. "And the humans blasphemed God from the affliction of hail, since it is very much a great affliction of him." He recapitulates again when he says: "And one of the seven angels came, and said to me, Come, I will show you the damnation of the great harlot, who sits over many waters, with whom the kings of the earth have fornicated," that is all the earthborn creatures. "And he brought me in the wilderness in the spirit, and I saw a woman sitting over the beast." In the beast all the evil populace is understood; in the woman corruption is shown: he says that the woman sits in the wilderness, because she would sit among the wicked, dead in spirit and deserted by God: in spirit, he said; because only in spirit is it able to seem a desertion of this kind. He said she was preciously decorated, on account of the decorations of luxury. For just as it was already said, the beast over which she sits, he says, is the populace, which the many waters are, just as he himself explains: "The water which you see, where the woman sits, is the peoples and the crowds, and the races and the languages." He says that corruption sits over the peoples in the wilderness. The harlot, beast, wilderness are one. The beast, as it was already said, is the body against the Lamb, in which body now the devil is, now the head just as if killed, which signifies the heretics, who just as they seem to take pride in the death of Christ, must be taken not only as the people of the haughty: because it all is Babylon. In the three spirits, which proceeding forth from the mouth of the dragon as of a frog: it is understood in one as the devil; in another, the pseudo-prophets or those put in charge of the heretics; in the third, the body of the devil, that is all the pretend, haughty, or wicked Christians, a great number of whom is contained in the Church. At last those who are of such a kind, according to the likeness of frogs, wallow in every filth and dirtinesses of luxury. Men are also similar to frogs, because they are not ashamed to be involved in sins or offenses, which others put aside through penitence or Baptism, saying to themselves, For the present I fulfill my wants; later, when those have been converted, [2441] I also will be converted to God. And suddenly when death comes upon confession perishes, damnation remains. What he says, that humans must be gathered for the great day; he says the great day is the entire time from the suffering of the Lord up to the end of the world. Indeed that day is pleasant for them, and those who, obedient in this to pleasure and luxury, seek wealth, are converted into great misery, because that of prophet must be fulfilled in those, "Woe to those desiring the day of the Lord!" Indeed through false and transitory sweetness they prepare for themselves an eternal bitterness. It is possible in this place that the great day is understood as that desolation, when Jerusalem was besieged by Titus and Vespasian, when with these excepted who were led into captivity, fifteen hundred thousand are referred to as dead. Because moreover he says, "He gathered those in the place of Armagedon," he wanted all the enemies of the Church to be understood. Finally he follows, and he says, "They surrounded the camp of the holy and the holy beloved city-state Apocalypse 20:8: that is, the Church. Because moreover there was thundering, and a great earthquake, and the great city-state was made into three parts; the great city-state, is understood as all the people, where one part is of the Pagans, another of heretics, a third of Christians, in which part there are also hypocrites. Since from that third part the good were separated, then those who are fictitious in the Church, receive the judgment of God when they have been joined to those two parts: that also in this time it is now fulfilled from another part. Indeed at that time Babylon falls, when the evil receive the power, to persecute the good who are the Churches. Moreover that the great hail the size of a silver dollar descends from the sky, in the hail the wrath of God is understood: and the one which also would come before the Day of Judgment is sent over the wicked and haughty spiritually within in the soul. The harlot woman, whom he sees in the spirit sitting over the beast sitting in the wilderness; therefore he says in the wilderness, because she would sit among the wicked, that is, dead in the soul and deserted by God. "In the Spirit," he says, because only spiritually is a desertion of this kind able to be seen, since it happens within in the soul. The harlot, the beast, the wilderness are one, because all of Babylonia is understood. The beast, as it was already said, is the body of the wicked against the Lamb; in this body now is the devil, now the head as if killed, which signifies the treachery of the heretics, who seem as if to glory in the death of Christ, when nevertheless they persecute the Church of Christ perpetually. And because not only the heretics or Pagans, but also the evil Catholics, that is the haughty and wicked persecute those whom they see in the Church as meek and humble; as much as we can, let us pray for the compassion of God, in order that he may both correct those from such evil acts according to the good, and grant to us fortunate perseverance in good works on behalf of his own piety, he who lives and rules with the Father and the Holy Spirit, etc.

Homily XIV.

[Apocalypse 17.] When the divine reading was just now read, dearest brothers, we have heard that the blessed John has said that he saw "a woman sitting over a scarlet beast": that is, a sinful, bloody one. "One full of blasphemy with names": he shows that there are many names in the beast that is in the wicked populace, as we have already said. "Having seven heads, and ten horns": that is, kings of the world and the kingdom, with whom the devil has been seen in the sky. "And the woman," that is, all the multitude of the haughty, "was surrounded with purple, and with scarlet, and was adorned with gold and precious stone": that is, with all the enticements of a simulated truth. What is finally within this beauty, he thus explains, saying: "And holding a golden goblet in her hand, full of abominations and of the impurities of her fornication." The gold is the imitation of the impurities; those who from the outside indeed obey the humans as if just, yet within are full of every impurity Matthew 23:28. "And on her forehead his name was written, Mystery, great Babylon, mother of fornications and abominations of the earth": there is no superstition, which gives a sign on the front, unless imitation. The spirit moreover told what was written on [2442] the front. For who places such a title openly? Indeed he said the mystery was, what he interpreted when he said, "And I saw a woman intoxicated from the blood of the saints and the martyrs of Jesus." One is indeed the body, which opposes the Church within and outside; that is, the fictitious Christians in the Church, and outside the Church the heretics or Pagans. Although this body seems separated from the place, in persecution of the Church nevertheless it attends the unity of the spirit the spirit attends the unity of the Church. It is impossible indeed that the Prophet perish in addition to Jerusalem who kills Prophets Luke 13:33-34; that is, it is not possible to happen that good Christians suffer any persecution without evil Christians. Thus the grandsons of ancestors with one accord, are accused to have stoned Zacharias Matthew 23:35, although they themselves didn't. "And the beast was and is not, and will be, and will ascend from

the abyss, and it will go into the perdition of the wrath of God":
that is, it is born from the populace, in order to be able to say, "The
beast from the beast, abyss from abyss. What is the beast from the
beast, and abyss from abyss, except an evil populace being born
from an evil populace? This may happen while evil sons imitate
very bad parents. And the one remaining ascends, and walks into
perdition, just as also his fathers, from whom he ascends. And
already they exist now, because others succeed them when some
die. And thus never are they lacking, either in a few or in many,
either secretly or as if openly, who will not plot against the Church
from the beginning. That moreover he says, a woman sitting over
a scarlet beast; he wanted to be understood as a sinful and bloody
plebs. That moreover he says she was surrounded with purple and
scarlet, and adorned with gold and a precious stone; he shows the
plebs of the haughty and wicked humans full of all the enticements
of simulated truth. That moreover she was holding a golden goblet
in her hand full of abominations and impurities of his fornication;
the hypocrites and false Christians are understood, who appear
from the outside indeed as if just, but within are full of every impurity. That moreover, she had written on her forehead, "Babylon
mother of fornications": there is no superstition which gives a sign
on the front, except an imitation, that is, they depict themselves as
good when they are evil. Moreover what he said, that the woman
was intoxicated with the blood of saints and of martyrs of Jesus; he
wanted one body of the evil ones to be understood, which it always
is opposed to the Church within and outside: because both in the
Church there are false Christians, and outside the Church heretics
or Pagans. And although they are meanwhile separated from the
body, yet in one mind they are joined in the persecution of the
Church. Moreover what he says, "There was a beast, and he is not,
and will be, and will ascend from the abyss": this is understood,
that an evil populace is born from an evil populace, in order that
it can be said, the beast from the beast, abyss from abyss. What
is the beast from the beast, except an evil populace being born
from an evil populace? This may be while the evil sons imitate
very bad parents: and thus while although some die others succeed, never are there lacking either in few, or in many, or secretly,
or openly, those who will not be against the Church always from
the beginning. Because from the company of these we are not able
by body to be separated in this age, let us beseech the compassion
of God, so that we may be separated in this way by customs, and
not perish with them from an eternal punishment: but more when

those have heard, "Depart from me, you who have been spoken ill of, into the perpetual fire"; let us be worthy of hearing, "Come, blessed ones of my Father, take up the kingdom" Matthew 25:41, 34; with the Lord our Jesus Christ being present. Amen.

Homily XV.

[Apocalypse 17 and 18.] In the reading which was recited, dearest brothers, those kings whom he spoke of because they persecute Jerusalem, are evil peoples, who persecute the Church of God: who are called as if kings, because they rule as if in dreams. Indeed every evil one who persecutes a good one, just as he does this in dreams: because the persecution of all the evil will not remain, but just like a dream will vanish, just as Isaiah says, "The riches of all races will be just as one dreaming in a dream" Isaiah 29:7. "These have one opinion": that is, they persecute the good with one mind. Therefore he says, "They have"; and not they will have: because the persecution of evil will be not only on the coming [2443] Day of Judgment, but also does not cease in the present. "And they will give both strength and their majesty to the devil": this he says therefore, because the wicked humans, themselves seem to give strength, with this urging they make evils. "These fight with the Lamb": that is, up until the end, until the holy take all the kingdom, they oppose the Church. "And the Lamb will conquer them": that is, in particular, because God does not permit those to be tried beyond that which they are able. Therefore he says, "And the Lamb will conquer them, since he is the Lord of Lords, and the King of Kings; and who are with him, have been called and chosen and are faithful": that is, the Church. On account of this moreover he said, "Called and chosen," because not all have been called and chosen: just as the Lord says, "Many have been called, few however chosen" Matthew 20:16. "And the angel said to me: You see the waters where the mother sits, these things are both the populace and the crowds, and nations and tongues: and the ten horns which you see, these have a harlot with hatred": that is, that woman. The harlot is indeed the luxurious life, which is lived by plunderings and pleasures. Therefore he said that they would have a harlot with hatred, because humans who are extravagant, haughty, desirous and proud, not only persecute the holy; but also hold themselves in hatred. And they hold themselves in hatred in another way, in whom it is fulfilled what was written, "He who esteems unfairness, hates his own soul" Psalms 10:6. "And they will make her deserted and nude." Indeed they themselves through the wrath of God and the just judgment, by which they are deserted by him, make the world deserted; while they have been dedicated to it and use it unjustly. "And he will eat its flesh." This therefore, because according to the Apostle they bite themselves in turn and are consumed Galatians 5:15. And therefore he added the reason when he said, "Indeed God gave into their hearts to do its opinion": that is, he instigated the afflictions, which he decided to afflict on the world with law and merit. "And they will give their kingdom to the beast, continuously while the words of God are finished": that is, evil humans obey the devil, until the Scriptures are fulfilled, and the Day of Judgment comes. After these things he follows, "The woman, whom you saw, is a great city-state, which holds a kingdom over the kings of the earth": that is, all the evil and wicked. Thus also it was said about the Church, "Come, I will show you the woman of the Lamb:" and he shows to me a city-state descending from the sky Apocalypse 21:9-10. Later I saw another angel descending from the sky, holding great power: and the earth was illuminated for his clarity. And he shouted in strength, saying: There has fallen, that great Babylon has fallen, and she has been made a habitation of demons, and the confinement of every unclean and defiled bird." Is the ruin of one city-state able to take all unclean spirits, or every unclean bird; or in that time when the city-state itself fell, was the whole world deserted from spirits and unclean birds, and in the ruin of one city-state will they live? There is no city-state which holds every unclean soul, except the city-state of the devil, in which every impurity in evil humans, abides through the whole world. The kings, whom he spoke of because they persecute Jersualem, are evil humans, who persecute the Church of God: who lives and rules, etc.

Homily XVI.

[Apocalypse 18-20.] As many times as you hear Babylonia named, do not understand that the city-state was made from stones; because Babylonia is interpreted as Confusion: but know that the name of the very one signifies haughty men, robbers, extravagant and wicked persevering in their own evils: just as on the contrary as many times as you have heard the name Jerusalem, which is said to be the Vision of peace, understand holy humans reaching to God. For because Babylonia bears an image of evil humans, therefore concerning them he says in the following, "Since all nations have drunk from the wine of the anger of its fornication, and the kings of the land who have fornicated with her": that is, with each other. Indeed not with one harlot are all kings able to fornicate, but while the extravagant ones, who are the limbs of the harlot, corrupt themselves in turn, with the harlot, that is with an extravagant familiarity they are said to fornicate. After these he follows, saying: "And all the merchants of the earth were made rich from the strength of her luxury." He speaks in this place of the rich by sins: for the excess of luxury makes poor men more than rich. "And I heard," he said, "another voice speaking from the sky: Go out from it, my people, so that you do not communicate with its sins [2444]; and are not harmed by its afflictions." In this place he shows Babylon to be divided into two parts: because while, with God assisting, the evil are converted to the good, Babylonia is divided; and that part which departed from that is made Jerusalem. Daily indeed they are transferred from Babylonia to Jerusalem, and from Jerusalem they are led astray to Babylonia; and while the evil are converted to the good, and those who seemed to be good in the imitation of good, are revealed publicly as evil. Finally for the good thus also the Scripture says through Isaiah, "Go out from the middle of them, and do not touch the unclean one: go out from the middle of them, and be separated, you who bring vases of the Lord Isaiah 52:11. The Apostle is mindful of this separation, saying: "Indeed the foundation of God remains firm; and God knew who are his, and he should depart from the iniqiuity everyone who names the name of the Lord" II Timothy 2:19. "Do not communicate," He says, "with his sins, and do not be harmed by his afflictions." Since it was written, "Whoever when involved in death was just, will be in refreshment" (Sap. 4. 7); how is a participant of sin able to be just, whom the fall of the city-state has brought forth with the wicked? Unless by chance when from the city-state of the devil, that is, from the extravagant and wicked conduct the good go out, if anyone of them wanted to remain and to take delight in the pleasures of Babylonia; if he did this, without a doubt he will be a participant of its affliction. What moreover he has said so often, "Go out," do not understand this related to the body, but spiritually. It is warded off from the middle of Babylonia, when the evil conduct is deserted. For also in one home and in one Church and in one city-state at the same time are Babylonians with the Jerusalemites: and yet as long as neither the good agree with the bad, nor the bad are converted to the good, both Jerusalem is recognized to be in the good, and Babylonia among the bad. At the same time they live in the body, but have been divided at a distance by the heart: because the conduct of the evil is always in the lands, because they esteem the land, and they establish every hope of theirs and all intention of their mind on the land; in truth the mind of the good according to the Apostle is always in the heavens, because they know what things are above Colossians 3:2. "Go out," he says, "from that, my people," that is, from Babylonia: "do not communicate with its sins, and do not be harmed by its afflictions. Since its sins have ascended all the way up to the sky, God has also remembered its iniquity. Return to her just as also she herself has returned to you, and double double things according to her works: in that goblet in which he has mixed, mix double for that one: as much as he has clarified and himself, give that much torture to him, and sorrow as his own goblet." All these things for good Christians, that is, God says for the Church: from the Church indeed visible and invisible afflictions go out into the world. "Since Babylon says in its heart," that is, the plebs of all evil or haughty ones, "I am sitting as a queen, and I am not a widow, and I will not see sorrow. Therefore its afflictions of death and sorrow and thunder will come in one day: and it will be consumed thoroughly by fire." If it will die in one day, and be consumed thoroughly, who will mourn the dead one in addition to those, or how much hunger is there able to be of one day? But he said the day was a short time of a present life, by which both spiritually and carnally they are afflicted: for over all the haughty and those devoted to pleasures, greater afflictions in the soul, than in the body is coming. Indeed at that time they are persecuted by a greater plague, when extolling themselves from their own wickednesses, thus they are allowed to do evil by a just judgment of God, in order that among the sons of God they do not deserve to be whipped, but there may be fulfilled among them that which was written: "In the labors of humans they are not, and they will not be whipped with humans; therefore their haughtiness has held them, Psalms 72:5-6. Since strong is Lord God, who will judge it. And they will weep and lament that they are over it like the kings of the earth, who have fornicated with it." What kings will lament it when overturned, if they as kings will overturn it? But what is the city-state; this is also the kings, who will lament it. They do not bewail the evil of extravagance because they sin with it, by doing penitence; but because they know the prosperity of the age, through which they will serve their pleasures, perishes: or because they begin to cease these things in them, which were pleasing before through extravagance, the extravagance are in turn consumed, "as if [2445] smoke of the present hell, while they stand far away on account of the fear of its penalty": standing afar not in body, but in mind; while each fears for himself, what he sees another suffer through trickeries and through the power of the haughty. "Saying, Woe, woe, the great city-state Babylon, a strong city-state, since your damnation came in one hour!" The spirit speaks the name of the city-state: those lament that the true world, when intercepted by a still scanty time of penalty, has ceased all weakened industry. "And the merchants of both horses and carts and pigs, who were enriched by it, will stand afar crying and saying, Woe, woe, great city-state!" Wherever he speaks of the spirits enriched by it, it signifies the riches of the sins. "Dressed in fine linen, and purple, and scarlet, and adorned with gold and precious stone and pearls." Is the city-state dressed in fine linen or purple, and not humans? They themselves therefore bewail themselves, while they are robbed by the words above. "And every governor, and each one who sails in ships, and the sailors, and however many work on the sea, have stood far away, and have shouted when they see the smoke of the fire." Does every governor and the sailors however many ply the sea, been able to have been present to see the burning of one city-state? But he says that all the lovers of the age and the workers of unfairness fear for themselves, seeing the ruin of their hope. After these things he says, "And I saw the beast and the kings of the land and their armies": in the beast he signifies the devil; in the kings of the land and in the army, all his people. "Gathered to make war with the one sitting over the horse, and with his army," that is with Christ and the Church. "And I saw another angel descending from the sky": he says is the Lord Christ in the first arrival. "Having the key of the abyss": that is, the power of the people; indeed he wants the abyss to be understood as the evil people. "And a great chain in his hand": this is, God gave the power in his hand. "And he held the dragon, an ancient serpent, which is the devil and Satan, and he bound him for a thousand years": especially at the first arrival, just as he himself says, "Who is able to enter into the home of a strong one and to steal his vases Matthew 12:29, unless he first has bound the strong one? Indeed when he excludes the devil from the people of believing ones, he sends him into the abyss, that is, into the evil people: and what he shows invisibly, when driving them out from the humans into pigs, who had been plunged into the abyss, he permits to go; which matter especially among heretics is fulfilled.

Homily XVII.

[Apocalypse 18-20.] Those things which your Charity has now heard from the reading of the Apocalypse, receive with an attentive mind according to your custom. Indeed the evangelist blessed John said that he had seen the sky opened. "And behold a white horse, and its rider is called Faithful and True, and his eyes as the flame of fire, and above his head were many diadems": indeed on that there is a multitude of crowners. "Having a name written, which no one knows except he himself": he himself especially and the things in that one are all the Church. "And he was surrounded by clothing sprinkled with blood": the garment of Christ is the Church which he is wearing; this is altered with the blood of sufferings. "And his name is said to be Sermon of God. The army which are in the sky were following him on white horses": that is, the Church in the white bodies represents him, just as it was said above, "These are the ones who follow the Lamb, wherever he has gone" Apocalypse 14:4. "Dressed in a white world of linen," by which he has defined the just deeds of the holy. "And from his mouth there comes forth a two-edged sword": it itself is the one from which the just are defended, the unjust are punished. "In order that he in this strike down the nations: and he himself will rule them in an iron rod. He himself tramples the winepress of wine of the indignation of the wrath of the omnipotent God": he also tramples now, when he permits the evil to do evil, and releases them in their pleasures; and later outside of the city-state, that is, outside the Church he will trample, when he will hand over those who did not give penitence, to the fires of hell. "This one has on his clothing, and over his thigh his name written [2446], King of Kings and Lord of Lords": this is the name which none of the haughty knows; because the Church by serving, rules in Christ, and is master of those dominating ones; that is, he conquers vices and sins. His thigh moreover is posterity, just as that "statement," "Let the prince not defect from the loins of Judah": and Abraham, lest his posterity be mixed with strangers, applies between himself and his slave, his thigh as a certain testimony Genesis 49:10, and 24:2-4. "And I saw," he says, "an angel standing in the sun": that is, a eulogist in the Church. "And he shouted in a great voice saying to all the birds, which are flying in the middle of the sky": we receive birds or beasts for the place as good and evil, just as there is that {statement}, "Let the beasts of the field bless me" Isaiah 43:20; and, "The lion from the tribe of Judah" Apocalypse 5:5: therefore the birds flying in the middle of the sky, he says are the Churches, which when he gathers into one body he had said was an eagle flying in the middle of the sky. "Come, be congregated at the great dinner of God, in order to eat the flesh of kings, and the flesh of tribunes and of the strong, and the flesh of horses and of those sitting above them, and the flesh of all freedmen and slaves both small and great": indeed all the nations, when the believing Churches are incorporated in Christ, spiritually are consumed thoroughly by the Church. And after these things he says concerning the devil: "And he shut and signed over him, lest he lead astray the nations: continuously while a thousand years are finished." Those thousand years are understood, which are done from the arrival of our Lord. In those therefore the Lord prohibited the devil to lead astray the nations; but the ones which were determined into life, which he was leading astray before, from being reconciled to God. "After these things it is necessary for him to be released for a little time": that is, in the time of the Antichrist, when the human of sin was revealed, when he received the total power of persecuting, such as he did not receive from the beginning. He said a thousand years, a part for the whole. Here he wanted to be understood that the remains [of the sixth] are called a thousand years of the sixth, in which the Lord was born and suffered. After these things he says: "Woe, woe, that great city-state, in which the enriched are all, those who had ships in the sea; since in one hour it [the city-state] was deserted! Rejoice, sky, over it and the holy, and the Apostles, and the Prophets." Does the city-state Babylonia alone in all the world persecute or has it alone persecuted the servants of God, in order that those extinguished things themselves of the universe may be revenged? Indeed in the whole world Babylonia is among evil humans, and in the whole world persecutes the good ones. "And one angel has brought a stone, like a great millstone, and sent it into the sea, saying: Thus will that great city-state Babylon be thrown down by force": therefore he says that Babylonia just as that great millstone which was thrown, because the revolution of times just as a millstone crushes all the lovers of the world just like a boulder, and sends it spinning, about which it was been written, "The wicked are walking round about" Psalms 11:9. The unhappy occupation of which is always as if it is beginning. "And it will not be found any more: and the voice of harpists, and of musicians, and of trumpeters, and of pipers will not be heard in it any more": he says the pleasantness of the wicked goes across and now is not found. And he added the reason, saying, "Since your merchants were the greatest of the earth": that is, since you reaped the good things in your life. "Since all the nations went astray in your malicious moral influences, and the blood of the Prophets and of the Holy was found by you of all the murderers over the land." Has the same city-state killed the Apostles, which [killed] both the Prophets and all the remaining martyrs? But this is the city-state of all the haughty, which Cain founded by the blood of his brother, and he called it his name by the name of his son Enoch Genesis 4:17, that is of posterity: because all the evil, in whom there is Babylonia, succeeding themselves, up until the end of the world persecute the Church of God. In the city-state therefore of Cain there is thrown down all the just blood by the blood of the just Able, up until the blood of Zacharias, that is, of the people and of the priest; "between the temple and the altar" Matthew 23:35, that is, between the people and the priests. This therefore was said, because not only the people, but also the priests conspired against the death of Zacharias. "Between the temple," he says, "and the altar": in the altar are understood the priests; in the temple, the peoples were signified [2447] for there was not another reason of naming the place. This is the city-state which kills the Prophets, and stones the ones sent to them. This is the city-state which is built by blood, just as it was written: "Woe, he who builds the city-state in bloods, and prepares a city-state among injustices" Habakkuk 2:12! On the white horse, about which it was spoken above, understand the Church: in its rider, Christ the Lord recognize. Moreover that he said, "Having its name written, which no one new except he himself": he himself in particular, and what is in that, all the Church. "In the garment sprinkled with blood," martyrs, who are in the Church, should be understood. That moreover, "the army which is in the sky, followed him on white horses"; the Church is in the white bodies. In the double-edged sword, the power of Christ is understood, from which the just are defended, the unjust are punished. "In an iron rod," his justice is recognized, about which the humble are instructed, the haughty as if earthen vases are broken. Moreover that he said, "The winepress itself of the wine of the anger of the omnipotent God": indeed it tramples also now, when he permits the evil to persecute the good, and he dismisses them in their pleasures; but afterwards he will require, when he will send those who did not pay penitence, will send into hell. Understand the angel standing in the sun, as preaching in the Church. Indeed therefore the Church is compared to the sun, because concerning it was written, "At that time the just will shine just as the sun, in the kingdom of their father" Matthew 13:43. That moreover, "He shouted to all the birds, which are flying in the middle of the sky"; those birds are understood to be the Church. That moreover it was said, "Be gathered for the great dinner, in order to eat the flesh of kings and the flesh of tribunes"; this we know happened in the Church in truth. For when all the nations of the Church are incorporated, spiritually they are consumed entirely: and those who having been devoured by the devil were the body of the devil, undertaken by the Church are made the limbs of Christ. What moreover concerning the devil he said, "And he closed and signed above him, that he not lead astray the nations, continuously while a thousand years are finished"; just as it was said, those thousand years are done from the suffering of the Lord, in which it is not permitted to the devil to do how much he wants; because God does not permit the servants to be tried beyond that which they are able to sustain I Corinthians 10:13. That moreover later in a little time he must be released, the time of Antichrist is designated, in which the devil will receive a greater power of being cruel. What moreover is said, "Woe, woe, great city-state!" is understood as Babylonia. Yet it should be known, that not only the city-state Babylonia persecutes the holy, in order that extinguished things themselves of the universe will be revenged. Indeed in the whole world Babylonia is among evil humans, and in the whole world she persecutes the good. Moreover that "a great stone like a millstone the angel sent into the sea, saying, Thus will Babylonia be sent"; therefore just as a millstone he says is Babylon, because the revolution of the times just as a millstone crushes the lovers of the world and sends them spinning. What moreover he said, "In your evil influences all the nations have gone astray, and the blood of the Prophets has been found by you of all the murderers over the earth": not indeed in one city-state were killed the Apostles and the prophets or the remaining Martyrs; but this is the citystate of haughty ones, which follows in the whole world the holy. The city-state itself is the one which Cain founded by the blood of his brother, and he called by the name of his son Enoch, that is, posterity: because all the evil ones in which Babylonia is, succeeding themselves up until the end of the world persecute the Church of God. From the persecu-

tion of them the Lord judges us worthy to free through his compassion, who with the Father and the Holy Spirit, etc.

Homily XVIII.

[Apocalypse 19-22.] In the reading which has been recited,
dearest brothers, the blessed evangelist John says thus: "I have
heard the great voice of a bountiful people, of those in the heaven
saying: Alleluia, Health, and clarity, and strength for our God:
since true and just are his judgments, since he has judged that
great harlot, who has corrupted the earth with her fornication,
and has revenged the blood of his servants from his hand. And
again they said, Alleluia."

This voice [2448] is of the Church, when the revolt was done,
and when all the evil ones exited from it [the church] for the eternal fire of burning up. "And their smoke ascended forever." Listen,
brothers, and panic, and know for certain because Babylonia and
the harlot, whose smoke ascends forever, are not understood unless as greedy humans, adulterous and haughty. And therefore if
you wish to evade these evil things, do not commit such serious
sins. "And their smoke," he says, "ascends": indeed does the smoke
of the visible destroyed city-state rise up forever, and not of humans holding out in haughtiness? "It ascends" however; and not,
it will ascend: for always even in the present time it goes into perdition. Babylon moreover is cremated in part, just as Jerusalem in
those holy ones who travel from the lifetime, goes across into paradise, with the Lord manifesting in the poor and the rich, Luke
16:19-22. "And I heard as a voice of the bountiful people, and as a
voice of the many waters, and as a voice of the strong thunderings,
them saying: Alleluia; since our Lord God omnipotent has ruled:
let us rejoice, and let us exult, and let us glorify his name; since the
nuptials of the Lamb have come, and his woman has prepared
herself": the woman of the Lamb is the church. "And it was given
to her to produce a splendid world of linen, for at Byssinus were
the just deeds of the saints done:" that is, it was given to her to
dress in her own deeds, just as it was written, "Your priests should
be clothed in justice" Psalms 131:9 "These," he says, "all have lived
and, have ruled with Christ for a thousand years": that is, in the
present century. And he has spoken correctly, "All both the surviving and the souls of the just": that is, both those who still live in

this world, and those who have already traveled from this life, should rule with Christ. "They have ruled" truly he said, just as, "They have divided my clothes for themselves" Psalms 21:19. For he was going to say, they will rule. In order to show however what those thousand years were in this life, he says, "This is the first resurrection." Indeed itself is by what we arise again through baptism, just as the Apostle says, "If you have arisen with Christ, seek what things are above" Colossians 3:2: and again, "Living as if from the dead" Romans 6:13. Indeed sin is a death [death is a sin], just as the Apostle said, "Since you died for dishonors and your sins" Ephesians 2:1. And just as the first death in this is the life through the sin, thus also the first resurrection in this is the life through the remission of sins. "Blessed and holy is the one who has a part in the first resurrection": that is, he who has served what he received when he was reborn in Baptism. "In this one the second death does not have power": that is, he will not feel eternal torments. "But there will be priests of God and of Christ, and they will rule with him for a thousand years." The spirit brought back when he wrote these things, that the Church would rule for a thousand years in this age up until the end of the world. It is manifest that it should not be doubted concerning the perpetual kingdom, when the holy ones will rule also in the present age. Indeed they are said to rule well, if they rule with the help of God also among the afflictions themselves of the world both themselves and others well. "And when a thousand years has ended, Satan will be loosed from his custody." He said ended, a part from the whole. For thus he will be loosed, in order that three years and six months of the very recent struggle remain in the times of the Antichrist. "And he will go out to lead astray the nations which are in the four corners of the earth." He says the whole from the part: for not all are able to be led astray. Only the wicked are led astray: because the true and humble Christians are not led astray. "For many have been called, few chosen" Matthew 20:16. "And the devil and his people ascended into the depth of the earth": that is, into the elation of the haughtiness. "And they surrounded the camps of the holy and the city-state of the beloved ones": that is, the Church. This is what he said above, that they were collected in Armagedon, Apocalypse 16:16. Indeed they were not able to be assembled into one city-state from the four corners of the earth; but in the four corners themselves each nation will be gathered into the fortress of the holy city-state, that is, for the persecution of the Church. "And fire descended from the sky from God": that is, from the Church. "And

he consumes them entirely": doubly in this place is fire understood: for either through the fire of the Holy Spirit they believe
into Christ, and spiritually [2449] they are thoroughly consumed
by the Church, that is, they are incorporated into the Church; or
they are thoroughly consumed by the fire of their sins, and they
perish. "And the devil, who was leading the very ones astray, was
sent into the pool of fire and sulfur, where both the beast and pseudoprophets": pseudoprophets are understood as either heretics or
false Christians. For from this the Lord suffered, the beast dies and
the pseudo prophets, also are sent into the fire, continuously while
a thousand years are finished from the arrival of the Lord. "And
they will be punished day and night forever. And I saw great and
small dead ones standing in the sight of the throne: and the books
were opened, and another book was opened, which is of the life of
each one." He says the opened books are the Testaments of God:
indeed according to each Testament the Church will be judged.
The book of life, he says is the memory of our deeds: not that a
witness should have a book as a record of secret things. "And the
dead have been judged for these things which were written in the
books according to their works": that is, they were judged from the
Testaments, according to what the precepts of God either did, or
did not command. "And the sea gave its dead": those whom this
Day of Judgment will find alive, they themselves are the dead of
the sea; because this age is the sea. "Death and the underworld
have given their dead": that is, those who will be found in the sepulchers on the Day of Judgment. "Death and the underworld have
been sent into the pool": death and the underworld he says are the
devil and his people. "And if there is anyone who has not been
found written in the book of life": and who was released to his
pleasures, through the timely examination in this age did not deserve to be judged by God while he was alive, "he was sent into the
pool of fire. And I saw the new heaven and the new earth. Indeed
the first heaven and the first earth went away, and the sea is no
longer. And I saw the new holy city-state of Jerusalem, descending
from the heaven from God, composed as if a bride, and adorned
for her husband. And I heard a great voice from the sky saying:
Behold the tabernacle of God with humans, and it will live with
themselves; and they themselves will be his people, and God himself will be with them as their God: and God wipes away every tear
from their eyes; and there will not be death any more, and there
will not be sorrow." He said this all concerning the glory of the
Church, what kind he will have after resurrection. "And he said,

Write; since those sermons are faithful and true. And he said to me; I am both the beginning and the end. I will give to the thirty from the fountain of the water of life freely;" that is, to the one desiring remission of sins through the fount of Baptism. "He, who conquers, will possess these things; and I will his God, and he himself will be my son. However for the timid, and unbelieving, and the detestable, and murders, and poisoners, and worshipers of idols, there will be a part of all liars in the burning pool of fire and sulfur, which is a second death." What was said above, "He has judged that great harlot who has corrupted the earth in her fornication, and he has revenged the blood of his servants from his hand"; this voice is of the Church, since all the evil ones went out from it on the Day of Judgment, to the eternal consuming of burning up. "And their smoke ascends forever." Indeed the smoke of the visible city-state does not forever, but of humans persisting in haughtiness. What however he says, "Because the nuptials of the Lamb came"; is understood concerning Christ, and concerning the Church. That in truth he says she was covered by fine linen; things covered in fine linen are understood as the just things of the holy, by which the just are dressed, according to what was said. "Let your priests be dressed in justice." What moreover he says, that they have ruled for a thousand years; is understood as the present time, in which the holy are said to rule justly, because they rule thus with the help of God, in order that they are not able to be conquered by sins. And in order to show this clearly, he continued saying: "This is the first resurrection." Indeed the first resurrection, by which the souls rise from the death of the sin to a life of justice, now is done in the whole time: in truth the second, by which they return from the dust of the earth to the life of the body, is expected in the future. For it itself [resurrection] is by which we rise again through Baptism. As the first death in this life is through sin, thus also the first resurrection is through the remission of sins. "Blessed [2450] and holy the one who has a part in the first resurrection": that is, he who has preserved what he has received when reborn in Baptism. Moreover what he says, the Church will rule for a thousand years; in this age it is understood up until the end of the world. Whence it is clear that it should not be doubted concerning the perpetual kingdom, since even in the present age the holy will rule. Indeed they are said to rule correctly, those who with the assistance of God, rule well also among the afflictions themselves of the world, both themselves and others. What moreover he says about the devil, "Because he leads astray the nations which are in the four corners of the earth," is understood as a whole from the part. For only the evil are led astray, according to that statement, "Many have been called, few chosen." Moreover what he says, that "the devil and angels surrounded the camps of the holy, and the city-state of the blessed ones": indeed they were not able to be gathered from the four corners of the earth into one city-state, but in the four corners themselves each race is gathered against the persecution of the Church. Moreover what he says, "The fire fell from the heaven and consumed them entirely," is understood doubly: for either through the fire of the holy spirit spiritually they are consumed entirely, while they are incorporated into the Church; or if they didn't want to be converted to God, they are consumed entirely by the fire of their sins, and they perish. Moreover what he says, that the books were opened, he wanted to be understood as the Testaments of God. Indeed according to each Testament the Church will be judged. The book in truth of each life, he says is the memory of our deeds, because on the Day of Judgment nothing will lie hidden, nor will anyone be able to hide his sins or his offenses. What he says, that "the sea gave its dead"; he says that they are those whom the arrival of Christ will have found alive in this world. They themselves are the dead of the sea, because this age is the sea. What he says, "Death and the under-world have given their dead"; those are understood, who will be found in sepulchers on the Day of Judgment. "And death and the underworld were sent into the pool of fire." In this place he want-ed to be understood death and underworld, as the devil and his people, who although they were released from their pleasures, were not worthy to be judged through the timely examination. Af-ter these things when the glory of the Church has been explained he adds and says, "I will give to the thirsting from the fountain of the water of life freely": that is, to the one desiring remission of sins through the font of Baptism. "He, who conquers, will possess these things, and I will be his God, and he will be my son": what he himself will consider worthy to offer, he who with God the Fa-ther, etc.

Homily XIX (a).

[Apocalypse 21 and 22.] Just as we have just now heard, dear-est brothers, the angel of the Lord spoke to blessed John, saying: "Come, I will show to you a bride, the wife of the Lamb. And he has brought me in spirit above a great and high mountain": the mountain he says is Christ: "And he showed to me the holy city-state of Jerusalem, descending from the heaven from God." This is the Church, a city-state established on the mountain, the bride of the Lamb. For the city-state itself at that time was established on the mountain, when it was called back on the shoulders of a shepherd, as if a sheep to its own sheep pen Luke 15:5. If indeed one is the Church, the other is a city-state descending from the sky; there will be two brides, a thing which is not able to happen entirely. And this city-state indeed he said was the bride of the Lamb. Whence it is clear that it itself is the Church, which he describes thus, saying: "The one having the clarity of God. His light is like a very precious stone." The very precious stone is Christ. "Having a great and high wall, having twelve gates, and over the gates twelve angels." He shows the twelve gates and twelve angels, to be the Apostles and the Prophets: since, just as it was written, we have been "built together above the foundation of the Apostles and the Prophets" Ephesians 2:20; just as also the Lord said to Peter, "Over this rock I will build my Church" Matthew 16:18. "From the east three gates, from the north three gates, from the south three gates, from the west three gates": and because that city-state which is described, is the Church spread in the whole world, therefore through four parts of the city-state there are said to be three gates each, because through all the four parts of the world, the mystery of the Trinity in the Church is preached. "And the wall of the city-state having twelve foundations and over them the twelve names of the Apostles of the Lamb": what are the gates, this the foundations; what is the city-state, this the wall, this the furniture? [2541] "And the one who was talking with me was holding a golden measure for a reed": in the golden staff, he shows the humans of the Church, indeed with fragile flesh, but founded on golden faith; just as the Apostle says, "Having a treasury in earthen vases" II Corinthians 4:7. "And the furniture of the wall and the city-state having a golden world, like a glass world": Indeed the Church is golden, because its faith shines as if gold; just as seven candelabra, and the golden altar and the golden saucers; this entire thing depicted the Church. The glass returned however to the purity of faith, because what is seen on the outside, this is also within, and nothing is simulated, but all is evident in the holy ones of the Church. "The foundations of the wall of the city-state are of every precious stone. The first foundation jasper, the second sapphire, the third chalcedon, the fourth emerald, the fifth of sardonyx, the sixth sardian

stone, the seventh of chyrsolite, the eighth of beryl, the ninth to-
paz, the tenth chrysoprasus, the eleventh jacinth, the twelfth am-
ethyst: therefore he wanted to name the diversity of the gems in
the foundations, in order to show the gifts of different thanks,
which were given to the Apostles; just as it was said from the Holy
Spirit, "Dividng for individuals as he wishes" I Corinthians 12:11.
"And twelve pearls individually: and every gate was from one
pearl": and in those pearls, just as it was said, he designated the
Apostles; and they are therefore said to be the gates, because they
open the door of eternal life through their teaching. "And the street
of the city-state has a golden world, as a clear glass: and I did not
see a temple in it; indeed the Lord God omnipotent is its temple
and the Lamb:" this therefore, because in God is the Church, and
in the Church is God. "The city-state does not need a sun nor
moon, to shine in it": because the Church is ruled not by light or
by the elements of the world, but is led by Christ the eternal sun
through the shadows of the world. "Indeed the clarity of God has
illuminated it: and its lamp is the Lamb": with the very one saying,
"I am the light of the world" John 8:12: and again, "I am the true
light, which illuminates every man coming into this world" John
1:9. "The nations will walk in his light," up to the end. "And the
kings of the land will bring glory": the kings of the land, he says
are the sons of God. "And its gates will not be closed by the day.
Indeed there is not a night there:" up until eternity. "And they will
bring in glory and the honor of nations": especially of those believing in Christ. "And there will not enter into this every kind of dirty
thing, or one making an abomination and lie, if they were not written in the book of the life of the Lamb. And he shows to me a river
of water, just like crystal, going out from the throne of God and of
the Lamb, in the middle of its street": he shows the fount of Baptism in the middle of the Church, coming from God and Christ.
For what kind of décor of the citystate can there be, if the river
descends through the middle of its street to the impediment of
those living there? "And from each part of the river the tree of life
making fruits through the individual twelve months, and restoring
its own fruit." Concerning the cross of the Lord he said this. There
is no tree which will bear fruit in every time, except the cross
which the faithful bear, who are washed by the water of the ecclesiastic river, and give back perpetual fruit in every time. "And the
throne of God and of the lamb will be in it" certainly from now
forever. "And his servants will obey him, and they will see his face":
just as he says, "He who sees me, sees also the Father John 14:9;

and, "Blessed with a clean heart, because they themselves will see God" Matthew 5:8. "And his name on their foreheads. And it will not be night any more, and they will not need the light of a lamp and the light of the sun; since the Lord God will illuminate over them, and they will rule forever." All of those things have begun from the suffering of the Lord. "And the angel said to me: Indeed you will have marked the words of the prophecy of this book: for the time is near. He who is unjust may do unjust things still, and the dirty one may still become dirty": those are the ones on account of whom he had said, "The signs which the seven thunderings spoke" Apocalypse 10:4. "And the just may do justice still, and the holy may be holy still:" those are the ones on account of whom he said, "Indeed you will not have marked the words of the prophecy of this book." And thus the divine Scriptures for all the haughty ones, and those loving the world more than God were signified: moreover they were opened for the humble and those fearing God. "Behold I come quickly, and my reward with me, to return to each according to his works. I am both the first and the most recent, the beginning and the end. The blessed who protect these commands, in order that there is power of them over the tree of life, may enter also through the gates [2452] into the city-state": indeed those who do not protect the mandates, do not enter through the gates, but into another part. The book was signified among those, concerning whom he aims at and says, "Outdoors are dogs, and the poisoners, and the fornicators, and the murderers, and the worshipers of idols, and every one loving and making a lie. I Jesus have sent my angel to bring to light to you these things in the Churches. I am the root and the race of David, a splendid star of morning. The Spirit and bride say, Come": especially the groom and bride, Christ and the Church. "He, who thirsts, let him come; he who wishes let him receive the water of life freely": that is, Baptism. "Therefore I bring to light each one hearing the sermons of the prophecy of this book": If anyone has added to these things, let God place over him the afflictions written in this book: and if anyone has withdrawn from the sermons of this prophecy, let God remove a part of him from the staff/tree of life and from the sacred citystate; written in the book." This he who gives proof of these things on account of the forgers of the sacred Scriptures; not on account of those who say simply what they believe. "Also I come quickly": a high mountain, on which the holy John said that he had climbed, is understood as the spirit. In the city-state of Jerusalem, which he said that he had seen there, the Church was signified. And this the Lord himself shows in the Gospel, when he said, "The city-state is not able to be hidden when placed above a mountain" Matthew 5:14. Moreover he says that, it has a light like a very precious stone: in that stone the clarity of Christ is shown. In the twelve gates and in the twelve angels, are understood the Apostles and the patriarchs, according to that statement, "Having been built on top of the foundation of the Apostles and of the Prophets": and because the city-state which is described, is the Church spread in the whole world, therefore through four parts of it on account of the mystery of the Trinity there are said to be three gates each. On the golden staff, it shows the humans of the Church, indeed with fragile flesh, but founded on golden faith, on account of that statement of the Apostle: "Having that treasury in earthen vases." What he says is the golden city-state, golden altar, and golden saucers: is the Church on account of correct faith. Moreover in the glass the purity of faith itself is signified. That moreover he wanted to name the names of the different gems in the foundations; he showed were the gifts of different thanks, which were given to the Apostles. In those pearls moreover he designated the Apostles, who therefore are said to be the gates, because they open the door of life through their teaching. What moreover he says, "Because I did not see a temple in it, because the omnipotent Lord is its temple and the Lamb"; therefore is this, because God is in the Church, and the Church in God. What in truth he says, "Because the city-state does not need the sun nor moon"; this therefore, because the Church is not illuminated with a visible sun, but by the eternal light of Christ among the shadows of that world spiritually, just as he himself says, "I am the light of the world." The kings of the earth, the sons of God, that is, he wanted to be understood as Christians. In the river of water, just like crystal, the font of Baptism in the middle of the Church coming from God and Christ. That moreover he said, "The staff next to the river through the twelve individual months gives fruit"; the cross is understood, which through the whole world not only in all the months, but also in all the days, among those who are baptized, will show the fruit to God. What moreover he says, "The Lord God will illuminate those, and will rule forever"; all those things began from the suffering of the Lord. What in truth in the upper part of the book he said, "The signs which the seven thunderings spoke"; he said on account of these, concerning whom he says: "In order that the dirty one still gets dirty, and the one who is unjust still does unjust things." Moreover that which he says, "You will certainly not have signified the words of the prophecy"; he wanted to be understood on account of the holy and the just. And thus the divine Scriptures were signified by all the haughty, and those loving the world more than God, moreover to the humble and those fearing God they were opened. And because thus the Apocalypse of John the evangelist concludes, in order that he says, "Behold I come quickly"; let us pray that the Lord Jesus Christ comes to us according to his promise, and frees us through his compassion from the prison of that world, and considers it worthy to lead to his blessedness for his piety: he who lives with the Father and the holy Spirit and rules forever. Amen."[335]

http://www.documentacatholicaomnia.eu/25_10_30-_Volumina.html

http://www.documentacatholicaomnia.eu/04z/z_0354-0430__Augustinus__Expositio_In_Apocalypsim_Beati_Joanni__MLT.pdf.html

---

[335] Saint Caesarius of Arles, (Augustini), *Expositio in Apocalypsim, B. Joannis,* Patrologia Latina, 1841, 35:2417-2452.

Appendix VIII

The Letters of Cassiodorus

[A selection of Letters and edicts by King
Theodoric the Great, King of the Ostrogoths]

507 A.D. – 511 A.D.
Book I – 9.

King Theodoric to Eustorgius, Bishop of Milan

'You will be glad to hear that we are satisfied that the Bishop
of Augusta [Turin or Aosta] has been falsely accused of betrayal
of his country. He is therefore to be restored to his previous rank.
His accusers, as they are themselves of the clerical order, are not
punished by us, but sent to your Holiness to be dealt with according to the ecclesiastical tradition. [The reflections in this letter
about the impropriety of believing readily accusations against a
Bishop,[336] and the course adopted of handling over the clerical
false accusers to be dealt with by their Bishop, have an obvious
bearing on the great Hildebrandic controversy. But as Dahn ('Konige der Germanen' iii. 191) points out, there is no abandonment
by the King of the ultimate right to punish an ecclesiastic.] Pg.
149–150.

---

[336] Nihil enim in tali honore temeraria cogitatione praesumendum est, ubi si
proposito creditor, etiam tacitus ab excessibus excusatur. Manifesta proinde
criminal in talibus vix capiunt fidem. Quidquid autem ex invidia dicitur, veritas
non putatur.'

508 June 24
Book I – 24.

King Theodoric to all the Goths

'To the Goths a hint of war rather than persuasion to the strife is needed, since a warlike race such as ours likes to prove its courage. In truth, he shuns no labor who hungers for the renown of valour. Therefore with the help of God, whose blessing along brings prosperity, we design to send our army to the Gaul's for the common benefit of all, that you may have an opportunity of promotion, and we the power of testing your merits; for in time of peace the courage which we admire lies hidden, and when men have no chance of showing what is in them, their relative merits are concealed. We have therefore given our Sajo,[337] Nandius, instructions to warn you that on the eighth day before the calends of next July, you move forward to the campaign in the name of God, sufficiently equipped, according to your old custom, with horses, arms, and every requisite for war. Thus will ye at the same time show that the old valour of your sires yet dwells in your hearts, and also successfully perform your Kings command. Bring forth your young men for the discipline of Mars. Let them see you do deeds which they may love to tell of to their children. For an art not learned in youth is an art missing in our riper years. The very hawk, whose food is plunder, thrusts her still weak and tender young ones out of the nest, that they may not become accustomed to soft repose. She strikes the lingerers with her wings; she forces her callow young to fly, that they may prove to be such in the future as her maternal fondness can be proud of. Do you therefore, lofty by nature, and stimulated yet more by the love of fame, study to leave such sons behind you as your fathers have left in leaving you.'

[We can hardly be wrong in referring this stirring proclamation to the year 508, when Theodoric sent troops into Gaul to save the remnants of the Visigothic Monarchy from the grasp of Clovis. The first sentence recalls the expression 'certaminis gaudia,' which Jordanes no doubt borrowed from Cassiodorus. For the simile at the end of the letter, cf. Deuteronomy xxxii. II, 'As an eagle stirreth up her nest'.] Pg. 157–158.

---

[337] See for the office of the Sajo, note on ii. 13

507 A.D.–511 A.D.
Book II – 16.

King Theodoric to the Senate of the City of Rome

This letter adds a little to the information contained in the preceding one, as to the career of Liberius, father of Venantius.

Liberius was a faithful servant of Odavacar, who adhered to his master to the last. 'He awaited incorruptly the Divine judgments, nor did he allow himself to seek a new King till he had first lost his old one. On the overthrow of his lord he was bowed by no terror; he bore unmoved the ruin of his Prince; nor did the revolution, at which even the proud hearts of the Barbarians trembled,[338] avail to move him from his calm.

'Prudently did he follow the common fortunes, in order that while fixedly bearing the Divine judgments he might with the more approbation find the Divine favour. We approved the faith of the man; he came over in sadness to our allegiance as one who has contrived [treacherously] that he should be conquered. We made him Praefectus Praetorio. He administered the finances admirably. By his economical management we felt the increased returns, while you knew nothing of added tributes.

'We especially like to remember how in the assignment of the [Gothic] thirds (in Tertiarum deputatione) he joined both the possessions and the hearts of the Goths and Romans alike. For whereas men are wont to come into collision on account of their being neighbours, with these men the common holding of their farms proved in practice a reason for concord. Thus it has happened that while the two nations have been living in common they have concurred in the same desires. Lo! A new fact, and one wholly laudable. The friendship of the lords has been joined with the division of the soil; amity has grown out of the loss of the Provincials, and by the land a defender has been gained whose occupation of part guarantees the quiet enjoyment of the whole. One law includes them: one equal administration rules them: for it is necessary that sweet affection should grow between those who always keep the boundaries which have been allotted them.

---

[338] 'Quam etiam ferocitas gentilis expavit.'

'All this the Roman Republic owes to Liberius, who to two such illustrious nations has imparted sentiments of mutual affection. See to it, Conscript Fathers, that his offspring does not go unrewarded.' Pg. 179– 180.

507 A.D.–511 A.D
Book II – 27.

King Theodoric to all the Jews living in Genoa

The Jews are permitted to roof in the old walls of their synagogue, but they are not to enlarge it beyond its old borders, nor to add any kind of ornament, under pain of the Kings sharp displeasure; and this leave it granted on the understanding that it does not conflict with the thirty years 'Statute of Limitations.'

'Why do ye desire what ye ought to shun? In truth we give the permission which you craved, but we suitably blame the desire on your wandering minds. *We cannot order a religion, because no one is forced to believe against his will.* Pg. 185–186.

507 A.D.–511 A.D.
Book II – 29.

King Theodoric to Adila, Senator and Comes

[Notice the Senatorial rank borne by a man with a Gothic name.]

'We wish to protect all our subjects,[339] but especially the Church, because by so doing we earn the favour of Heaven. Therefore, in accordance with the petition of the blessed Eustorguis,[340] Bishop of Milan, we desire you to accord all necessary protection to the men and farms belonging to the Milanese Church in Sicily: always understanding, however, that they are not to refuse to plead in answer to any public or private suit that may be brought against them. They are to be protected from wrong, but are not themselves to deviate from the path of justice.' Pg. 186–187.

---

[339] 'Quia Regnantes est Gloria, subjectorum otiose tranquillitas.'
[340] For Eustorgius, cf. Letter i. 9.

507 A.D.–511 A.D.
Book II – 37.

King Theodoric to Faustus, Praetorian Praefect

'As our Kingdom and revenues prosper, we wish to increase
our liberality. Let your Magnificence therefore give to the citizens
of Spoletium another "millena" for extraordinary gratuitous ad-
missions to the baths.[341] We wish to pay freely for anything that
tends to the health of our citizens, because the praise of our times
is the celebration.'

[The 'millena' probably means 1,000 solidi, or 600#. Pg. 190–
191.

507 A.D
Book II – 41.

King Theodoric to Luduin [Clovis], King of the Franks

Congratulates him on his recent victories over the Alamanni.
Refers to the ties of affinity between them (Theodoric having married the sister of Clovis). Clovis has stirred up the nation of the
Franks, 'prisca aetate reside,' to new and successful encounters.
'It is a memorable triumph that the impetuous Alaman should be
struck with such terror as given to beg for his life. Let it suffice
that the King with all the pride of his race should have fallen: let
it suffice that an innumerable people should have been doomed
either to the sword or to slavery.'

He recommends (almost orders) Clovis not to touch the pan-
ic-stricken refugees who have fled to the territory of Theodoric.
Theodoric himself has always found that those wars were pros-
perously waged which were ended moderately.

Theodoric sends 'illum et illum' as ambassadors, to take certain verbal counsels from himself, to bring this letter and carry
back the reply, and also to introduce the Citharoedus of whom we
heard in the preceding letter.[342]

---

[341] 'Ad exhibitionem thermarum supra consuetudinem.'
[342] There are two allusions to the relationship between the Kings: 'vestrae virtutis

[This campaing of Clovis against the Alamanni, referred to in this letter, is not mentioned by Gregory of Tours. Ennodius, however, in his Panegyric on Theodoric, and Agathias in his History, make distinct allusions to this event, and to Theodoric's reception of the vanquished Alamanni in his own dominions, probably in the valleys of Raetia.

This letter is very fully discussed by Von Schubert. At pp. 32-43 of his 'Unterwerfung der Alamannen' (Strassburg, 1884). I may also refer to 'Italy and her Invaders' iii. 390-91.

The date of the letter is probably 504.] Pg. 194–195.

507 A.D.
Book III – 1.

King Theodoric to Alaric, King of the Visigoths

'Surrounded as you are by an innumerable multitude of subjects, and strong in the remembrance of their having turned back Attila,[343] still do not fight with Clovis. War is a terrible thing, and a terrible risk. The long peace may have softened the hearts of your people, and your soldiers from want of practice may have lost the habit of working together on the battlefield. Ere yet blood is shed, draw back if possible. We are sending ambassadors to the King of the Franks to try to prevent this war between our relatives; and the ambassadors whom we are sending to you will go on to Gundibad, King of the Burgundians, to get him to interpose on behalf of peace. Your enemy will be mine also.'

[The battle of Vougle, in which Alaric was overthrown by Clovis, was fought in 507; but the date of the letter is probably 506 (Dahn's date) rather than 507, as there were no doubt some premonitory symptoms before the war broke out.

Binding i. 181 (n.608), and Pallmann ii. 55 n. I, and 135 n. 2, incline to a date somewhat earlier even than 506, thinking that there may have been earlier threatening of war, which Theodoric succeeded for the time in averting.

The earlier the date the better will it suit the allusion to Clovis (and Alaric) as 'Regii Juvenes' in the following letter. Clovis was born in 466, and was therefore 41 years of age at the battle of

---

(Cont.)

affinitate' (line I), and 'ad parentum vestrorum defensionem confugisse' (line 10).

[343] Quamvis Attilam potentem reminiscamini Visigothorum viribus inclinatum.'

Vougle.] Pg. 196–197.

507 A.D.
Book III – 4.

King Theodoric to Luduin (Ludwig, or Clovis), King of the Franks

[On the same subject.]

'The affinities of Kings ought to keep their subjects from the plague of war. We are grieved to hear of the paltry caused which are giving rise to rumours of war between you and our son Alaric, rumours which gladden the hearts of the enemies of both of you. Let me say with all frankness, but with all affection, just what I think: "It is the act of a passionate man to get his troops ready for action at the first embassy which he sends." Instead of that refer the matter to our arbitration. It would be a delight to me to choose men capable of mediating between you. What would you yourselves think of me if I could hear unmoved of your murderous intentions towards one another? Away with this conflict, in which one of you will probably be utterly destroyed. Throw away the sword which you wield for my humiliation. By what right do I thus threaten you? By the right of a father and a friend. He who shall despise this advise of ours will have to reckon us and our friends as his adversaries.

'I send two ambassadors to you, as I have to my son Alaric, and hope that they may be able so to arrange matters that no alien malignity may sow the seeds of dissention between you, and that your nations, which under your fathers have long enjoyed the blessings of peace, may not now be laid waste by sudden collision. You ought to believe him who, as you know, has rejoiced in your prosperity. No true friend is he who launches his associates, unwarned, into the headlong dangers of war.' Pg. 198–199.

507 A.D.–511 A.D.
Book III – 7.

King Theodoric to the Venerable Januarius, Bishop of Salona

'The lamentable petition of John says that you have taken sixty tuns of oil from him, and never paid him for them. It is especially important that the preachers of righteousness should be righteous themselves. We cannot suppose that God is ignorant whence come the offerings which we make before Him [and He must therefore hate robbery for a burnt offering]. Pray enquire into this matter, and if the complaint be well founded remedy it promptly. You who preach to us our duty in great things should not be caught tripping in little ones.' Pg. 201.

507A.D.–511 A.D.
Book III – 15.

King Theodoric to Theodahad, Senator

'It is the extreme of insolence in anyone not to execute our "sacred orders." A certain person whom we commanded to attend before the judgment- seat of the Illustrious Sona, has with inveterate cunning withdrawn himself there from. We therefore hand him over to you, that your fame may grow by your skilful management of a difficult case like this.' Pg. 205.

507 A.D.–511 A.D
Book III – 20.

King Theodoric to the Sajo Grimoda and to the Apparitor Ferrocinctus.

. . . . 'No powers of any kind, be they Praetorian Praefects or what they may, shall be permitted to trample on the lowly.' Pg. 207–208.

507 A.D.–511 A.D.
Book III – 23.

King Theodoric to Colossaeus, Vir Illustris and Comes (Cir. A.D. 505)

Show forth the justice of the Goths, a nation happily situated for praise, since it is theirs to unite the forethought of the Romans and the virtue of the Barbarians. Remove all ill planted customs,[344] and impress upon all your subordinates that we would rather our treasury lost a suit than it gained one wrongfully, rather that we lost money that the tax payer was driven to suicide.'

[Cf. Muchar, 'Gescgichte der Steiermark' iv. 131.] Pg. 209.

507 A.D.–511 A.D.
Book III – 37.

King Theodoric to Bishop Peter.

[See the full explanation of this letter in Dahn, 'Konige der Germanen' iii. 193-4. Cf. also Var. iii. 14. Observe how marginal note (in the edition of the Benedictine, Garet) strains the doctrine of this letter in favour of the clergy.[345]]

'Germanus , in his "flebilis allegation," informs us that you detain from him a part of the property of his father Thomas. As it is proper that causes which concern you should first be remitted to you (so often employed as judges to settle the disputes of others), we call upon you to inquire into this claim, and if it be a just one to satisfy it. Know that if you fail to do justice yourself to the petitioner, his cause will be carried through to our own audience chamber.' Pg. 216 – 217.

---

[344] Consuetudines abominanter inolitas.' Fornerius thinks this means 'all extortionate taxes.' Compare the English use of the word 'customs.

[345] 'Causae sacerdotum a sacerdotibus debent terminari.'

508 A.D.
Book III – 43.

King Theodoric to Unigis, the Sword Bearer
[Spatarius]

. . . . 'We delight to live after the law of the Romans, whom we seek to defend with our arms'. Pg. 219.

507 A.D.–511 A.D.
Book III – 48.

King Theodoric to all Goths and Romans living near the Fort of Verruca

Examples of gulls, who fly inland when they foresee a storm; of dolphins, which seek the shallower waters; of the edible sea urchin, 'that honey of flesh, that dainty of the deep,' who anchors himself to a little pebble to prevent being dashed about by the waves; of birds, who change their dwellings of when winter draws nigh; of beasts, who adapt their lair to the time of year. And shall man alone be improvident? Shall he not imitate the higher Providence by which the world is governed? Pg. 222–223.

507 A.D.–511 A.D.
Book IV – 1.

King Theodoric to Herminafrid, King of the Thuringians.

'Desiring to unite you to ourselves by the bonds of kindred, we bestow upon you our niece [Amalabirga, daughter of Theodoric's sister; see 'Anon. Valesii 70], so that you, who descend from Royal stock, may now far more conspicuoiusly shine by the splendor of Imperial blood.'[346] [A remarkable passage, as showing that Theodoric did in a sense consider himself to be filling the place of the Emperors of the West.] Pg. 235.

---

[346] Nunc etiam longius claritate Imperialis sanguinis fulgeatis.'

507 A.D.–511 A.D.
Book IV – 2.

King Theodoric to the King of the Heruli.

[Adopting him as his son by right of arms]

'It has been always held amongst the nations a great honour to be adopted as "filius per arma." Our children by nature often disappoint our expectations, but to say that we esteem a man worthy to be our son is indeed praise. As such, after the manner of the nations and in manly fashion, do we now beget you.[347]

'We send you horses, spears, and shields, and the rest of the trappings of the warrior; but above all we send you our judgment that you are worthy to be our son.[348] Highest among the nations will you be considered who are thus approved by the mind of Theodoric.

'And though the son should die rather than see his father suffer aught of harm, we in adopting you are also throwing round you the shield of our protection. The Heruli have known the value of Gothic help in old times, and that help will now be yours. A and B, the bearers of these letters, will explain to you in Gothic (patrio sermon) the rest of our message to you.[349] Pg. 236.

508 A.D.–511 A.D.
Book IV – 12.

King Theodoric to Marabad, Vir Illustris and Comes; and Gemellus, Senator

. . . . 'It is our purpose not only to defend by arms but

---

[347] Notice the strong expression, 'Et ideo more gentium et conditione virili filium te praesenti munere procreamus.'

[348] Damus quidem tibi equos, enses clypeus, et reliqua instramenta bellorum, sed quae sunt omnimodis fortiori, largimur tibi nostra judicia.'

[349] In 512, says Marcellinus Comes, 'Gens Erulorum in terras atque civitates Romanorum jussu Anastasii Caesaris introducta.' But what relation that entry of the Heruli into Roman territory may bear to this letter is a very difficult question. See Dahn, Konige der Germanen ii. 8, n. 2.

to govern by just laws the Provinces which God has sub-
jected to us.' Pg. 241.

509 A.D.–510 A.D.
Book IV – 13.

King Theodoric to Senarius, Vir Illustris, Comes Privatarum

. . . . 'A hungry army cannot be expected to preserve discipline, since the armed man will always help himself to that which
he requires. Let him have the chance of buying, that he may not
be forced to think what he can plunder. Necessity loves not a
law2, nor is it right to command the many to observe a moderation which even the few can barely practice.' Pg. 242.
2 'Necessitas moderamen non diligit.'

507 A.D.–511 A.D.
Book IV – 20.

King Theodoric to Geberich, Senator

'If we are willing to enrich the Church by our own liberality,
a fortiori will we not allow it to be despoiled of the gifts received
from pious princes in the past.

'The supplication of the Venerable Bishop Constantius informs us that a jugum [=jugerum, about two-thirds of an English
acre] of land so bestowed on the "sacrosanct' Church has been
taken away from her, and is unlawfully held by the despoiler.

'See that right is done, and that the Church has her own restored to her without any diminution.' Pg. 245.

510 A.D.–511 A.D.
Book IV – 23.

King Theodoric to Arigern, Vir Illustris and Comes

Theodoric who says that he will not suffer any such acts of

treason against the Divine Majesty, and that it is not lawful for
Christian times to deal in magical arts, orders the recapture of the
offenders, who are to be handed over to a Quinque-viral Board,
consisting of the Patricians Symmachus, Decius, Volusianus, and
Caelianus, with the Iluustrious Maximian, and by them examined;
if guilty to be punished (probably with confiscation and exile); if
innocent, of course to be discharged.[350] Pg. 246.

507 A.D.–511 A.D.
Book IV – 32.

King Theodoric to Duda the Sajo.

'We are anxious strictly to obey the laws, and to take no advantage over our subjects in courts of justice. If a man knows he
can get his own by legal process, even from the Sovereign, he is
the less likely to seek it by the armed hand. Pg. 250.

507 A.D.–511 A.D.
Book IV – 33.

King Theodoric to all the Jews of Genoa.

'The true mark of civilitas is the observance of law. It is this
which makes life in communities possible, and which separates
man from the brutes. We therefore gladly accede to your request
that all the privileges which the foresight of antiquity conferred
upon the Jewish customs shall be renewed to you,[351] for in truth
it is our great desire that the laws of the ancients shall be kept in
force to secure the reverence due to us.[352] Everything which has
been found to conduce to civilitas should be held fast with endur-

---

[350] At the beginning of the first letter occurs the remarkable expression 'Abscedat
ritus de medio jam profanes; conticescat poenale murmur animarum,' which the
commentator interprets of the ventriloquistic sounds produced by soothsayers. Cf.
Milton's Christmas Hymn: 'No voice or hideous hum Runs through the arched roof
in words deceiving.'

[351] 'Privilegia debere servari quae Judaicis institutis legume provida decrevit
antiquitas.'

[352] 'Quod nos libenter annuimus qui jura veterum as nostrum cupimus reverentiam
custodiri.'

ing devotion.' Pg. 251.

509 September 1.
Book IV – 36

King Theodoric to Faustus, Praetorian Praefect.

'A wise ruler will always lessen the weight of taxation when his subjects are weighed down by temporary poverty. Pg. 253.

507 A.D.–511 A.D.
Book IV – 38.

King Theodoric to Faustus, Praetorian Praefect.

'The inhabitants of Gravasi (?) and Ponto (?) complain that they have been overloaded with taxes by the Assessors (discussores) Probus and Januarius. They have bad land, and say that they really cannot cope with the taxes imposed upon them [at the last Indiction?]. The former practice is to be reverted to, and they are not to be called upon to pay more than they did in the days of Odoacer.' [An evidence that in one case at least the fiscal yoke of Odoacer was lighter than that of his successor.] Pg. 254.

507 A.D.–511 A.D.
Book IV – 39.

King Theodoric to Theodahad, Vir Illustris
[and Nephew of the King]

'A high-born man should ever act according to well ordered civilitas. Any neglect of this principle brings upon him odium, proportioned to the oppression which the man of humbler rank conceives himself to have suffered at his hands.' Pg. 254–255.

509 A.D.–511 A.D.
Book IV – 43.

King Theodoric to the Senate of the City of Rome

[On the burning of the Jewish synagogue. This synagogue of the Jews was in the Trastevere. See Gregorovius I. 296-298 for a description of it. I do not know what authority he assigns 521 for the date of the tumult in which it was burned.]

'The propriety of manners which is characteristic of the City of Rome must be upheld. To fall into the follies of popular tumult, and to set about burning their own City, is not like the Roman disposition.[353]

'But we are informed by Count Arigern[354] that the populace of Rome, enraged at the punishment inflicted on some Christian servants who had murdered their Jewish masters, has risen in fury and burned their synagogue to the ground,[355] idly venting on innocent buildings their anger against the men who used them.

'Be pleased to inquire into this matter, and severely punish the authors of the tumult, who are probably few in number.

'At the same time inquire into the complaints which are brought against the Jews, and if you find that there is any foundation for them, punish accordingly.' Pg. 256–257."[356]

---

[353] 'Levitates quipped seditionum et ambire propriae civitatis incendium, non est velle Romanum.'

[354] It happens that one of the letters addressed to Count Arigern also refers to a Jewish synagogue. See iii. 45.

[355] Quod in dominorum caede proruperit servilis audacia: in quibus cum fuisset pro districtione publica resecatum, statim plebis inflammata contentio synagogam temerario duxerunt incendio concremandam.' The above is Gregorovius' explanation of the somewhat enigmatical language of Cassiodorus.

[356] Cassiodorus, Magnus Aurelius, Hodgkin, Thomas, The Letters of Cassiodorus. London: Henry Frowde, 1886.

We invite you to view the complete
selection of titles we publish at:

www.TEACHServices.com

or write or email us your praises,
reactions, or thoughts about this
or any other book we publish at:

TEACH Services, Inc.
P.O. Box 954
Ringgold, GA 30736

info@TEACHServices.com

Finally, if you are interested in seeing
your own book in print, please contact us at

publishing@teachservices.com.

We would be happy to review your manuscript for free.

CPSIA information can be obtained at www.ICGtesting.com
Printed in the USA

266330BV00006B/16/P